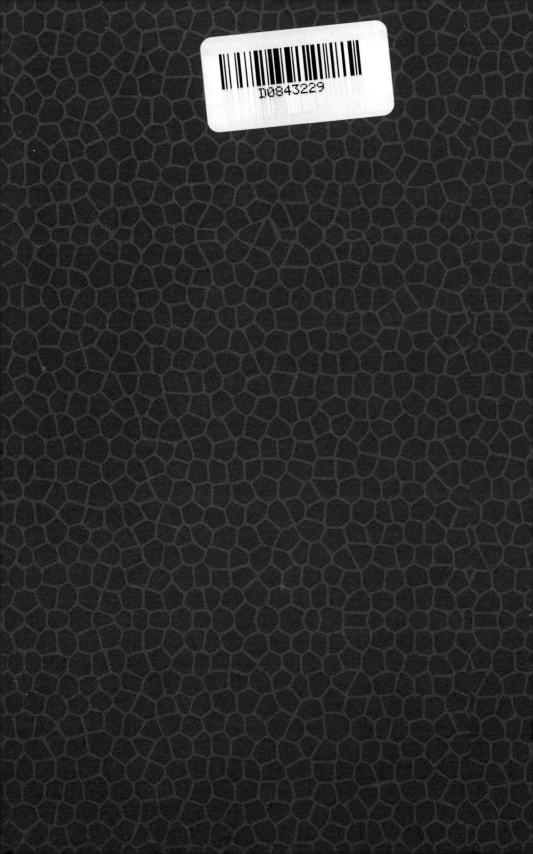

UPON A
עלי עשור

Ten-Stringed
Harp

MOSAICA PRESS

UPON A
Ten-Stringed
Harp

עֲלֵי עָשׂוֹר

*How Torah
and Mitzvos Prepare
the Soul for Eternity*

RABBI YAAKOV WOLBE

Published by Mosaica Press, Inc.
www.mosaicapress.com
info@mosaicapress.com

בס"ד

שמואל קמנצקי

Rabbi S. Kamenetsky

2018 Upland Way
Philadelphia, PA 19131

Home: 215-473-2798
Study: 215-473-1212

בס"ד י"ג לחדש ניסן תשפ"א

אל כבוד הרב ר' יעקב וולבה שליט"א

ואחדשה"ט באהבה רבה

חז"ל מגלים לנו שהמצות לא ניתנו אלא

לצרף בהם את הבריות ומה שמצרפים את עצמנו

ע"י המצות מזומן לחיי עוה"ב.

כוללת את ספרו המיוחד עלי שור המחולק

בדין טעם ודעת הפוסקים הנשגבה הכל מבוסס

על פי חז"ל ודברי על פי גדרי רבינו המשגיח

ר' שלמה וולבה זצוק"ל.

יהי רצון שספריו יתקבלו ויפוצו וישגה

שירבה הדעת ויזכה כב' דס"פ הוצאות לקרב

אחב"י לאבינו שבשמים.

בב"ח הכותב

שמואל קמנצקי

Table of Contents

Introduction 1

Part I

Chapter 1: The Pre-Birth Instruction. 11

Chapter 2: The Head-Mounted Beacon 18

Chapter 3: Know Your Enemy 26

Chapter 4: A Yetzer Hara–Free World 32

Chapter 5: Dual Dangers 37

Chapter 6: The Enemy Within. 42

Chapter 7: 903 Ways to Die 49

Part II

Chapter 8: A Changed Man 59

Chapter 9: Lifeline to God 63

Chapter 10: Miracle Drugs and Superfoods. 69

Chapter 11: The Two Realms of Emunah. 78

Chapter 12: Faith of the Farmer 85

Chapter 13: Rungs of Righteousness 91

Chapter 14: The Love Formula 98

Chapter 15: The Cocoon of Selfishness 104

Summary of Parts One and Two 113

Part III

Chapter 16: The Art of War with the Yetzer Hara 119

Chapter 17: Vanquishing the Villain. 128

Chapter 18: Elixir of Life 133

Chapter 19: The Shema 143

Chapter 20: Remember the Day of Death 152

Chapter 21: The Scope of Victory 158

Part IV

Chapter 22: The Values Hierarchy 167

Chapter 23: The Stature of Avraham 174

Chapter 24: The Greatest Man Who Ever Lived 183

Chapter 25: Angelic Man 188

Chapter 26: The Stature of Moshe 197

Part V

Chapter 27: Spiritual Pleasure and Olam Haba. 207

Chapter 28: Surveying Olam Haba 213

Chapter 29: Crossover to Eternity 222

Chapter 30: A Kernel of Eternity 230

Chapter 31: Spiritual Shortcuts. 237

Chapter 32: Just One Mitzvah 247

Chapter 33: From Adam to Moshe 253

Acknowledgments 258

Introduction

And He banished Adam, and stationed cherubs on the
east of the Garden of Eden, and the flaming, turning
sword to guard the path of the tree of life.[1]

*I*t is hard to imagine Adam's depths of despair after being evicted from the Garden of Eden. Previously, he had been a towering figure, one that the angels mistook for God and sought to worship—a man of unhindered vision and clairvoyance. After his sin (and the resultant punishment), his stature was severely diminished and God banished him from the Garden. To ensure that no one will enter unauthorized, God stationed angels to guard the Garden's gates, and placed a swirling, flaming sword over its door, barring entry to all but the worthiest.

Despondent and forlorn, Adam resolved to find a way back in. After searching in vain, he stumbled upon a cave that bore the distinctive aroma of the Garden, and he began digging furiously, searching for an entrance, for a portal; maybe he could finally return home. Amidst his excavations, a Heavenly voice thundered: "Stop! You may dig no further." Adam had discovered one of the entrances to the Garden, but again his entry was denied.

---

1   *Bereishis* 3:24.

When Chavah died, Adam buried her in that very cave, and left instructions that he be buried there as well. A thousand years later, Avraham also discovered that cave, and ultimately, Avraham and Sarah, Yitzchak and Rivkah, and Yaakov and Leah were also interred in what became known as the Cave of the Patriarchs, or the Cave of Machpelah.

Adam's agony is reenacted every time a Soul enters this world. Like Adam, Souls originate in a Heavenly and spiritual realm and are evicted from their home and cast into a foreign and dangerous world. Like Adam, the Soul is singularly and desperately seeking a portal to get back—to return to its familiar, safe abode; to restore its equilibrium. That portal lies at the end of this world. To get home, the Soul must skillfully navigate through this world. For the spiritual Soul, this physical world is laden with innumerable dangers threatening to imperil its journey. Should the Soul arrive at the portal unprepared, unarmed with the tools of passage, or irreparably damaged from its journey, entry to the palace gates will be denied. If the Soul is to safely return home, assiduous preparation in this world is imperative.

The Roadmap Home

The world that the Soul so deeply covets is called "Olam Haba" (lit., the next world) in Jewish literature. A life well-lived will result in the Soul basking in Divine pleasure in Olam Haba. But eligibility for Olam Haba hinges upon successful preparation in this world. Our Sages teach us that Torah and Mitzvos are the keys to prime a person for Olam Haba. This book is an attempt to rigorously study and examine how that works:

- Part I is diagnostic: To properly understand how Torah and Mitzvos improve man, we must first identify his maladies. What are his flaws that necessitate Torah and Mitzvos? Why must he prepare in this world in order to enter the next one? Part I attempts to answer these questions.
- Based on our recognition of *why* man needs Torah and Mitzvos, in Part II we will examine *how* they are a tailored remedy to the problem.

- In Part III, we will study some of the strategies and tactics of how the objectives of Torah and Mitzvos can be practically implemented.
- Part IV will dissect the ascent to greatness and study the stature of history's most outstanding exemplars of Torah, and see how that dovetails into the framework of the previous three parts.
- Part V ventures a peek beyond the palace gates of Olam Haba, and examines how Torah and Mitzvos make man worthy of entry to—and of distinction in—that world. The book will conclude with a study of the various ways to ensure that we access and flourish in Olam Haba.

Along the way, we will address many important aspects of Jewish life and practice, and the reader can learn practical lessons that will enrich their personal connection to Torah and Mitzvos. But the main objective of the book is to build a comprehensive framework for understanding the interrelationship between man and Torah and Mitzvos, and the consequences thereof. To facilitate a focused read, we have tried to resist the temptation to encumber the reader with corroborating sources to the core concepts of the book and tangential points that do not contribute toward its objective.

Why Read This Book?

Needless to say, the question of how Torah and Mitzvos impact us has been broached before, and by far greater Torah scholars than me. This book seeks to add novelty in two ways: First, it attempts to offer a complete picture in a single volume. Scattered throughout various Scriptural, Mishnaic, Midrashic, and Talmudic sources, the Torah itself addresses all aspects of our pursuit, and it was continually discussed by our Sages throughout the ages. This book seeks to identify the interlocking puzzle pieces of this construct, examine and dissect those teachings, and assemble from them a complete picture of what a person stands to gain with observance of Torah and Mitzvos. I surmise that even readers who are deeply steeped in Jewish learning and are aware of many of the concepts detailed within in isolation will benefit from seeing a unified, encompassing tapestry. I am not aware of a book that does this—certainly not one in English.

A second unique aspect of the book is the methodology employed to arrive at the results. We will not suffice with delineating the reasons and the benefits of Torah and Mitzvos; instead we will try to demonstrate said benefits by presenting Torah sources and analyzing and parsing them in the rigorous question-and-answer learning style found in the great yeshivos, and finally extracting from them conclusions that, taken together, comprise a cohesive framework.

It is my sincerest hope that this volume and its conclusions will deepen the reader's appreciation for the meaning and indispensability of Torah and Mitzvos, but perhaps equally as beneficial to the reader is experiencing a flavor of the joy and beauty of Talmudic inquiry through which those conclusions are reached.

How to Read This Book

This book is designed to be read in three different ways: The ideal way to absorb and digest this work is to read it sequentially. Although most chapters can be studied in isolation, the order in which these ideas are presented follow a logical sequence; each successive chapter is built upon the ideas and conclusions of the preceding ones, and the book's five parts are also organized to chronologically follow man as he is impacted and transformed by Torah and Mitzvos. By reading it in order, a complete, cohesive picture emerges. To make it easier for the reader to keep track of the building blocks of the framework that the book seeks to depict, I've included the key takeaways of each chapter at its conclusion.

There is a second way to enjoy the book. Each of the five parts of the book addresses a central aspect of Jewish philosophy and can be consumed independently:

- To understand the architecture of the conflict that embroils our lives in this world and the imperative for Torah, read Part I.
- If you want to learn how Torah and Mitzvos refine us and cleanse our flaws, Part II is for you.
- Part III is a study of the Talmud's prescriptions for battling the Yetzer Hara, and it can be a valuable, stand-alone read.

- Part IV is dedicated to the spiritual accomplishments of Avraham, Moshe, and prophets in general, and is the appropriate read for those who want to understand the stature of these giants—and for aspiring prophets!
- If you are interested in the tantalizing eschatological subjects of what happens after you die, and reward and punishment in Heaven, and the Resurrection of the dead, our explication of those topics are self-contained in Part V.

A third way to enjoy the book is by reading chapters piecemeal. Almost all the chapters revolve around one idea—frequently based upon a statement from the Talmud—that can be pondered in isolation. This is the way that the book was conceived, and it is a good option for someone who wants to dip their toe into this work.

Regardless of the above approaches, the reader is reminded that this work is oriented around the examination, analysis, and explication of sources, often via critically probing the source's structure and precise word usage. To maximize the value of this volume, the reader is encouraged to analyze and ruminate upon the sources on their own, if possible, in their original language and without the paraphrasing that I frequently employed in the text to aid readability.

Explanation of the Book Title

The book's title is based upon *Tehillim* 92: "It is good to thank God and to sing to Your exalted Name. To proclaim Your kindness in the morning and Your faith in the night. Upon a ten-stringed harp..."[2] I found this a fitting title for a couple of reasons.

First, the Talmud[3] teaches that the verse in *Tehillim* is referring to Olam Haba: The harp played in the Temple had seven strings, the harp that will be played in the Messianic days will have eight strings, and the harp that will be played in Olam Haba will have ten strings, as the verse states, "Upon a ten-stringed harp..." This book is about how to be

---

2   *Tehillim* 92:2–4.
3   *Arachin* 13b.

included in the rarified class of people who merit to thank God and to sing His praises upon a ten-stringed harp in Olam Haba.

Second, the book title evokes the original premise of this project. During a series of lectures that I gave several years ago on the core beliefs of Judaism, I discovered that there are many different levels of Emunah—by my count at least ten—and I began to sketch out an outline of a book about the finer aspects of the various levels and how to advance from one to another. However, as I deepened my study and research into the subject, the scope continuously expanded until it encompassed the study of the impact of Torah and Mitzvos at large. The original "Ten Levels of Emunah" are subsumed in the current volume and form its backbone.

Although the book is in English, I decided to assign it a Hebrew-language title, עֲלֵי עָשׂוֹר, which means, "upon a ten-stringed harp." For one, the words עֲלֵי עָשׂוֹר share the precise *gematria* of my name, יעקב בה"ר אברהם וולבה. In addition, עֲלֵי עָשׂוֹר pays tribute to my venerated grandfather, Rabbi Shlomo Wolbe, *zt"l*, and his magnum opus, עֲלֵי שׁוּר. Although my grandfather passed away more than a decade before I began writing this book, I can say with confidence that he is the person to whom credit for this work is most due. Many of the concepts and insights herein were borrowed from his voluminous vaults of Torah teachings, and even the ideas that are not attributed to him are influenced by his method of approaching and dissecting cryptic Talmudic teaching. My grandfather always reminded us that the words of our Sages were written with laser-like precision, but in a way that their true intent is masked. To unlock a Talmudic teaching, you must dwell in it; you must live with it; you must allow it to germinate within you until its hidden wisdom sprouts forth. I have tried to employ this approach in the book.

On a personal note, ever since I was a young child, my grandfather was deeply invested in my well-being and development. He prayed for me; he monitored my growth and maturation; he ensured that I received the finest education; he urged me to write down my novel Torah insights; and he encouraged us all to pursue careers in Jewish education and outreach. Even from his hospital bed, on the night of the Pesach Seder 2005—less than two days before he transitioned to the Heavenly

Academy—my grandfather placed his hand on my head and blessed me to become a well-rounded Torah scholar: "May you study Chumash well, may you study Mishnah well, may you study Talmud well." I am convinced that what little I have accomplished in Torah scholarship is thanks to his merit, together with the merit of my other illustrious antecedents, and I sincerely hope that this work bestows pride and honor to them in Heaven.

Note on Word Usage

A large portion of the book is dedicated to defining and clarifying the nature of several central entities in Torah philosophy, such as Tzaddik (a righteous person), Rasha (a wicked person), Mitzvah (Torah commandment), Yetzer Hara (evil inclination), Emunah (faith), and Olam Haba (the World to Come). These things constitute the main "characters" of the book, and I have opted to utilize their Hebrew names and to capitalize them. The Soul is the book's main protagonist and it will be capitalized as well, but in an effort to avoid addressing the dizzyingly complex question of the Soul's nature, I opted for the ambiguous English term in lieu of the Hebrew, "Neshamah" or "Nefesh."

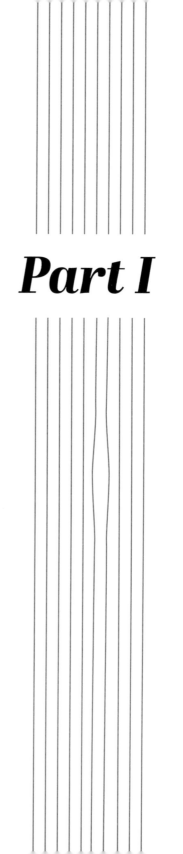

Part I

The Pre-Birth Instruction

*B*y the time a child is born, its Soul already has a long history. Our Sages teach that there are a finite amount of Souls in existence.[1] No new ones have been created since the Six Days of Creation. A day-old child bears a Soul that has been extant for millennia. What the Soul has been occupied with during those eons is surely a tantalizing matter to ponder, and we are truly incapable of fully knowing the answer, but our Sages provided us with several vivid teachings in the Talmud and in the Midrash relating to an unborn child and his Soul during four distinct stages preceding birth:

- Prior to conception, when the Soul is being housed in a Heavenly chamber together with all the other Souls designated for future bodies
- At the moment of conception, when the spiritual Soul is inserted into the biological matter soon to develop into a body
- During the months of gestation
- Immediately preceding birth, when the child is given a dramatic parting message

---

1   Quoted in *Rashi, Yevamos* 63b, s.v. *guf.*

The Sages never inundate us with trivial, useless information. The existence of these descriptions of what transpires to a child and his Soul pre-birth indicate that they contain valuable wisdom for the living. In our analysis of these teachings, it will become evident that during these pre-birth stages, the child and his Soul undergo seismic changes that lay the groundwork for the conflict of life. To fully understand how man benefits from Torah and Mitzvos, we have to understand his genesis: Where does man come from? What are the elements of which he is comprised and how were they assembled? Then, we will be able to definitively identify the critical flaw in man that Torah is designed to fix, and begin to understand how Torah is precisely tailored to rectify that problem. Let us dissect these sources, beginning with what occurs right before birth, and see what insights they contain.

The Pre-Birth Instruction

The Talmud teaches that immediately prior to birth a child is informed what he must accomplish. His mission:

> *Be a Tzaddik and don't be a Rasha! Although the entire world may tell you, "You are a Tzaddik!" you must nevertheless consider yourself to be a Rasha! You must know that the Holy One, blessed is He, is pure; His angels are pure; and the Soul that He placed within you is pure. If you safeguard its purity, good. If not, behold I will take it from you.*[2]

This pre-birth instruction will serve as a guiding light for us as we try to understand the goal of Torah and Mitzvos and the problems they are designed to fix. Over the course of the book, this pre-birth instruction will be referenced numerous times. Let us examine it piece by piece.

The first part succinctly distills man's mission into a binary directive: be a Tzaddik and do not be a Rasha.[3] Evidently, the *only* variable of life that is not predetermined—and thus remains in the hands of the

---

2   *Niddah* 30b.

3   This precise binary formulation is found in another Talmudic source (*Niddah* 16b).

person alone—is whether he will be a Tzaddik or a Rasha. All free-will decisions move a person closer to one of these two results, and the pre-birth instruction urges the Soul immediately before birth to choose the Tzaddik option.

Absent from the text, however, are clear definitions. What are the parameters of "Tzaddik" and "Rasha"? What are the characteristics or behaviors that cause a person to fall into one category or the other? Also, what are the means to becoming a Tzaddik or a Rasha?

The next part of the pre-birth instruction, when the soon-to-be-born child is told not to rely on the affirmation of others, must likewise be pondered. Other people, whose perspectives are untainted by bias or self-delusion, tend to have a more objective and accurate sense of a person's true character. Why should someone still consider themselves a Rasha even if everyone affirms that they are, in fact, a Tzaddik? (This question will only be answered in Chapter 7.)

The third section of the pre-birth instruction begins with a preamble regarding the purity of the Soul:

> You must know that the Holy One, blessed is He, is pure; His angels are pure; and the Soul that He placed within you is pure.

After the astonishing statement that a Soul's purity parallels the purity of the Almighty and His angels, an instruction is administered to the child to preserve and maintain that purity, or else suffer dire consequences:

> If you safeguard its purity, good. If not, behold I will take it from you.

This, too, raises questions:

- First, what is the connection between being a Tzaddik and safeguarding the purity of the Soul?
- Furthermore, the Instruction indicates that at this juncture, the Soul is to a certain degree akin to God and God's angels in purity, but *maintaining* that purity going forward is not assured. For the time being the Soul is scintillatingly pure, but factors exist that

may cause it to become impure. What are these potential causes for the decline in the purity of our Soul?

- Most critically, how does one ensure that the purity of his Soul is not compromised?

Timing the Arrival of the Soul and the Yetzer Hara

The key to deciphering this enigmatic Talmudic teaching lies in the timing of the pre-birth instruction. Immediately prior to entering the world, the instruction to be a Tzaddik and not a Rasha and to prevent the Soul from becoming impure is conveyed. We can infer from this that only from birth onwards is there a risk of the Soul getting sullied; before birth, the Soul is uncorrupted and *incorruptible*. Evidently, the conflict of our life, *and the flaw that Torah and Mitzvos are engineered to remedy*, comes into being only at birth. At that "crossover moment" of birth, something changes that imperils the Soul's purity and kickstarts the question of whether this child will be a Tzaddik or a Rasha.

What happens at birth that creates the possibility of being a Tzaddik or a Rasha and makes the Soul susceptible to becoming impure?

We find the answer in another Talmudic teaching in the form of a debate between Rabbi Yehudah Hanassi and the Roman Emperor Antoninus regarding the precise timetable of the pre-birth development of man.[4] The first issue they tackle is the question of when does the Soul bind with the body. Elsewhere, the Talmud informs us that all the Souls were created during the week of Creation and are encased in a Heavenly vault named *"Guf"* awaiting their turn to be fused with a body.[5] At what point does this fusion happen? After a short debate, Rabbi Yehudah Hanassi concedes to Antoninus' position that body and Soul are bound together at the moment of *conception*. From conception forward, the Soul is implanted within the zygote that will eventually comprise the body.

With that question settled, Rabbi Yehudah Hanassi and Antoninus proceed to debate when a child begins to be influenced by the Yetzer

---

4   *Sanhedrin* 91b.
5   *Yevamos* 62a, 63b; and *Rashi s.v. guf.*

Hara. Once again, Rabbi Yehudah Hanassi ultimately accedes to Antoninus' position, concluding that the Yetzer Hara is only foisted upon a person at *birth*. The Talmudic narrative ends with a proclamation of Rabbi Yehudah Hanassi:

> *This matter was taught to me by Antoninus, and a verse in Scripture supports him, as it states: "At the entrance, sin crouches."*[6]

The notion that the Yetzer Hara is added to the cauldron only at birth is buttressed by the verse, "At the entrance sin crouches," implying that at the entrance of a child into the world, sin is ready to pounce upon him because the force that instigates sin, the Yetzer Hara, begins operations at birth.

The Curse of Birth

The revelation that the Soul is present from conception but the Yetzer Hara arrives at the scene only at birth sheds light on the aforementioned pre-birth instruction. Prior to the advent of the Yetzer Hara, the Soul is entirely pure (to some extent on par with the Almighty and His angels!) and its purity is unchallenged. This idyllic utopia is shattered at birth with the introduction of the Soul's primary antagonist—"At the entrance sin crouches." The Yetzer Hara is the cause for the newfound potential for sin, which would diminish the purity of the Soul. Therefore, immediately prior to the beginning of the Yetzer Hara's assault on the purity of the Soul, a child is informed of their life's mission: *To safeguard and maintain the purity of his Soul by resisting and repulsing the Yetzer Hara's advances.* The binary options of Tzaddik and Rasha only begin from the moment that sin becomes feasible due to the arrival of the Yetzer Hara at birth.

A Soul Freed of the Yetzer Hara

The conclusions of the two debates between Rabbi Yehudah Hanassi and Antoninus teach us that the Soul is present from conception until

---

6   *Bereishis* 4:7.

birth, free of any influences of the Yetzer Hara. The period of gestation is thus particularly instructive and worthy of inquiry. For those brief nine months in utero, a Soul does not yet suffer from the influences of the Yetzer Hara; it is pure and untainted. This knowledge will aid us in our next task: There is a series of intriguing—and on the surface quite incomprehensible—Talmudic teachings regarding a child during the months of gestation. They describe the child in strange ways and capable of unimaginable powers. What those intrauterine teachings reveal is the sheer force of a pure and untethered Soul, unhindered by the Yetzer Hara. The time period between when a Soul is present and when the Yetzer Hara arrives is an excellent window into understanding the Soul's nature when freed from detractors.

Contrasting the state of the Soul before and after it comes into contact with the Yetzer Hara also reveals the destructive powers and methods of the Yetzer Hara, knowledge that will come in handy in crafting a strategy to engage with it.

Last, the descriptions of a fetus influenced only by the Soul can serve as an illustration of the spiritual makeup of a man who reversed the curse of birth and defeated his Yetzer Hara entirely. Though completely eliminating our Yetzer Hara and cleansing ourselves of its noxious presence is probably unachievable, our Sages taught that Avraham, Yitzchak, and Yaakov were successful in doing so, and we are tasked with resisting and neutralizing the Yetzer Hara as best we can. Examining the state of the Soul of a person before the arrival of the Yetzer Hara is thus learning about both the *original* state of the Soul, and the best and most aspirational *future* for it.

What does it look like when man's Soul is not subject to the Yetzer Hara? What happens when a Soul is liberated from the inhibitors that define its existence in our world? Let us examine and analyze the sources describing the Soul in utero and find out.

Chapter 1 Takeaways

- A child bears a Soul from conception and absorbs the negative influence of the Yetzer Hara only at birth.

- The central conflict of life is to protect the Soul from the Yetzer Hara.
- Immediately before birth, the child is given his marching orders that contain his life mission—to be a Tzaddik and to protect the purity of his Soul.

The Head-Mounted Beacon

What transpires to a fetus and its Soul over the course of the nine months of gestation? That question is the subject of a long discussion in the Talmud. It begins by addressing matters relating to the physical environment of child in the womb; it describes his placement in fetal position, how the food that the mother eats sustains her baby as well, and we read about the phenomena of the child's closed orifices opening at birth as its umbilical connection to the mother gets sealed.

The Talmud continues by listing several enigmatic statements regarding the child's *spiritual* status during the months of gestation:

> *A candle is lit on his head and he sees from one end of the world to the other...Those days are the best days of his life...They teach him the entire Torah...At birth an angel comes and hits him on his mouth and causes him to forget it, as Scripture states: "At the entrance sin crouches."* [1]

---

1   *Niddah* 30b.

These puzzling teachings clearly require some explanation.

- The Talmud says that during the months of gestation a child has a candle on his head. The Talmud is obviously not referring to a literal candle, but rather the candle is a euphemism. What is the nature of this "candle"?
- Also, the placement of the candle atop his *head* is unusual. Candles are typically handheld; why is this candle on the child's head?
- Next, we are told that the child sees from one end of the world to the other. This, too, is certainly not referencing vision as we know it. What does it mean?
- Then, the Talmud states that these days are the pinnacle of a child's life. At that stage, he has not yet accomplished anything. How can those days be labeled as the best?
- Also, we read how a child is taught the entire Torah until an angel strikes his mouth at birth, causing him to forget it. What is the meaning of the child's Torah study? Also, who teaches it to him?
- Furthermore, why does the angel cause him to forget it? Why teach the child Torah to begin with if he will invariably forget it at birth?
- Finally, the method that the angel employs to make the child forget the Torah—smacking him on the mouth—is odd. Striking the head, which is the venue where the knowledge ostensibly lies—seems more appropriate. How does the angel erase the Torah by hitting him on the mouth?

The teaching also has, upon initial assessment, a technical problem: It showcases the verse, "At the entrance sin crouches," to prove its assertion that a child forgets the Torah at birth. The problem is that we have already seen in the previous chapter that the Talmud deploys this verse to teach us an entirely different lesson. In settling the debate of Rabbi Yehudah Hanassi and Antoninus, the Talmud cites it as Scriptural proof that the Yetzer Hara arrives at *birth* and not earlier in the child's development.[2] Using this same verse to teach that a child forgets the Torah

---

at birth violates a Talmudic principle that only *one lesson* can be derived from one verse. Once a verse is used for one application, its deductive capacities are exhausted and no further applications can be drawn from it. Apparently, the Talmud concludes that *both* the arrival of the Yetzer Hara at birth and the forgetting of Torah at birth are deduced from the *same verse* of "At the entrance sin crouches." How can one verse furnish two seemingly unrelated teachings?

In the previous chapter, we discovered that for the duration of gestation, a child is influenced only by an astounding spiritual force of purity, a Soul, and faces no resistance from the Yetzer Hara. Understanding that the Soul is unencumbered during the child's stint in his mother's womb will help us answer these questions.

The Candle on the Head

Let us start with the puzzling idea that the fetus has a candle on his head. In Torah parlance, a "candle" is a euphemism for the Soul. The verse states:

> The candle of God is the Soul of man, which searches out the chambers of one's innards.[3]

The perceptive reader will notice that this verse reveals two vital insights for understanding the concept of the candle on the head:

- One, that the word "candle" is a reference to the Soul of man.
- Two, it reveals the *typical location* of the Soul ("which searches out the chambers of one's innards").

The Talmudic piece we saw above places the *fetus's* "candle" (Soul) in a different location: Unlike a *man's* Soul, which is harbored deep within his innermost chambers, the Soul of a child in utero is *not* buried deep within him, but rather is prominently perched atop his *head*.

This distinction cannot be overstated. The "head" refers to a person's consciousness, his purview and focus. In utero, the Soul is at the forefront of the child's world. It maintains the dominant influence over the

3   *Mishlei* 20:27.

child. His connection to the spiritual realm is primary; everything else is secondary.

The Soul's prominence is upended at birth. At that time, the Soul is buried deep within him. Thenceforth it begins "searching within the chambers of his innards." It is demoted from being on his head and is moved into his stomach; from that point forward, it is hard to access. In other words, before birth, a child *is* a Soul; afterwards he *has* a Soul, but his identity is something entirely different. For a child in utero, ignoring the Soul is impossible; its existence is palpable, its supreme importance undeniable. After birth, the Soul is no longer the candle on the head; its primacy in man's consciousness gets replaced and it is submerged deep within him. From birth on, man's connection to his Soul is abstract and theoretical. At that point, it becomes feasible for a person to question its very existence.

The relationship between man and his Soul after birth is indeed comparable to his relationship with his internal organs. Suppose a person underwent abdominal surgery, and while his abdominal cavity is open, the surgeon chose to remove his appendix as well. Would the patient be able to feel or sense, post-op, in any way that his appendix is missing? Of course not! Our connection to our innards is not *sensory*. Intellectually, we are aware of the existence—and perhaps the functions and indispensability—of our intestines, but we've likely never seen them, and they don't occupy much of our headspace. Unless something goes horribly wrong, man is unlikely to think deeply about his internal organs. That is what happens to the Soul at birth. *Theoretically*, we may be aware of its existence and importance, but it is no longer at the forefront of our minds, and it is possible to live an entire life ignoring the Soul completely. However, before birth, during the months of gestation, the Soul is dominant. *The candle is on his head.*

Through this prism, the rest of the narrative of the child in utero comes into focus: A fetus has superlative vision—"He sees from one end of the world to the other." What specifically this means is a hard question to answer, but this transcendental ability is a reflection of the power of an unfettered Soul. The Talmud uses similar words to depict Adam pre-sin in the Garden of Eden: "He was from one end of the world to the other end of the world."[4] Both Adam before his sin and a child in utero harbor Souls whose powers have yet to be contaminated by the Yetzer Hara's venom. Uncorrupted Souls do not suffer from the rigid limitations of our world. Though the true stature of a Soul in such a state is beyond our comprehension—after all, the Talmud in the pre-birth instruction finds parallels between a pure Soul and the Almighty Himself,[5] Who is surely beyond our comprehension—we can at least recognize that the descriptions of the superlative vision of the fetus is a reflection of his Soul in that pure state. The transformation of the Soul at birth mirrors Adam's demotion and eviction from the Garden because both are marked with the advent of the Yetzer Hara. Once the Yetzer Hara is ensconced in man, the Soul is immediately suppressed and its powers curtailed.

Given the Soul's demotion at birth, the next statement of the pre-birth narrative rings true: The months of gestation are certainly the highlight of a child's life because the Soul is unencumbered and not diminished. There is no joy that matches the sublimity of bearing an unmolested Soul. During this interim period, where a child is positively influenced by the Soul and not yet adversely affected by the Yetzer Hara, he is indeed at the acme of human primacy.

Intrauterine Torah

Finally, we are told that the child before birth is taught the entire Torah, only to be struck on the mouth by an angel at birth causing him to forget it. This famous anecdote is often erroneously misquoted as, "an *angel* teaches the child Torah." In the actual text, the only job of the angel is to make the child *forget* the Torah at birth. The source does not actually mention *who* teaches it to him. The truth is that *a child in utero knows the Torah innately without a standalone teacher.*[6] Before the Soul's counterbalance, i.e., the Yetzer Hara, is introduced, the Soul's power is unrestrained. It is absolutely pure—comparable to God and

---

4   *Sanhedrin* 38b.
5   See also *Berachos* 10b for a list of five commonalities between God and the Soul of man.
6   See *Maharal's* commentary to *Niddah* 30b.

the angels—and knows Torah instinctively without needing a teacher, just as the body does not need to be taught how to breathe and swallow. The "candle" that is upon his head comes preloaded with all of Torah, and because the child before birth is connected to his Soul on a sensory level, he knows Torah as well.

At birth, an angel blankets the child with a Yetzer Hara. Instantly, the Soul is supplanted from its primacy by the Yetzer Hara. The utopia of an unchallenged Soul is over. No longer is the Soul "on his head"; no longer is it the dominant force of influence on his life. Thenceforth the Soul is "searching out the chambers of his innards"; its voice and impact have been muffled by the Yetzer Hara, if not muted entirely. With the demotion of the Soul, the child loses all the powers that he had when his Soul reigned supreme. According to the Midrash, this terrible loss of stature is the reason why babies cry at birth.[7]

Thenceforth he can no longer see from one end of the world to the other, the best days of his life are behind him, and he forgets the entire Torah. Why does he forget it? Not because the Torah was *deleted* from the "candle." The Soul, with its implanted power and Torah, is still extant, intact, pure, and unadulterated. Now, though, it's buried within him, the child's *access* to it is severed, and for all *practical* purposes, the Torah is forgotten. However, deep within the innermost chambers of man lies a Soul that is totally pure and undefiled, bursting with Torah, and awaiting to be unearthed.

The Yetzer Hara's Venom and Its Byproducts

Thanks to this fundamental insight (that the arrival of the Yetzer Hara causes the demotion of the Soul and the concomitant forgetting of the erstwhile Torah knowledge), we can now reconcile the problem of deriving two separate lessons from a single verse—"At the entrance sin crouches." It is true that we can only derive a single lesson per verse, and *indeed at birth only one* transformation occurs: the introduction of the Yetzer Hara. However, as a *byproduct* of that, the Soul gets demoted and consequently the Torah that it contains gets forgotten by the child.

---

7   *Tanchuma, Pekudei* 3.

The forgetting of Torah is *not independent of the child gaining a Yetzer Hara*, but rather it's the direct *result* of the child gaining a Yetzer Hara. Thus, one verse suffices to teach "both" lessons.

In other words, the description of an angel hitting the mouth is not directed at the forgetting of the Torah but at the infusion of the Yetzer Hara that causes it. Why is the mouth the conduit by which the Yetzer Hara is inserted into man? A common motif in Jewish literature is that the touchpoint of the physical and spiritual in man is his capacity of verbal speech. Speech is the quintessential human activity because it is a synthesis of the physical and spiritual. To speak, man must utilize his body—throat, teeth, tongue, lips—to produce the sounds, but it has spiritual characteristics too; it's invisible, intangible, and hard to define and quantify. Speech is a confluence of the two divergent worlds that unite in a human.[8] The angel striking the fetus' mouth is referring to the fusion of these opposites. From this point forward, the human will be a fusion of physical and spiritual; of angel and beast; of Soul and Yetzer Hara. This marriage is cemented at birth with the insertion of the Yetzer Hara into a person.

The relevance of the pre-birth teachings is now abundantly clear: Our Sages are providing invaluable insight into the nature and power of our Soul, and into the transformation that occurs at birth that sets the stage for the challenge and mission of life. Due to the arrival of the Yetzer Hara at birth, the Soul is no longer in charge. Instead, it will be exiled to the deepest abysses of man's innards, and the conditions to potentially sully the Soul are thenceforth in place.

Though the Soul *itself* is untainted by these transformations, and for the meantime its purity remains intact, once the Yetzer Hara assumes control it becomes *susceptible* to impurity. Immediately prior to the advent of the Yetzer Hara, the child is exhorted to be a Tzaddik and to safeguard the purity of his Soul. In truth, these two are one and the same:

---

8   See *Targum, Bereishis* 2:7.

- A Tzaddik is someone who successfully maintains the purity of his Soul in the face of the Yetzer Hara's fierce attacks.
- A Rasha is someone who allows his Soul to be rendered impure by his Yetzer Hara.

It is our life's mission to be a Tzaddik by maintaining the purity of our Soul. That is achieved via Torah and Mitzvos, as we shall yet see.

But first, we will attempt to understand what the Yetzer Hara is, how it operates, and how it threatens the purity of the Soul in a devastating and terrifying way. Those important questions are the subject of the five upcoming chapters.

Chapter 2 Takeaways

- During the months of gestation, the child operates as a Soul whose power has yet to be diminished.
- Consequently, the child knows all the Torah that his Soul knows, and is capable of Adam-like spiritual powers.
- With the arrival of the Yetzer Hara at birth, the child's sensory connection to his Soul is severed, and the Yetzer Hara now controls his worldview and perspective.

Know Your Enemy

"The war with the Yetzer Hara." That is the term used in Jewish sources to describe man's engagement with his most formidable foe.[1] The Talmud employs military terminology by comparing the Yetzer Hara to a powerful king who besieges a city with sin.[2] The Mishnah teaches: "Who is truly mighty? He who conquers his Yetzer Hara!"[3]

As in conventional warfare, the stakes of the battle with the Yetzer Hara are life and death. Unlike conventional warfare, it is the eternal Soul, not of the ephemeral body, whose life is at risk. In this war, the Yetzer Hara is the force attempting to infiltrate the Soul, defile its purity, and (effectively) "kill" it. As such, the consequences of losing this war are even more grave than that of a physical war, and its effects linger upon the Soul beyond its stint in this world.

Thinking of the engagement with the Yetzer Hara in a military paradigm helps explain why our Sages dedicated significant attention to detailing its nature and methodologies. To effectively wage war against a skilled enemy, one must study his modi operandi, and with that knowledge devise strategies and tactics to combat and counteract him. It is thus critical to understand precisely how the Yetzer Hara operates.

---

1 See, for example, *Chovos Halevavos, Shaar Yichud Hamaaseh* 5.
2 *Nedarim* 32b.
3 *Avos* 4:1.

It is also imperative to understand how the Yetzer Hara can affect the Soul. Our life instruction is to ward off the Yetzer Hara from breeding impurity into our Soul. What is the interplay between the Soul and its great antagonist, and how could the Soul's purity be impacted?

Multifaceted Enemy

Attempting to identify the precise nature of the Yetzer Hara is tricky because our Sages offer varied and disparate depictions of it. Let us examine a selection of sources classifying the Yetzer Hara and see what we can discover.

The first source is in the text of a post-prayer supplication of one of the Sages of the Talmud. Upon conclusion of the canonized prayer, Rabbi Alexandri would add:

> *Master of the world, it is revealed and known before You that it is our will to fulfill Your will. What inhibits that? The leaven in the bread (Rashi: the Yetzer Hara within us) and our sub-servience to foreign rulers. May it be the will before You that You will save us from them and we will return to do Your will wholeheartedly.*[4]

In this source, the Yetzer Hara is described as "the leaven in the bread." What does the force that compels man to sin and threatens to damage his Soul have to do with the agent that makes dough rise?

Elsewhere in the Talmud, a decidedly different description of the Yetzer Hara is found:

> *Rav Avin said: What is [the meaning of] the verse, "You shall not have within you a foreign god and you shall not bow down to an alien god"?*[5] *Which is the foreign god that exists within the body of a person? Invariably the answer is: the Yetzer Hara.*[6]

---

4   *Berachos* 17a.
5   *Tehillim* 81:10.
6   *Shabbos* 105b.

Here, the Yetzer Hara is portrayed as a foreign god that exists within a person. What does this mean?

There are more sources to consider: The Talmud presents the Yetzer Hara as both a *renewing* force and an *overpowering* force:[7]

> Rabbi Yitzchak said: A person's Yetzer Hara renews itself upon him every day.
>
> Rabbi Shimon Ben Lakish said: A person's Yetzer Hara overpowers him every day.

What are these aspects of the Yetzer Hara?

In the aforementioned debate between Antoninus and Rabbi Yehudah Hanassi regarding when the Yetzer Hara is foisted upon a child,[8] the Talmud describes the Yetzer Hara as causing suicidal impulses:

> Antoninus said to Rabbi [Yehudah Hanassi], "From when [in the development stages of the child] does the Yetzer Hara control the person: from conception or from exit (birth)?" He said to him, "From conception." He responded, "If so, he would kick [the womb of] his mother until he exited; it must be that it is from the exit." Rabbi [Yehudah Hanassi] said, "This matter I studied from Antoninus, and a verse supports him, as it states, 'At the entrance sin crouches.'"[9]

Antoninus argued, and Rabbi Yehudah Hanassi agreed, that had the child in utero been placed under the dominion of the Yetzer Hara, he would kick his way out and be miscarried. This is truly perplexing; the baby in utero has all its needs taken care of, and is blissfully unaware of the world outside the confines of the womb. Why would the presence of the Yetzer Hara compel it to fatally kick its way out to a world that it has not yet experienced?

Amid all these questions, it seems like there is one thing that we know for sure: The Yetzer Hara is a nefarious foe determined to derail our

---

7   *Kiddushin* 30b, *Sukkah* 52a.
8   See Chapter 2.
9   *Sanhedrin* 91b.

lives. Its very name is *"evil"* inclination. Yet even this basic assumption is challenged by the Midrash[10] in its exegesis of the verse, "And God saw all that He did and behold it was exceedingly good"[11]:

> *[What is intended by the words] "and behold it was exceedingly good"? This refers to the Yetzer Hara. Is the Yetzer Hara exceedingly good?! Indeed, for if not for the Yetzer Hara, a man would not build a house, nor marry a woman, nor bear children, nor engage in commerce.*

This throws another monkey wrench into our quest. The Yetzer Hara is labeled as *evil* by God, yet it can also be classified as *exceedingly good* because it propels man to build houses, marry, procreate, and engage in commerce. How can the Yetzer Hara be simultaneously evil and good?

What is particularly confounding is the Midrash's assertion that without the Yetzer Hara, man would not seek to bear children. Without the Yetzer Hara, our Soul would have little resistance in implementing its agenda and pursuing Mitzvos. The first Mitzvah in the Torah is to be fruitful and multiply,[12] yet the Midrash posits that without a Yetzer Hara, we would not seek to bear children. Why not? Our Soul is motivated to do Mitzvos. Why would a Soul free of a Yetzer Hara refrain from the Mitzvah of procreation?

Dynamic Danger

To further complicate our efforts, the sources maintain that the Yetzer Hara is not a static entity; it changes depending on a person's choices. But how precisely it changes is unclear, and indeed the sources, upon initial analysis, appear *contradictory*. One Talmudic source demonstrates that as a person gets ensnared into its traps, the Yetzer Hara *grows and expands*:

---

10   *Bereishis Rabbah* 9:7.
11   *Bereishis* 1:31.
12   Ibid. 1:28.

> *Rav Asi said: The Yetzer Hara is initially comparable to a spi-*
> *der's web, and in the end it is comparable to a thick rope that*
> *fastens an ox to a plow.*[13]

Rashi explains that as a person follows its sinful agenda, the Yetzer Hara gets progressively stronger and larger. It begins as an easily thwarted strand of cobweb rope. Tzaddikim who resist the Yetzer Hara's sinful overtures do not allow it to grow, and thus it remains flimsy and feeble; but the Resha'im capitulate to its seductions and sin, and thereby allow it to balloon into something much larger and more formidable. It would seem therefore that the Yetzer Hara of a Rasha is larger than the one of a Tzaddik.

However, the very same Talmudic page indicates the *exact opposite*—that the Yetzer Hara gets *larger* for the *righteous* and *smaller* for the *wicked*:

> *Rabbi Yehudah taught: In the future, the Holy One, blessed*
> *is He, will bring the Yetzer Hara and slaughter it before the*
> *Tzaddikim and before the Resha'im. To the Tzaddikim, it will*
> *appear as a tall mountain, and to the Resha'im it will appear*
> *as a strand of hair. Both groups will cry. The Tzaddikim will cry*
> *and say, "How were we able to conquer such a tall mountain?";*
> *the Resha'im will cry and say, "How were we unable to conquer*
> *this strand of hair?"*

From this futuristic narrative, it seems that the Yetzer Hara of the Rasha progressively *shrinks* (the Yetzer Hara he sees is a *minimal strand of hair*), but for the Tzaddik it grows larger (to him the Yetzer Hara appears to be a *large mountain*). The notion that the Yetzer Hara of the Tzaddik is larger is reinforced by the Talmud's remarkable statement:

> *Whoever is greater than his friend has a greater Yetzer Hara.*[14]

---

13   *Sukkah* 52a.
14   Ibid.

Again, we see that the Yetzer Hara of the righteous is larger than that of the wicked, in direct contradiction to description that we saw above—that with sin, the Yetzer Hara grows from a spider's web to a thick rope. Which is it? Does the Yetzer Hara expand with righteousness or wickedness? Who has a larger Yetzer Hara, the Tzaddik or the Rasha?

Putting the seeming contradiction in the sources aside for a moment, the mechanism of the Yetzer Hara's change evokes questions of its own: Is it malleable? Does it grow itself? When it shrinks, does a portion of it get lopped off? Does it become denser? How exactly the Yetzer Hara metastasizes is, initially, a great mystery.

All told, the sources have provided a bevy of descriptions of the Yetzer Hara and its methods:

- The leaven in the bread
- A foreign god within a person
- A force that renews each day
- A force that overpowers each day
- A suicidal force that would compel a baby to kick its way out of utero
- A force that is exceedingly good because it spurs man to marry, procreate, build houses, and do business
- Conflicting sources regarding if it expands or contracts for Tzaddikim and Resha'im

Each of these attributes is a piece of the puzzle needed to create a comprehensive assessment of the enemy. We will now attempt to assemble all these sources and offer a clear, cogent, and convincing description of the Yetzer Hara, how it operates, and how it changes.

Chapter 3 Takeaways

- The Yetzer Hara is an enemy that demands military-like planning and execution to defeat.
- Our Sages provide us with a variety of descriptions of the nature of the Yetzer Hara that initially appear to be unclear and even contradictory.

A Yetzer Hara–
Free World

The proper place to start the effort to discover the nature of the Yetzer Hara is the Midrash that states that without a Yetzer Hara, a person would not build a house, engage in commerce, marry, or procreate. That teaching opens for us a window into a world wherein the Yetzer Hara does not exist. By probing how man would operate in that hypothetical world and contrasting it with common behavior in ours, we can isolate the central way that man is affected by the Yetzer Hara.

The Attitudes of an Uncorrupted Soul

Recall that the child in utero knows Torah intuitively because the Soul innately knows Torah, and the Soul is a person's consciousness (the candle is on his head during the months of gestation). In other words, Torah is the natural law of the Soul. An isolated Soul would naturally abide by the Torah's Mitzvos and live by its values *without* instruction. It is only due to the existence of the Yetzer Hara that demotes our Soul and shifts our identity and consciousness to the body that renders the Torah, its Mitzvos, and its values "external" to us. Once under the dominion of the Yetzer Hara, the Soul is viewed as an abstract concept—if its existence is even acknowledged—and its attitudes cease to resonate. But in this hypothetical world wherein man was not subject to the

Yetzer Hara, he would still be dominated by the Soul, and all Mitzvos and Torah values would be natural.

Such a person would innately recognize the primacy of Olam Haba over this world, and would naturally follow Rabbi Yaakov's dictum:

> *This world is like a corridor before the next world; prepare*
> *yourself in the corridor so that you may enter the palace.*[1]

This characterization not only references a world beyond ours, but it also demonstrates a hierarchy of the two worlds. In the Mishnah's perspective, relative to Olam Haba our world is merely a corridor of *preparation*, a path leading to the ultimate destination. Calling Olam Haba "the Afterlife" belies its true value. The term "the Afterlife" suggests that *this world is primary*—it is "life"—and what comes afterwards is only *after* life. In the Mishnah's view, Olam Haba is "life," and our world is but the "pre-life" corridor to get there. With only the Soul informing man's perspectives, the hypothetical person without a Yetzer Hara would accord this world with no absolute value; its only value would be relative to its capacity to prepare a person for Olam Haba.

Such a person would not sin. At the core of the issue, to sin is to opt for the choice that betters man's existence as a body and advances his interests in this world, and to do a Mitzvah is to choose the option desired by the Soul that best optimizes the person for Olam Haba. The Yetzer Hara is the force engineered to urge us to sin and to refrain from Mitzvos. It causes us to identify with our body and thus to pursue its sinful agenda. In the hypothetical world where the Yetzer Hara does not exist, man would innately follow the Soul's preferred behavior as outlined in the comprehensive manual for living as a Soul, the Torah.

It is only due to the Yetzer Hara spinning its fiction that we must be reminded to resist sin in teachings such as the hallowed Mishnah of Akavia Ben Mahalalel:

---

1   *Avos* 4:15.

Visualize three things and you will not sin: Know from where you came, to where you are heading, and before Whom you are destined to give an accounting and a reckoning.

From where you came—from a putrid drop.

To where you are heading—to a place of dust, worms, and maggots.

Before Whom you are destined to give an accounting and a reckoning—before the King of all kings, the Holy One, blessed is He.[2]

Tactics to avoid sinning, such as remembering the shameful origin of our body and our pending reckoning before God, are only needed because we are influenced by the Yetzer Hara. In our hypothetical scenario where man has only the Soul informing his outlook, he would innately find sin revolting. He would have a palpable sense of the futility and preposterousness of embracing as one's identity the body that comes from such lowly and shameful origins (a putrid drop), and eschewing the Soul and its preeminently holy and lofty roots. He would realize that the body is a rapidly depreciating entity that relatively soon will be buried in the ground and decompose. A Yetzer Hara–free and Soul-dominated man would also live with the weight of the future accounting and reckoning before God looming over him. To the Soul, this is patently obvious and self-evident. Behaving in a way that favors the ephemeral body and world over the permanent Soul and Olam Haba would be asinine for a man unaffected by the Yetzer Hara.

Choosing between Two Mitzvos

Without the Yetzer Hara, a person would naturally and effortlessly reject any activity that favors this world, and instead act with singular focus to be best positioned for life in Olam Haba. All decisions would filter through this flowchart: Which of the choices would better prepare me for Olam Haba? Sins would be rejected out of hand and only Mitzvos would be pursued.

---

2   Ibid. 3:1.

But what if there was a choice not between a Mitzvah and a sin but between two different Mitzvos? How would a person who is not affected by the Yetzer Hara decide between the two? It would follow that he would assess the situation in the same way: Which of these two Mitzvos is a *better* candidate to achieve the desired outcome of preparing its doer for Olam Haba? Even with respect to two Mitzvos that both contribute toward advancing the Olam Haba agenda, the preference would be the one that is *best* suited for that purpose.

The Midrash states that without a Yetzer Hara a person would not invest in this world by building a house, engaging in commerce, marrying, or procreating. When the Soul looks at the body, it sees an origin of a putrid drop and a destiny of worms and maggots. If it would be in charge, advancing the body's agenda by building houses and doing business would not register as worthy uses of its time and opportunities.

The Midrash adds further that such a person would not marry or procreate. Though to be fruitful and multiply is indeed a Mitzvah, a man who harbors no influence of the Yetzer Hara would calculate that other Mitzvos are better options. In his view, the Mitzvah to procreate has two drawbacks that make other Mitzvos preferable:

- First, a significant amount of time elapses between the action that precipitates the Mitzvah and the actualization of the Mitzvah itself.
- Second, it is not guaranteed that the action intended to yield the desired results will in fact succeed.

Therefore, if the only metric used to determine which action to choose was a strict and cold assessment of the two options regarding which is likelier to prepare a person for Olam Haba, such a person would choose a Mitzvah that can certainly be achieved and is immediately fulfilled, such as Torah study, and forgo procreation. Thus, without the Yetzer Hara, the sole quest of man would be Olam Haba, and people would not procreate.[3]

---

3   For an example of a Sage who made that calculation, see *Yevamos* 63b regarding Ben Azzai.

How different is this worldview from ours! We are influenced by a Yetzer Hara that weaponizes our body to be used as a vehicle of sin and mutes the perspective of our Soul. It deludes us into ascribing value into this world as an ends instead of as a means. It causes us to see ourselves as a body and to seek its agenda in this world. It transforms the corridor into the destination. The Midrash notes that a certain degree of the Yetzer Hara's influence is "exceedingly good." Thanks to it, we are motivated to build houses, marry, bear children, and do business. The world's continuity hinges upon the Yetzer Hara successfully lobbying man to build an earth-based legacy. But in aggregate, it is a harmful influence because it drives us to sin and to thereby taint our Soul.

This Midrash shows us a sharpened contrast between life with and without a Yetzer Hara. The Yetzer Hara causes a person to ascribe value to this world and to identify as a body, and once cast under its spell, the person becomes likely to sin. That is the overall objective of the enemy; next, we will see the tactics it uses to achieve its goal.

Chapter 4 Takeaways

- A Soul freed from a Yetzer Hara's influences would be single-minded in pursuing Olam Haba to the complete exclusion of any priorities and agenda of this world.
- The essence of the Yetzer Hara is to make us see this world as a "palace" instead of as a "corridor."

Dual Dangers

What tactics does the Yetzer Hara use to distort our sense of reality? How can it delude us into favoring a temporary world while neglecting an eternal world?

Two-Front War

The Gaon of Vilna writes that the Yetzer Hara exists on two planes: There is an *external* and an *internal* Yetzer Hara. This does not mean that there are two distinct entities—a fixed external Yetzer Hara and a fixed internal one; rather, the Yetzer Hara is a single entity of which a portion operates within a person and a portion operates outside of him, the ratio of the two changing constantly. More precisely, the Yetzer Hara contains an *external* aspect operating outside of man that attempts to *initiate* sin, and thereby infiltrate and corrupt his Soul. The *internal* aspect is the *result* of the earlier sin that continues to sabotage the Soul from within.[1] We will now try to explain the nature, interplay, and consequences of these two aspects of the Yetzer Hara.

The external Yetzer Hara operates as an *outside solicitor* for sin. Logic dictates that a person cannot be blamed for actions and circumstances beyond his control. Man cannot be held accountable for simply being *desirous* of sin due to the Yetzer Hara being placed upon him at birth. The mere *inclination* to sin alone is not indicative of a person's failings.

---

1   *Even Sheleimah* 4:19.

Man did not choose to have these impulses and cannot be liable for them. For the external Yetzer Hara, man is truly blameless. Moreover, the external Yetzer Hara is *not part of a person's being*. A person is a fusion of Soul and body, and the external Yetzer Hara is only an external force that is attempting to make inroads into the person.

All this changes when a person sins. As a result of sin, a portion of the Yetzer Hara infects and infiltrates man's Soul (causing the Soul to become impure) and is now part of the *internal* Yetzer Hara. Once that part of the Yetzer Hara transforms from being an *external influence* to being *part of the person's essence*, it is an entirely different beast. No longer does it need to attempt to influence the person as an outsider, but now it is securely ensconced within him and can more easily and effectively impel sin. For the *internal* Yetzer Hara, the person is not blameless. Due to his choices, he welcomed the Yetzer Hara into his being and allowed his Soul to become corrupted.

In subsequent statements, the Talmud classifies these two elements of the Yetzer Hara:

> *Rabbi Yitzchak said: A person's Yetzer Hara renews itself upon him every day.*
>
> *Rabbi Shimon Ben Lakish said: A person's Yetzer Hara overpowers him every day.*[2]

The first statement is referring to the external Yetzer Hara—it is a *renewing* force; and the latter to the internal Yetzer Hara, an *overpowering* force. Let's us examine their properties.

The External Yetzer Hara

The only way that the external Yetzer Hara can entice sin is by changing the world outside of man. Regarding this world, Scripture testifies that, in truth, "there is nothing *new* under the sun."[3] How does the Yetzer Hara tempt a person to indulge in this old and stale world? "Rabbi Yitzchak said: A person's Yetzer Hara *renews* itself upon him every day."

---

2   *Kiddushin* 30b.
3   *Koheles* 1:9.

The power of the *external* Yetzer Hara is that it transforms an old, tired, and boring world and the agenda of the rapidly depreciating body into something shiny and exciting. It injects newness into a world in which there is really nothing new under the sun.

The excitement that the Yetzer Hara injects into this world and the body is comparable to leaven in the dough, the agent that converts "matzah" into "*chametz*." The Soul views this world as a corridor to prepare for Olam Haba. Its *ultimate* objective is the spiritual, eternal world. The physical world is only a means to achieve that. The body and the physical world are thus accorded relative importance because of their capacity to help prepare man for Olam Haba. As vital tools in achieving the ultimate objective, the body and the physical realm must be properly maintained, but they are ascribed no value other than their utility as implements to bring about the ultimate goal.

That attitude is embodied by matzah. It serves no purpose other than providing fuel and nourishment. It has no independent allure. The Soul has a matzah-perspective regarding partaking in this world; it is all but fuel to enable its journey home to Olam Haba. But the Yetzer Hara is the yeast in that dough. It spices up the matzah and converts it into a fluffy and enticing bread. It transforms this world and the body's agenda into an independent platform worthy of being pursued on its own.

If we did not have the Yetzer Hara, all this world's pursuits would have the appeal of matzah: old and stale with the taste of sawdust. Without the Yetzer Hara, we would truly feel like there is "nothing new under the sun." Nothing under the sun would be worthy of our efforts. We would seek and yearn exclusively for spiritual and lasting matters (things that are "above the sun"). Building a house would have zero appeal; engaging in commerce would be unthinkable; and even marrying and procreating would be ignored. Torah and Mitzvos would be the sole objects of our attention. Certainly, we would take steps to ensure that our physical needs are met—otherwise our true goals will be imperiled—but we would minimize those interactions to the bare minimum needed to fuel and energize our journey through the corridor to our destination. We would dutifully and passionlessly "chew the matzah" as needed.

But the Yetzer Hara arrives and injects leaven into the yeast. The person captivated by the allure and pizzazz of this world is liable to neglect the pursuit of the permanent and instead view *this* world as the destination. The proverbial "leavened bread" that the external Yetzer Hara creates inside the corridor tantalizes man and distracts him from his true objective that lies at the end of the corridor.

Artificial Needs

Nutritionally, the matzah and the leavened bread are the same, the only difference being in their respective appeal. If all we needed was fuel for our journey down the corridor, matzah would be sufficient. But the Yetzer Hara convinces us that we *need* the chametz, and thus must pursue it.

Our Sages demonstrate that the agenda supported by the Yetzer Hara is falsely peddled as real needs by commenting:

> *A small organ exists in the person—if he satiates it, it is starved; if he starves it, it is satiated.*[4]

When a *real* need is addressed and fed, the desires subside. The Yetzer Hara creates *artificial* needs that the only way to quell them is to *avoid* fulfilling them. This is the power of the external Yetzer Hara: It *renews every day*, creating illusions that cause us to become entrenched in this world, and thus to sin.

This transformative power is hinted in its very name. The words "*Yatzar*" and "*Barah*" are both used to describe the creation of Genesis. The commentaries note that *Barah* refers to creation *ex nihilo,* something from nothing, and *Yatzar* refers to creation of something from something else. Truthfully, this world is neither new nor exciting, but the Yetzer Hara acts as virtual-reality goggles that create a new, alternative reality that obscures that truth. Seeing the world through the lenses of the external Yetzer Hara shows a world replete with new things under the sun begging to be consumed and embraced. Scripture

---

4   *Sanhedrin* 107a.

labels the Yetzer Hara as a wily king.[5] Its deception is clever, its virtual reality executed flawlessly, and seeing through its nefarious indoctrination is maddeningly difficult.

Once a person willfully drinks the external Yetzer Hara's Kool-Aid, and commits the sin, he is ingesting some of its venom. As a result, a part of the external Yetzer Hara internalizes and embeds itself into his Soul and defiles its purity. This force will continue trying to compel sin, but now, operating from within, it is even more lethal; it is much harder to resist; and it is nearly impossible to extricate. Allowing the Yetzer Hara to migrate internally and cleave to the Soul like a parasite has disastrous consequences.

Chapter 5 Takeaways

- The Yetzer Hara operates on two planes: external and internal.
- The external Yetzer Hara is a force of "renewal" that tries to tempt the person to sin by inflating the value of sin like leaven in the dough.

---

5   *Koheles* 4:13, see *Rashi.*

The Enemy Within

T he very nature of the Yetzer Hara—and consequently the nature of the person's Soul—is altered as a result of sin. With every sin, a portion of the external Yetzer Hara infiltrates and infects the Soul. Regarding this defilement, a child is warned about in the pre-birth instruction ("Safeguard the purity of your Soul!"). The Yetzer Hara changes too. Part of it is now cleaving to the Soul, transforming it from being an *external influence* into being attached to the person's *essence*.

There is an important difference between how the internal and external Yetzer Hara operate. Both of them attempt to instigate sin. However, when it is external, the Yetzer Hara must employ subterfuge to entice a person into desiring something that they do not need and that will ultimately harm them. Once the Yetzer Hara establishes a beachhead in the Soul, its erstwhile fantasies become *actual physiological needs*. With each passing sin, the Yetzer Hara embeds itself deeper and deeper into the Soul, and as it increases its hostile takeover of the Soul, the more basic its needs become.

A Powerless Addict

The Talmud likens this transformation to an addiction that creates a chemical dependency.[1] Prior to the initial exposure to the harmful substance, a person is not dependent at all on the drug. With continued

---

1   See *Avodah Zarah* 17a.

exposure, however, the chemicals progressively alter the person's physiology, and he develops a chemical dependency for the substance. Withholding the addictive substance from the addict cannot be done without disastrous consequences.

That is how the internal Yetzer Hara operates: Once it becomes entrenched into a person's Soul, the actions that it previously advocated for as an outsider become real needs, and the person can suffer terrible withdrawal symptoms without them.[2] Unlike the external Yetzer Hara, the internal variety causes sin not by creating a *desire* that *obscures* the truth; rather, given the new composition of the person's essence, sins become *basic needs*. As is the case by an addict, capitulation to the *internal* Yetzer Hara can happen without temptation and pleasure other than that of addressing a pressing need.

Regarding the *internal* Yetzer Hara, the Talmud remarks:[3]

> *Rabbi Shimon Ben Lakish said: A person's Yetzer Hara overpowers him every day.*

Once the Yetzer Hara infects the Soul from within, it no longer needs the power of "renewal" to make sin appealing. It does not need to puff up sin like the yeast in the dough to generate compliance. Thenceforth, it wields *power* over the person and can compel him to sin out of need.

In the Talmud, this kind of Yetzer Hara is referred to as "a foreign god within a person." The Talmud goes on to demonstrate the transformation of the Yetzer Hara from being an external influence to an internal master:

> *Rabbi Shimon Ben Elazar said in the name of Chilfa Bar Agra, who repeated in the name of Rabbi Yochanan Ben Nuri: Someone who rips his clothing while angered, and one who smashes his vessels while angered, and one who scatters his money while angered should be considered as an idol worshipper. For this is the methodology of the Yetzer Hara: Today he*

---

2   See above Talmud for stories of extreme cases where sin-withdrawal caused death.

3   *Kiddushin* 30b.

> *tells him "do this," and tomorrow he tells him "do that," until*
> *he tells him, "worship idols," and the man goes and worships.*
>
> *Rav Avin said: What is the verse [that sources this idea]? "You*
> *shall not have within you a foreign god, and you shall not bow*
> *down to an alien god."[4] Which is the foreign god that exists*
> *within the body of a person? Invariably the answer is—the*
> *Yetzer Hara.[5]*

Initially, the person who is ripping clothing and smashing vessels is committing self-harm due to anger. This reflects the *external* Yetzer Hara that is capable of deluding someone into the notion that damaging one's own possessions is appropriate due to the circumstances. With each subsequent sin, it increasingly infects the inner sanctums of the Soul and becomes more and more of an *internal* master over the person. The Talmud forecasts that such a person is well on his way to committing idolatry. Ultimately, the Yetzer Hara will have complete mastery over him, and with the escalation of its rogue dominion, it will proceed to demand compliance to commit increasingly severe sins.

This force is appropriately called an internal, foreign god. Under the dominion of the newfound deity, the person will dutifully obey the instruction of the master, and he will sin repeatedly even without temptation. The Yetzer Hara will lord over him, he will become subjugated to it, and enslaved into doing its bidding irrespective of any desire or passion.

With the knowledge of the Yetzer Hara's dual modi operandi, the words of the prayer of Rav Alexandri become ever more meaningful:

> *Master of the world, it is revealed and known before You that*
> *it is our will to fulfill Your will. What inhibits that? The leaven*
> *in the bread and our subservience to foreign rulers. May it be*
> *the will before You that You will save us from them and we will*
> *return to do Your will wholeheartedly.*

---

4   *Tehillim* 81:10.
5   *Shabbos* 105b.

Both inhibitors to fulfilling the will of God wholeheartedly are the Yetzer Hara:

- The "leaven in the bread" refers to the external, renewing variety.
- The "subservience to *foreign rulers*" is the internal, overpowering one—the foreign god within.

Death Grip

This duality of the Yetzer Hara can also explain its suicidal streak. When we began our analysis of the Yetzer Hara several chapters ago, we were bothered by the Talmud's assertion that had the Yetzer Hara existed in utero it would have caused the child to kick his way out notwithstanding the entailed peril.[6] Why would a child who is unaware of the outside world and who has all his needs met try to force its way out? What could possibly motivate this gestational deathwish?

Given our discovery of its dual elements, at every invocation of the term "Yetzer Hara," we must discern if it is referring to the Yetzer Hara in general, the *external* Yetzer Hara that *renews*, or the *internal* Yetzer Hara that *overpowers*. The Talmudic excerpt in question begins:

> *Antoninus said to Rebbi [Rabbi Yehudah Hanassi], "From when [in the development stages of the child] does the Yetzer Hara control the person?"*

The words of our Sages were written with extreme precision. The question was regarding the *internal Yetzer Hara that **controls** its host*. That force does not utilize pursuit of pleasure as motivation, but rather it demands absolute fealty from those subject to its power. That force is the foreign *god*. It loathes the notion of being subject to anyone or anything. The overpowering, internal Yetzer Hara desires control and abhors (and thus resists) being subject to the will of others. To such a force, God and His Torah are anathema. It wants and needs to be in charge and does not want to be told by God how to behave.

---

6   *Sanhedrin* 91b.

How far does the internal, overpowering Yetzer Hara's recalcitrance extend? The Talmud reveals that if this force was present in utero, it would cause the child to fatally force its way out. In the womb, he is totally subject to the will of the mother and dependent upon her for everything. Had the *controlling* Yetzer Hara been present, it would orchestrate a rebellion against her control and kick his way out. The terrifying reality of the internal Yetzer Hara is that it would prefer to maintain its mantle of control over an underdeveloped fetus than to be subject to the will of another, even if that would spell the child's death.

This insight gives new meaning to the teaching in the Talmud:

> *Rabbi Shimon Ben Levi said: The Yetzer Hara of a person overpowers him every day and seeks to kill him…and if not for God helping him, he would not survive.*[7]

This statement need not be understood metaphorically. The internal, *overpowering* Yetzer Hara cannot coexist with any other power, and, left unchecked, it will seek to literally kill the person to unshackle itself from anyone else's control—and end its misery.

Sin as Rebellion against God

With each sin, the ratio of the Yetzer Hara that is internal increases. The internalization of the Yetzer Hara is described in the Talmud:

> *Rav Huna said: Once a person sins and repeats the sin a second time, it becomes permitted. [Asks the Gemara:] Does this really mean that it becomes permitted?! Rather [the intention is that] it becomes for him as if it were permitted.*[8]

There is a dramatic attitude change resulting from repeated sins. Initially, the sins are caused by the desires fomented by the external, renewing Yetzer Hara. During those sins, a person may be aware of the severity of their actions, but they nonetheless submit to the temptation. However, after repeated sins they become "as if permitted." With each

---

7   *Kiddushin* 30b.
8   Ibid. 40a.

ensuing sin, the Yetzer Hara infiltrates the Soul, and once the enemy gets its foot in the door of the Soul, it acts as a foreign god who dictates to the person, and the person obeys even without lustfully desiring the sin. Capitulation to the external Yetzer Hara is bad, but obeying the internal Yetzer Hara amounts to a degree of idolatry. To the degree that the Yetzer Hara is internal, God is removed from our purview. After repeated sins, it is as if permitted, because the person is now heeding the will of the foreign god and obeying his newfound master religiously.

Rambam writes that when calculating a person's sins, God ignores the first two times the person commits a particular sin, and only judges and punishes the sinner from the third sin on.[9] Why is a person afforded such an allowance? Why does the Almighty follow a "three-strikes-you're-out" policy? *Maharsha* links this principle to the teaching of Rav Huna cited above that "after two sins it becomes for him as if permitted."[10] Sins resulting from the internal Yetzer Hara are a far worse betrayal of God than those done under the influence of the external Yetzer Hara. When a person is tempted to sin and loses the battle to his temptations, it is a terrible development, but it does not constitute an act of mutiny against God. The first two sins are caused by the external Yetzer Hara. The person knows that it is forbidden but he, sadly, lost the battle and caved to the (external) Yetzer Hara. In His kindness and benevolence, the Almighty overlooks such sins and forgives him. However, once we sin twice, it becomes as if permitted. Thenceforth it is a sin resulting from the Yetzer Hara overtaking his Soul and, like a foreign god, mandating his behavior. A sin caused by the internal Yetzer Hara is an open rebellion against God and is therefore intolerable unless the person repents and dethrones the foreign god from within.

In the next chapter, we will conclude our assessment of the Yetzer Hara by addressing the yet-unanswered questions regarding the interplay between the external and internal components of the Yetzer Hara, and learning about the frightening consequences of allowing the purity of our Soul to be compromised.

---

9   *Rambam*, Laws of Repentance 3:5.

10   *Yoma* 86b.

Chapter 6 Takeaways

- With each sin, a bit of the external Yetzer Hara infects the Soul and becomes part of the internal Yetzer Hara.
- The internal Yetzer Hara is a force of "overpowering" that compels sin like a foreign god.

903 Ways to Die

Who has a larger Yetzer Hara: the Tzaddik who mostly resists sin, or the Rasha who frequently sins? On the very same page of Talmud, we observed conflicting answers: In one, the Yetzer Hara *grows* with sin and hence it is *larger* for the Rasha:

> Rav Asi said: The Yetzer Hara is initially comparable to a spider's web and in the end is comparable to a thick rope that fastens an ox to a plow.

In the second citation, it is much larger for the Tzaddikim:

> Rabbi Yehudah taught: In the future, the Holy One, blessed is He, will bring the Yetzer Hara and slaughter it before the Tzaddikim and before the Resha'im; to the Tzaddikim, it will appear as a tall mountain; and to the Resha'im, it will appear as a strand of hair.

Further evidence that the Tzaddik has a larger Yetzer Hara is found on that same Talmudic page:

> Whoever is greater than his friend, his Yetzer Hara is larger.[1]

---

1   *Sukkah* 52a.

The Tzaddik's Yetzer Hara vs. the Rasha's

Given our discovery that the Yetzer Hara is not a static entity, but rather operates both inside and outside of a person, we can now reconcile these statements. The relative size of the Yetzer Hara of the Tzaddik and Rasha respectively depends on which aspect of the Yetzer Hara is being addressed. The Tzaddik who resists sin and the consequential invasion of the Yetzer Hara has a greater proportion of his Yetzer Hara that remains external. Internally, his Yetzer Hara is, like the one of a child who has not yet allowed it to infiltrate, is only minimally bound to the Soul as it was at birth—"the Yetzer Hara is initially comparable to a spider's web." Moreover, every Mitzvah and resistance to sin that the Tzaddik does actively evicts the Yetzer Hara outward. Thus, regarding the *external* Yetzer Hara, it is appropriate to declare: "Whoever is greater than his friend, his Yetzer Hara is larger." Externally, his Yetzer Hara is a formidable, seemingly unconquerable mountain; internally, it is only a flimsy strand.

For the Rasha, the opposite is true: For him, too, the internal Yetzer Hara was initially as negligible as a spider's web. Through sin, however, the Rasha allowed the Yetzer Hara to penetrate and infect his Soul, and with each subsequent sin, the Yetzer Hara further embedded itself within him until the internal portion becomes as formidable as a rope that fastens an ox to a plow. Concurrent with the Rasha's Yetzer Hara's *internal expansion* is its *external contraction*. Thus, when the Almighty slaughters the *external* Yetzer Hara (the fate of the internal Yetzer Hara is addressed below), all that is left external for the Rasha is comparable to a feeble strand of hair.

In other words, the Yetzer Hara does not objectively grow or shrink; it simply moves in or out. With each Mitzvah or resistance to sin, a bit of the internal Yetzer Hara uncoils from upon his Soul and slides outwardly, and each sin moves the Yetzer Hara inward. The Yetzer Hara is never totally of the external, renewing variety, nor totally internal: "Rabbi Yitzchak said: 'A person's Yetzer Hara renews itself upon him **every day**.' Rabbi Shimon Ben Lakish said: 'A person's Yetzer Hara overpowers him **every day**.'" We always have a bit of both.

Put simply, the greater the Tzaddik, the more external the Yetzer Hara. With the exception of the select few that actually *eliminated* their

Yetzer Hara, a Tzaddik on the most righteous part of the spectrum will have a Yetzer Hara that is externally comparable to a mountain, and internally to a hair.

For the most wicked Rasha on the spectrum, the distribution will be reversed: The Yetzer Hara will be like an *internal mountain and an external hair*. The struggle of our lives exists in between these two extremes, and the battle lines are always moving. With every Mitzvah and resistance to the Yetzer Hara, we are moving slightly toward the complete Tzaddik and expelling our Yetzer Hara outward, and with every sin we are inviting the Yetzer Hara inward.

Vigor Mortis

The consequences of allowing the Soul to be infiltrated by the Yetzer Hara are manifested at death. The Talmud gives us a fascinating—and downright frightening—portrayal of how the purity level of the Soul affects the harshness of death:

> *Nine hundred and three types of death were created in the world…The harshest one is azkera, the mildest one is neshika.*
>
> *Azkera is like yanking out branches of thorns that are entangled in a clump of wool…Neshika is like pulling a hair out of milk.*[2]

Ostensibly, death is simply the separation of the Soul from the body. All deaths should therefore be uniform. However, here we are told that there are many different types of death, ranging from *azkera* to *neshika*. Why are there different forms of death, and what is the meaning of these strange descriptions (plucking thorns from wool and gliding hair out of milk)?

This Talmudic teaching reveals that death is a bit more complicated than extracting the Soul from the body. The Midrash teaches us that left to its own devices, the Soul needs no coaxing to return to Heaven.[3] Death for it amounts to liberation from bodily confinement. For the Soul, death is the actualization of its wish to return home. In fact, the

---

2   *Berachos* 8a.
3   *Tanchuma, Pekudei* 3.

Midrash informs us that while the child is in utero, the Soul seeks to escape and the Almighty stations two angels to guard against that.

However, after birth, the Midrash notes, the Soul becomes acculturated to this world and will only agree to leave it if it is coerced by angels. What causes the Soul's sudden change in attitude? Why does it need angels to prevent it from escaping back home before birth, and yet after birth it will only go home if forced by angels?

The answer should be obvious: The Soul *itself* does not change at the crossover point of birth; it still wants nothing more than to flee from its misery in the body and go back home to its spiritual place of origin. But at birth, a bit of the Yetzer Hara's venom is implanted into the Soul. It does not necessarily begin to prefer this world over Olam Haba, but it tolerates it enough to not escape. From birth on, there is no need to appoint angels to prevent the Soul from escaping, it is *the internal Yetzer Hara itself that stops that from happening.* To allow the Soul to slip free of the body, the internal Yetzer Hara that is enmeshed within it must first be removed, restoring the Soul to its purity and its homesickness.

When the Talmud notes that there are 903 different types of death, it is not referring to varying degrees of removal of the Soul from the body, rather to the 903 different types of extrication of the internal Yetzer Hara from the Soul to enable the Soul to leave. A critical reading of the Talmud's parable makes it evident that *it is not addressing the removal of the Soul but rather the removal of its contaminants*: In both examples (removing hair from milk and thorns from wool) the *waste* is being removed from the *desired elements.* If the Talmud was referencing the removal of the Soul from the body, the example is inverted: The desired elements ought to be extracted from the waste. Clearly, the aspect of death being referenced is the removal of the Soul's contaminants, and the harshness of that process hinges on the strength of the Yetzer Hara's vise on the Soul at that time.

The Soul of a Tzaddik who resists the efforts of the Yetzer Hara to penetrate its essence looks the same way it did at birth: pure, affording the Yetzer Hara only a minimal, hair-like foothold within it. When the internal Yetzer Hara is removed at death it is as seamless as extracting a strand of hair from a glass of milk.

Not so for the Resha'im. They, too, were given a pure Soul at conception and a Yetzer Hara at birth. Unfortunately, they allowed their Yetzer Hara to infiltrate their Soul and render it impure. As their Yetzer Hara made its way inward, its hair-like bind to their Soul progressively became thicker until eventually it became akin to a thick rope. The Yetzer Hara and Soul became hopelessly entangled as thorns in tufts of wool. Separating the two at death is not pleasant. Flecks of their Soul will get removed along with their thorn-like Yetzer Hara, and little bits of their Yetzer Hara will remain clinging to their Soul, necessitating a post-mortem cleansing. Terrifying indeed.

Spectrum of Righteousness

In telling us that 903 different types of death exist and that the severity of the death is a reflection of the degree that the Yetzer Hara has infiltrated the Soul, our Sages revealed another fundamental insight: Being a Tzaddik or a Rasha is *not binary*. There exists a spectrum with 903 possible levels spanning from a complete Tzaddik whose Yetzer Hara can be removed as easily as slipping a hair out of milk to a complete Rasha whose Yetzer Hara has mangled his Soul like thorns to wool.

Now we can finally understand the caveat of the pre-birth instruction:

> Be a Tzaddik and don't be a Rasha! Although the entire world
> may tell you, "You are a Tzaddik!" you must nevertheless con-
> sider yourself to be a Rasha!

At first glance, this seems to be encouraging us to treat the observations of others with skepticism. However, thanks to our discovery of the many levels of righteousness, the statement can be understood quite simply: Others may claim that you already are a Tzaddik, and their assessment may be accurate on a relative scale, but nevertheless, there are many more levels to aspire toward, and viewing yourself as a Rasha will help you achieve them.

Believing the plaudits of others also leads to complacency that invariably results in regression. Regardless of where along the 903 junctures of righteousness a person may be presently located, unless he consciously resists the Yetzer Hara's attempts to draw him toward sin and impurity, it will gain headway. The Mishnah teaches:

> *Run to [even] minor Mitzvos as you would stringent Mitzvos, and flee from sin.*[4]

The Mishnah is exhorting us to embrace Mitzvos and avoid sin, but the wording indicates that we need to run in pursuit of Mitzvos *because they are fleeing from us*, and we must escape sin, *which is chasing us*. The implication is that we default to sin. As soon as a child is born, sin is crouching, ready to pounce and attack. If he does nothing, the Yetzer Hara will surely infect the Soul and spread within it like a cancerous tumor. Only the paranoid will survive its assault. Unless a person actively and concertedly chooses to resist, he is on the fast track to becoming a Rasha. The assumption of righteousness, regardless of its relative veracity, is therefore harmful.

Gearing Up for Battle

Our analysis of the enemy is now complete. The bevy of Talmudic sources portray the Yetzer Hara as a skillful, multi-faceted, and deadly adversary that seeks to defile man's Soul, and cause him to abandon his Creator in favor of its fraudulent, pitiful rule. Should it succeed, the consequences will be devastating and eternal. The imperative to resist and defeat the Yetzer Hara and thereby preserve the purity of our Soul is now undeniable. Appropriately, when our Sages reveal the ultimate objective of life in the pre-birth instruction, it is oriented around resisting and defeating the Yetzer Hara's attempts to pollute man's Soul and turn him into a Rasha:

> *Be a Tzaddik and don't be a Rasha! Although the entire world may tell you "You are a Tzaddik!" you must nevertheless consider yourself to be a Rasha! You must know that the Holy One, blessed is He, is pure; His angels are pure; and the Soul that He*

---

4   *Avos* 4:2.

placed within you is pure. If you safeguard its purity, good. If not, behold I will take it from you.

The next step is figuring out how to maintain the purity of our Soul. Broadly speaking, the means to accomplish this goal are the 613 Mitzvos. The Midrash flatly states that this is the *sole* purpose of Mitzvos: "Mitzvos were only given in order to purify people."[5]

In Part II, we will probe how Mitzvos act as the battle plans for defeating the Yetzer Hara, and what is the mechanism of the transformation that they engender.

Chapter 7 Takeaways

- With every deed, the Yetzer Hara will move: internally with a sin, and externally with a Mitzvah.
- Death is the process of disentangling the Soul from the Yetzer Hara to facilitate its removal from the body.
- The changing nature of the Soul determines the kind of death that a person has.

---

5   *Vayikra Rabbah* 13:3.

Part II

A Changed Man

*I*n Part I, we learned that the primary mission of man is to preserve the purity of his Soul from the defilement that would result from the Yetzer Hara infiltrating it. Part II is dedicated to understanding how Torah and Mitzvos are the means through which we can counteract the Yetzer Hara and spare the Soul from its venom.

It should come as no surprise that we find Talmudic and Rabbinic teachings that expressly place thwarting the Yetzer Hara as the reason why we were given the Torah and its Mitzvos. For example, the Talmud compares the Yetzer Hara to a fatal disease, and Torah to a medicine for that malady:

> *The Holy One, blessed is He, said to Israel: "My son, I created the Yetzer Hara, and I created the Torah as an antidote. If you engage in Torah you will not succumb to it."*[1]

Just as a medicine has no utility other than to treat the illness, the reason why we were given Torah is to remedy the Yetzer Hara. Elsewhere, the Talmud compares Torah and Mitzvos to tools helping a person navigate a perilous world replete with Yetzer Hara–produced obstacles.[2] Along these lines, *Rambam* comments that the degree of

---

1   *Kiddushin* 30b.
2   *Sotah* 21a.

a person's successful conquest of his Yetzer Hara is the sole indicator of his greatness.[3]

Using the Talmud's analogy of the Yetzer Hara as a disease and Torah as its medicine, in Part I we studied the pathology of the "disease," and now we will study the pharmacology of the "medicine."

Emunah

To begin our immersion into the subject, let us examine several Talmudic and Rabbinic teachings that seem to offer other reasons why we were given Torah and Mitzvos. The first source contends that the overall objective of Mitzvos is to achieve Emunah (commonly translated as "faith"). The Talmud relates that with the decline of the spiritual acuity of the Jewish nation over time, its great leaders in each generation bundled the 613 Mitzvos of the Torah into increasingly smaller lists of core objectives. David pared all 613 down to eleven core principles; some time later, Yeshayah sifted them down to six; Michah into three; and finally the prophet Chavakuk distilled all of Torah into one short verse that encapsulates the objective of all the Mitzvos: "And a Tzaddik lives with Emunah." The Talmud thus canonizes living with Emunah as the end goal of all Mitzvos.[4]

This conclusion is echoed in a critical teaching from *Ramban's* Commentary on the Torah, where he sets out to reveal the purpose of Mitzvos. After a comprehensive treatment of the subject, he concludes:

> *The purpose of all the Mitzvos is that we have Emunah in Hashem our God and recognize that He created us. This is the objective of creation; for we have no other reason for the initial creation, and the Lofty God only desires of lowly man to know and to acknowledge his God Who created him.*[5]

---

3   *Rambam*, Laws of Repentance 7:4.
4   *Makkos* 23b–24a.
5   *Ramban, Shemos* 13:16.

This seems like a new answer to the question of why we have Torah and Mitzvos: Without them man cannot live with Emunah. This raises several questions:

- What is Emunah, why does man not have it initially, and how do Mitzvos engender it?
- Further, the verse from Chavakuk stresses that the end goal is a Tzaddik who *lives* with Emunah. Faith is typically understood as something you *have*, not something you *live with*. What is implied by the word usage of *living* with Emunah?
- Also in need of an explanation is how this coexists with what we have hitherto learned—that Torah and Mitzvos are given to us to ensure the purity of Soul in the face of the venomous Yetzer Hara. Is that the goal or is Emunah the goal?

Loving Your Fellow as Yourself

To complicate the matter further, there is another candidate vying for the mantle of being the goal of Torah and Mitzvos. The Talmud tells of a non-Jew who approached Hillel the Elder and asked to convert, provided that Hillel taught him all of Torah while balancing on one foot. In essence, this potential convert was asking our question: What is the overarching goal of Mitzvos? Hillel responded with a reformulation of the Mitzvah of "You shall love your fellow as yourself,"[6] by saying: "Do not unto others what you do not wish done to you. This is all of Torah, the rest is commentary. Go study!"[7] Here, loving your fellow as yourself is presented as the goal of Torah and Mitzvos. Rabbi Akiva seconds this by exclaiming, "You shall love your fellow as yourself—this is a great principle of Torah."[8]

As with Emunah, we need to properly understand what it means to love your fellow as yourself and how it is the great principle underpinning all of Torah. The Mitzvah itself sounds hyperbolic and impractical:

---

6   *Vayikra* 19:18.
7   *Shabbos* 31a.
8   *Bereishis Rabbah* 24:8; *Yerushalmi, Nedarim* 30b.

- Can we truly love others as we love ourselves?
- Moreover, this seems to contradict the earlier sources claiming that Torah and Mitzvos are ultimately about battling the Yetzer Hara and acquiring Emunah.
- Lastly, how can Emunah and loving your fellow as yourself, themselves listed among the 613 Mitzvos, be considered to be the goal of them all?

A Changed Man

The premise of this book is that *man himself changes* via Torah and Mitzvos. In Part II, we posit that Emunah, loving your fellow as yourself, and conquering the Yetzer Hara are three dimensions of the same holistic transformation:

- Emunah reflects the idealized relationship between man and God.
- Loving your fellow as yourself is the ultimate interpersonal achievement.
- Successful war with the Yetzer Hara is man triumphing over his internal nemesis.

All three are intertwined; each one necessitates the other two, and none are achievable alone. If man fundamentally changes in any of these three domains that would be immediately reflected in the other two. We will begin by laying out the skeletal outline of this transformation. We will then add flesh to the bones by examining how Mitzvos accomplish this transformation, and how Emunah and loving your fellow as yourself fit in.

Chapter 8 Takeaways

- The purpose of Torah and Mitzvos is to counter the Yetzer Hara.
- The Talmud describes various end goals of Torah: resisting the Yetzer Hara, acquiring Emunah, loving your fellow as yourself.
- These three goals are different manifestations of the same holistic transformation that Torah and Mitzvos engender.

CHAPTER 9

Lifeline to God

*I*n a remarkable and profound Midrashic teaching regarding the Mitzvah of tzitzis, which is a microcosm of all 613 Mitzvos,[1] we get a snapshot of life from the Torah's perspective. The Midrash portrays dangers inherent in life, and offers an illustration of the process of how Torah and Mitzvos purify a person and foil the Yetzer Hara's assault on the Soul.

The verse states:

> *And it shall be tzitzis for you, and you shall see it and remember all the Mitzvos of Hashem, and you shall perform them, and you shall not deviate after your hearts and your eyes that lead you astray. So that you remember and perform all My Mitzvos and you shall be holy to your God.*[2]

By looking at his tzitzis, man will remember and perform all the Mitzvos of Hashem and become holy, and thereby mitigate the risk of deviating after his hearts and eyes. How do tzitzis evoke this grand transformation?

---

1   See *Rashi's* comment to *Bamidbar* 15:41.

2   *Bamidbar* 15:39–40.

Saving the Man Overboard

The Midrash offers an analogy:

> [This can be explained with] a parable of a man who was cast into the sea. The captain threw him a rope and said, "Grab this rope and do not release it; if you release it you will die." Similarly, the Holy One, blessed is He, said to Israel, "So long as you cleave to Mitzvos [it will be a fulfillment of the verse], 'And you who cling to Hashem your God, you will have life the entire day.'"[3]

The Midrash's analogy portrays a man tossed from the deck of a ship into a deadly sea, and the strings of the tzitzis are like a life-saving line being thrown to him by the ship's captain. What is the meaning of this analogy?

Before we parse the analogy and deconstruct the worldview that it depicts, it is important to remember that it reflects the Torah's perspective on the conflict of our life, but due to man's current orientation and composition, he is not necessarily inclined to share it.

The analogy is describing man's Soul as a sailor who was previously aboard the ship and in close proximity to the captain (the Almighty), but was cast overboard into the perilous and turbulent sea (i.e., a body in a physical world replete with sins made tantalizing by the Yetzer Hara), and is now distant from the captain and very well may drown (i.e., allow the Yetzer Hara to overwhelm him and kill his Soul). But in his magnanimity, the captain extends the flailing sailor a Divine lifeline of the 613 Mitzvos to save him from death and provide the opportunity to be reeled in and resume being close to God.

Thus, the rope-like tzitzis remind us of *all* the Mitzvos, because they embody the goal of Mitzvos: to be saved from the Yetzer Hara and be brought back to God. The man overboard faces a choice: To grasp the lifeline and save his Soul or to ignore it and drown. This mirrors the two

---

3   *Bamidbar Rabbah* 17:6; verse from *Devarim* 4:4.

options in the pre-birth instruction: Be a Tzaddik by safeguarding the purity of your Soul, or be a Rasha and allow it to become defiled.

This analogy also reveals the diametrically opposite perspectives of how our Soul experiences life and how the Yetzer Hara makes us feel. While harbored in a body, the Soul is out of place and in a state of mortal distress. Like the sailor in the analogy who initially was aboard and adjacent to the captain, *our Soul originates from the world of close proximity to God and has no business being distant from Him.* For the Soul, being placed in this physical world that is replete with sin is like being taken from the safety and security of the ship deck and chucked into a raging, menacing, deadly sea.

The Yetzer Hara makes us think otherwise. While our Soul is thrashing about in fear of drowning, we tend to feel at home and supremely comfortable in this world, and indeed find it quite appealing. To the contrary, the spiritual world of the Soul—the ship deck—is alien and a bit terrifying to us. If we even acknowledge the existence of our Soul and the world from which it originates and desperately seeks to return to, they are theoretical, abstract concepts. The Yetzer Hara's power stems from its ability to distort our reality and delude us into feeling more comfortable amidst what is, for the eternal Soul, a roaring, dangerous sea, than in the safety of the spiritual world—the ship deck—the Soul's homeland.

At birth, the purity of man's Soul comes under assault due to the Yetzer Hara. In the analogy, we begin life being thrown from the ship deck into the proverbial waters. All the conditions that can potentially lead to the Soul drowning are present, and if strong measures are not undertaken that will be the inevitable result, but for the time being the Soul is still alive (pure). The way to avoid that catastrophic result is by seizing the lifeline of Mitzvos. Absent the lifeline, the Soul will surely drown. Man's life mission is to maintain the purity of the Soul—to seize the ropes of the Mitzvos and not relinquish them and be pulled by God close to Him and away from danger.

The Midrash highlights an important insight—that the Almighty plays a crucial role in effectuating this transformation. All the sailor must do is seize the lifeline and not relinquish it, and the captain will rope him in. Our purification through Mitzvos is likewise a partnership between us and the Almighty. We must obey the instruction to cling to the lifeline with all our strength, and He will do the "heavy lifting" to draw us closer.

Salvation and Elevation

This Midrash reveals another dimension of our life's objective. Hitherto, we have presented life's battle in strictly *defensive* terms: The Yetzer Hara seeks to contaminate our Souls and we can prevent that with Torah and Mitzvos. In this Midrash, we discover that Mitzvos are much more than a Divine prophylactic; they yield an incredible benefit in *bringing man closer to his Creator.* Mitzvos are a lifeline that both save man from spiritual devastation and usher him into God's proximity.

If we dig a bit deeper into the subject, it becomes evident that these are not two disparate qualities of Mitzvos. Mitzvos nudge man toward purity, and thus both *preserve* the existing purity of the Soul and *increase* it.

Ramchal explains how man can increase his purity: Man is an animal/angel hybrid. With respect to his body, man is not distinct from animals; the Soul—provided that it is not corrupted—is *spiritually loftier than angels.* An angel and an animal are different things. Which is man? The answer is that at any given time, man is a mix of the two, the ratio of which is determined by his behavior: So long as he is grasping the lifeline, *part of his hitherto body becomes Soul-like* and he pivots up the rope toward God. Mitzvos *preserve* the purity of the Soul and *introduce purity to the body by making it Soul-like.* By seizing the lifeline of Mitzvos, man is chipping away at the soul's would-be antagonist and harmonizing it with the Soul.[4]

A profound insight emerges: *The body and Soul will invariably acclimate and meld into each other; the only question is: In which direction will the change go?* In embracing the lifeline, man converts the physical into spiritual and thereby becomes a Tzaddik. Whoever makes the regrettable decision to release the lifeline is a Rasha. In choosing that unfortunate

---

4   *Ramchal, Daas Tevunos* 70.

option, the Yetzer Hara will have its way and dominate them, and their Soul and body harmonize as well, but in this instance the Soul tragically loses its angelic nature and becomes animalistic and body-like.

This dynamic is comprehensive, zero-sum, and never static. Every decision moves the needle in one direction or the other. If it is an action of the Soul (a Mitzvah) or even if man refrains from an action of the body promoted by the Yetzer Hara (sin), the collective man edges toward purity; his Soul subsumes a portion of his previously mundane body and expands, and as a result he ascends the lifeline and becomes closer to God. The more the Tzaddik purifies his body and converts it to being Soul-like, the more distance he places between himself and the raging Yetzer Hara below, and by extension the closer he gets to God. Of course, the opposite is also true. With each sin, man slips a bit down the lifeline, away from God and closer to eternal death.[5]

Literally Altering Your Physiology

The terms "personal transformation" and "personal change" have become platitudes devoid of meaning, but this understanding demonstrates how Mitzvos *literally* transform a person. The Tzaddik and Rasha are not just *behaviorally* different; they are fundamentally different in their very composition. The "sailor on board" is a pure Soul untethered to a body whose lofty stature exceeds angels, and by dint of that he is close to God. That status is the origin of every Soul, and we yearn to once again return to it. Sadly, those who submit to the Yetzer Hara's demands descend progressively deeper into the abyss of sin, thereby defiling their Soul and distancing themselves from God, perhaps even rendering their Soul beyond repair.

We begin life between these two poles. We are a *drowning*—but not yet *drowned*—sailor. Our Soul is implanted in a body and we are enticed by the Yetzer Hara to commit Soulicide-by-sin—but it has not yet done so. Depending upon whether and how he seizes the lifeline, man is,

---

5   This dynamic is the same as the one described in Part I regarding the Yetzer Hara shifting internally or externally as a result of man's behavior, only that here it is presented from the perspective of the Soul and there from the perspective of the Yetzer Hara.

at every point in life, somewhere along this spectrum spanning these two extremes.

The premise of Torah and Mitzvos is that the drowning sailor can once again get aboard and resume being close to God. The Soul *can* return home. It is possible to purify the body and once again exist entirely as a Soul. This personal transformation, changing not only *who we are*, but changing *what we are*—converting a portion of our body into being like our Soul—is enabled by Torah and Mitzvos.

Ramchal advises a person seeking character perfection to engage in self-contemplation for a minimum of an hour a day.[6] As a tactic, *Ramchal* suggests asking oneself probing questions, and lists several sample questions including, "what are you?" A man pondering *what* he is makes sense if he can be different things. Man can revert back to being a pure, uncorrupted Soul that is loftier than angels, and that same man can descend to being a total animal, all body bereft of Soul. Mitzvos are the actions that literally change the composition of man from being animalistic to angelic and thereby prevent man from drowning and usher him toward closeness to God. Next, we will try to probe how exactly this transformation works.

Chapter 9 Takeaways

- The Soul of man originally was like a sailor aboard a ship in close proximity to the captain (God).
- At birth, the Soul is thrown into the dangerous waters of this world, and without intervention it would drown in the sea of sin.
- Mitzvos are akin to a lifeline thrown to the imperiled sailor by the captain.
- Man's identity as a Soul and body is dynamic: with sins, the Soul becomes more body-like, and with Mitzvos, the body becomes more Soul-like.

---

6   *Derech Eitz Chaim.*

CHAPTER 10

Miracle Drugs and Superfoods

*I*n the previous chapter, we discovered a foundational insight: Man is a fusion of polar opposites—an animalistic body and an angelic Soul—that are temporarily bound in this world by Divine decree. Though man is a hybrid of the two, the ratio of body to Soul in the makeup of his overall composition is in constant flux, depending upon his choices:

- Mitzvos purify man by making him more Soul-like and less body-like, and consequently he ascends the lifeline away from the Yetzer Hara and closer to God.
- The Yetzer Hara seeks to steer us in the opposite direction—infiltrating the Soul and making it body-like and consequently drowning the Soul in the "waters of sin" and pushing it further away from God.

Spiritual Replica

What is still unexplained is the notion of man's pliable identity. What does it mean that man can exist as a body or as a Soul and everywhere in between? Also, we need to understand the relationship between that identity and both Mitzvos and sins, and the dynamics of the transformation of Mitzvos.

To begin, let us examine an intriguing overlap between Mitzvos and man. The Talmud calculates that the Torah contains 613 Mitzvos, 248 positive commandments, and 365 negative commandments.[1] These numbers are not coincidental: The 248 positive Mitzvos correspond to the 248 limbs of man, and the 365 negative Mitzvos correspond to the days of the year. The *Zohar* adds another wrinkle, writing that the 365 negative Mitzvos also correlate to man's makeup in that they parallel the 365 sinews that support and bind the limbs together.[2]

An interesting picture emerges: The human body consisting of 613 parts, 248 limbs and 365 sinews, and, correspondingly, 613 Mitzvos, 248 positive and 365 negative. That each Mitzvah is connected to a corresponding limb or sinew should come as no surprise. If Mitzvos are the tools to change man's identity from being a body to being a Soul, it would seem appropriate that the tools fit whatever it is that they must fix.

This dynamic extends a step further. It is not only the human *body* that parallels Mitzvos, the sources maintain that the Soul is also composed of 248 *spiritual* limbs and 365 *spiritual* sinews.[3] Man's body is akin to a fleshy garment that temporarily enshrouds the Soul, and must therefore be tailored to clothe the Soul encased within it. The body has 248 limbs and 365 sinews *specifically because* the Soul that permeates it is comprised of 248 spiritual limbs and 365 spiritual sinews.[4]

The principle that our body is made compatible with our Soul and not vice versa may strike us as odd. Thanks to the Yetzer Hara shaping our default mindset, we tend to view our body as our essence, and the existence of a Soul within our body as an ancillary aspect of being human. Instead of recognizing that the body is merely a garment for the Soul, we erroneously treat the Soul as an accessory to our body. In the Torah's perspective, a body is merely a vessel that holds the Soul during its temporary sojourn in this world.

---

1   *Makkos* 23b.
2   *Zohar, Vayishlach* 170b.
3   *Reishis Chochmah, Shaar Hayirah, Shaarei Kedushah* 1:1.
4   See also *Berachos* 10b.

Regardless of whether the body services the Soul or vice versa, this revelation that the Soul architecturally mirrors the body and the 613 Mitzvos sheds light on the transformation of identity that Mitzvos can bring about: The Soul has 613 parts; the body has 613 parts, and there are 613 Mitzvos. But what is *man*? What comprises *his* identity? Does he have 1226 (613+613) parts? The answer is that man too has 613 parts, no more no less, but the nature of those 613 parts is changeable. The Torah contains 613 Mitzvos because each Mitzvah affords an opportunity to convert one aspect of our identity from being body-like to Soul-like. The lifeline of Mitzvos is really 613 ropes that combined together shift the entirety of our identity from being contained in the 613 parts of the body to the 613 parts of the Soul. Over the course of life, using the power of the 613 Mitzvos, we can reinvent our identity to begin seeing the body as a mere vessel that hosts us for our journey back to Olam Haba.

Eternal Nourishment

How do Mitzvos engender this transformation? Several sources liken Mitzvos to food for the Soul.[5] Both body and Soul are living organisms that need sustenance and nourishment or else they will wilt and die. A body needs oxygen, food, and water at regular intervals in order to not perish. The Soul also needs various forms of nourishment or else it will weaken and die. Unlike physical bodies that are fed using physical means, spiritual Souls can only be nurtured via spiritual sustenance, namely the Mitzvos.

A Mitzvah is vital sustenance for our Soul in the exact way that physical food is for our body. We do not eat breakfast begrudgingly as if it is a burden, or ritualistically because of Divine mandate; we recognize that *we* need it for our own benefit. Mitzvos are exactly the same. They, too, are necessary nourishment for our Soul. On a more granular level, each of the 613 parts of the Soul are nourished by its corresponding Mitzvah.[6]

---

5   *Nefesh Hachaim* 4:29; *Shaarei Kedushah* 1:1.
6   See *Maharsha, Makkos* 24a, who writes that the heart corresponds to the Mitzvah of

The only problem is that, by default, we do not *feel* the hunger of our Soul. When we go twenty hours without physical food, our stomach grumbles and we are cranky until fed. But our physical senses don't register the hunger of our Soul. A person can go a lifetime without Mitzvos and feel no existential lacking. The reason is that we start off life under the influence of the Yetzer Hara and therefore identify entirely as a body and feel only its senses and instincts. The Soul and its agenda do not register in a visceral way. Our Soul is starving but we feel nothing! And even when we do a Mitzvah, it often feels awkward and out of character. Mitzvos are acts of the Soul that *do not resonate with the body*. Mitzvos are critical nourishment that the Soul depends upon, but man, by default, is not interested in them and does not realize their value and necessity. How can man overcome this obstacle?

Prescriptions of Purity

There is another dimension of Mitzvos that helps man break out of this cycle. Scripture states:

Emunah: just as the heart pumps blood that nourishes all the limbs and organs, Emunah pumps spiritual lifeblood into all aspects of our Soul. As a general rule, though, we were not given a definitive guide as to which Mitzvah corresponds to which limb; see *Avos* 2:1.

What about the Mitzvos that we are incapable of fulfilling, like sacrifices and laws related to agriculture in Israel, laws pertinent to only men or women or Kohanim or kings etc.? How do we nourish those spiritual limbs? The Talmud (*Menachos* 100b) teaches that if you study the Torah related to sacrifices, it is considered as if you actually offered a sacrifice and that particular limb is strengthened. Study of the Torah portions related to a given Mitzvah achieves the same end as performance of that particular Mitzvah and thereby we can fill in all the gaps.

More broadly, see *Nefesh Hachaim* 4:29, who writes that Torah study is a panacea for all limbs. Every individual Mitzvah feeds its parallel organ or sinew. The Mishnah (*Peah* 1:1) teaches that Torah study is equal to all the Mitzvos. Torah study is a multivitamin that sustains all organs and sinews. References to the cure-all properties of Torah study are found throughout the Talmud. "There is no bread but Torah" (*Tanna D'bei Eliyahu Rabbah* 25); "there is no water but Torah" (*Bava Kamma* 17a); "Torah is akin to oxygen" (*Berachos* 61b); "Torah is an elixir of life for the meritorious" (*Yoma* 72b). Perhaps this is the reason why someone who is engaged in Torah study is absolved from all other Mitzvos (*Rambam, Ishus* 15:2). It would be unwise for someone to forgo an activity that sustains the entirety of his spiritual self in favor of a Mitzvah that addressed the needs of one aspect alone.

And he said, "If you will truly listen to the voice of Hashem
your God, and you will do what is just in His eyes, and you will
hearken to His Mitzvos, and you will guard all His laws, all the
illness that I placed upon Egypt I will not place upon you for
I am Hashem, your Healer."[7]

Here, Mitzvos are portrayed as medicines for illnesses, both curative
and preventative.[8] This seems to contradict the earlier assertion that
Mitzvos are spiritual food. Everyone needs food, but medicine is only
used to treat the sick. Are Mitzvos food or medicine?

There is a subtlety in the answer: Mitzvos are miracle drugs that
heal *man,* and superfoods that nourish his *Soul.* By default, man is
unwell due to his identification with the ephemeral body—the Soul's
garment—while neglecting the permanent Soul itself. A symptom of
the sickness is the lack of an appetite for the needs of the Soul, causing
him to harm his Soul by not nurturing and sustaining it, and thereby
jeopardizing its wellbeing. This illness permeates his entire existence;
each of his 613 parts of identity needs to be healed.

To that end, the greatest Physician gave us a detailed prescription
of 613 different supplements, vitamins, and medicines to treat and
heal each aspect of our existence. He knows that our Soul is starving
for Mitzvos, and in His kindness instructed us to force-feed ourselves
Mitzvos, even though we do not initially have an appetite or a desire for
them. By following the Doctor's orders, we can strengthen our Soul and
regain our appetite for spiritual food.

The Virtuous Cycle of Mitzvos

At the beginning of his foray into the world of Mitzvos, man is not
inclined to desire them at all. This is the illness that plagues all of
mankind by default due to the Yetzer Hara's absurd notion that man's
body is his essence and true identity. Under the Yetzer Hara's influence,
man neither connects to his Soul instinctively nor senses its needs. This

---

7   *Shemos* 15:26.
8   See *Rashi* ad loc.

results in a vicious cycle by which man continually ignores "feeding" the Soul with Mitzvos, which in turn exacerbates the illness by further weakening its influence, which makes him even less inclined to feed it. The negative effects of the illness and starving the Soul compound upon each other, and man gradually drifts away from God, and deeper into the sea of sin of the Yetzer Hara, bringing his Soul closer and closer to death.

But something dramatic happens when the Soul is fed. It is empowered and its place in a person's identity is augmented, and concurrently the Yetzer Hara's influence is weakened. A virtuous cycle results wherein one Mitzvah makes the second Mitzvah more likely. Initially, the Mitzvos need to be force-fed—like feeding a sickly patient who refuses food. The earlier Mitzvos create a medicine-like transformation because by feeding the Soul, it captures a larger share of his identity and its needs become a bit more instinctual, leading man to naturally desire more Mitzvos and be drawn to them with magnetic attraction.

In his magisterial commentary, Rabbeinu Yonah features this insight to explain a strange property of Mitzvos found in *Avos*:

> *Ben Azzai says: Run toward a minor Mitzvah as you would a stringent Mitzvah, and flee from sin, because a Mitzvah begets another Mitzvah, and a sin begets another sin; for the reward of a Mitzvah is [another] Mitzvah, and the reward of a sin is [another] sin.*[9]

Every Mitzvah *begets* another Mitzvah, and the *reward* for every Mitzvah is another one. Both statements inform of the principle that Mitzvos lead to Mitzvos, and saying it twice seems redundant.

Rabbeinu Yonah explains that indeed Mitzvah A leads to Mitzvah B in two different ways—one natural and one supernatural. As *reward* for one Mitzvah, the Almighty supernaturally enables another one, as the Talmud teaches, "He who seeks purity we will helped [from Above]."[10] When it states that a Mitzvah *begets* a Mitzvah, that is not supernatural

---

9   *Avos* 4:2.

10   *Yoma* 38b.

at all; rather, a Mitzvah spurs another in its wake because the first Mitzvah makes the person more of a Soul, who is *naturally more inclined to desire the second Mitzvah.*

The opposite goes for sins: The sin is favoring the Yetzer Hara and reinforcing its fiction that the body is an end unto its own. That weakens the influence of the Soul within him, and, due to that internal change, the second sin is more naturally desirous.

Preparing Your Spiritual Being for the Spiritual World

The effect of Mitzvos on the health of the Soul has eternal consequences. The Talmud makes two puzzling pronouncements regarding Tzaddikim and Resha'im:

> *Tzaddikim are deemed alive even when dead...Resha'im are deemed dead even when alive.*[11]

At face value, the teachings are self-contradictory. If it is acknowledged that someone is alive, how they can be considered dead, and vice versa?

The answer is that this teaching is referring to the health of their respective *Souls*. While living in our current configuration—i.e., a Soul wrapped inside a garment-like body—a raging conflict exists: Will man identify as a Soul and feed it Mitzvos, or will he identify as a body and starve the Soul and allow it to shrivel and die? When a person dies, the proverbial garment enshrouding their Soul is stripped away. Thenceforth no conflict exists; only the Soul remains. The condition of the Soul at that juncture, however, depends upon whether the person fed it adequately with Mitzvos during his lifetime. Thus, declares the Talmud, the Tzaddikim who properly nurtured their Soul with Mitzvos are still alive, even after their Soul is extracted from their body. By contrast, the Resha'im allowed their Soul to die by chronic malnourishment and neglect. For them, even while they are alive in body, they are truly deemed dead, because their Soul is dead within them.

---

11   *Berachos* 18a–b.

The recognition that Mitzvos correspond to the 613 parts of man's spiritual persona also explains their variability. Some of the body's physical limbs and sinews are more vital for life than others. A body lacking a heart, brain, or liver cannot function at all, whereas if it was missing a toe it can live with relatively minimal disruption. This hierarchy is true on the spiritual side as well. There are Mitzvos that if a person were to, God forbid, refrain from their observance, their Soul cannot live at all. These Mitzvos are categorized as ones that are punishable by *kareis* (spiritual death) and by losing Olam Haba, meaning that without them the Soul is incapable of maintaining spiritual life. Other transgressions are less severe and will not imperil their spiritual lives entirely, and only render them a spiritual cripple.

This revelation that Mitzvos are responsible for the health and well-being of our Soul for eternity should serve as a clarion call for embracing *all* the Mitzvos, and seeking ways to perform them in their highest and best manner. My grandfather would explain the aforementioned Mishnah that teaches us to run in pursuit of even a minor Mitzvah in accordance with this principle: While it is true that we do not need five toes on each foot to survive and live in this world, we would not be inclined to volunteer to part with any one of them or even agree to have one of our fingernails pried off. Merely thinking about that makes us wince. Man views his body as more than an assortment of disjointed limbs; it is a single, indivisible unit that is *him*, and he is unwilling to compromise on even the relatively minor parts of himself. That is precisely why we must pursue even the minor Mitzvos. Even a minor Mitzvah is precious because it nurtures one of the spiritual limbs that is part of the greater whole that is us. We must therefore cherish every Mitzvah and passionately pursue them in the same manner that we cherish and care for even the more minor parts of our physical selves.

Extending this principle further demonstrates the value and importance of perfecting the Mitzvos themselves. A physical limb can have impaired functionality and operate at suboptimal performance levels. So too our spiritual halves. It is possible for a spiritual limb to exist but work suboptimally. The *quality* of the Mitzvah that empowers it determines the operational vitality of each spiritual limb. Righteous motivations and a greater degree of difficulty raise the quality of the spiritual limbs that the Mitzvos spawn.

In short, via observance of the 613 Mitzvos, man can infuse life into his 613 spiritual parts, and thereby gradually identify as a Soul in lieu of his body, and in opposition to the will of the Yetzer Hara. This concept is succinctly expressed in the verse:

> *You shall guard My statutes and My laws that a man performs and through them he lives, I am Hashem.*[12]

When the prophet Chavakuk sought to distill the goal of Torah and its Mitzvos into one verse, he couched it in terms of Emunah: "And a Tzaddik lives with Emunah." From what we have seen thus far, the Mitzvos are the food and medicine needed to transform man into being Soul-like. What exactly is Emunah and how does it relate to man being Soul-like? That question is the subject of the three upcoming chapters.

Chapter 10 Takeaways

- The 613 Mitzvos are perfectly correlated to man's identity: Man's body and Soul are each comprised of 613 parts.
- Each Mitzvah transforms one part of man from being a body to being a Soul.
- Mitzvos are nourishment for the Soul that empower it and create a medicine-like transformation of man's identity.
- The health of man's Soul depends upon how well it is fed and maintained with Mitzvos, the consequences of which become noticeable only after the Soul is removed from the body.

12 *Vayikra* 18:5.

The Two Realms
of Emunah

*T*he prophet Chavakuk distilled the goal of all of Torah into a short verse: "And a Tzaddik lives with Emunah." Establishing Emunah as the end goal of the Torah and its Mitzvos raises several questions: First, in his enumeration of Mitzvos, *Rambam* counts only three Mitzvos that are directly related to Emunah:

1. Know that Hashem exists.
2. Do not entertain the possibility that He does not exist.
3. Do not worship other gods.

While there are many others that are tangentially associated with Emunah, for instance, the many laws pertaining to idolatry, it seems like a stretch to suggest that *all* 613 Mitzvos relate to Emunah.

Moreover, this suggests that to achieve Emunah, all 613 Mitzvos are necessary. If 612 of them, or for that matter 213, were enough to gain Emunah, the remainder would be superfluous. Every single Mitzvah on its own relates to Emunah, yet, all 613 are necessary. In common parlance, a person is either a believer or not. Ostensibly, once Emunah is gained, the person completed that task and can proceed to other pursuits.

From these sources, it is apparent that many levels of Emunah exist. What is Emunah, what are its various levels, how are they achieved, and what is the relationship between Emunah and man identifying as a Soul?

Complete Emunah vs. Limited Emunah

Let us begin by analyzing Emunah in general. Our Sages assign the label, "a person of limited Emunah," to several people. The first is Noach. According to our Sages, he spent many decades building the Ark, an enormous boat that had no utility aside from being a refuge from the pending Flood that God foretold. If Emunah was simply about "believing in God," Noach's decades-long commitment to fulfilling the Almighty's instruction should quiet all doubts regarding his Emunah credentials. To the contrary, Noach ought to be a paragon of unflapping, resolute Emunah! Yet, the sources cast aspersions on it. The verse tells that God instructed him to enter the Ark,[1] but when he actually entered it was "because of the waters of the flood."[2] *Rashi* quotes our Sages' criticism of Noach's conduct:

> *Noach, too, was of limited Emunah. He believed—but he did not fully believe—that the Flood will come, and he only entered the Ark when he was compelled to by the waters.*

How can Noach, a prophet who dedicated a lifetime working on a project solely due to his belief in God, be characterized as a "man of limited Emunah"?

A second person characterized as having "limited Emunah" is found in the Talmud. That citation is based upon a Mishnah that lists the spiritual downgrades that resulted from the destruction of the Temple. Among the negative developments is that "men of Emunah ceased." What constitutes a "man of Emunah"? The Talmud explains:

> *Rabbi Yitzchak said: This refers to people who believe (have Emunah) in the Holy One, blessed is He, as it states in a Beraisa, "Rabbi Eliezer the Great says: Whoever has bread in his basket and says, 'What will I eat tomorrow?' is a man of limited Emunah."*[3]

---

1   *Bereishis* 7:1.
2   Ibid. 7:7.
3   *Sotah* 48b.

Notice the metric for determining if someone has complete Emunah: if the person has bread for today but not tomorrow, he is unfazed and does not worry, "What will I eat tomorrow?" Merely *wondering* what he will eat tomorrow demonstrates that his Emunah is limited.

Had Noach been a man of complete Emunah, he would have entered the Ark immediately when instructed to by God, irrespective of the rising waters. Also, a man of complete Emunah would be so confident that God will provide tomorrow's food, despite having no concrete plans of how to obtain it, that he would not even consider the matter. We need to understand these classifications of complete Emunah and limited Emunah.

Finally, we have to probe the Talmud's curious comparison between Emunah and agriculture. The Talmud connects the six words from the verse in *Yeshayah*—"And it shall be the Emunah of your times, the strength of salvation, wisdom and knowledge, the fear of Hashem is his treasure"[4]—to the six Orders of the Mishnah.[5] The word "Emunah" is compared to *Seder Zera'im*, the section of Mishnah relating to agricultural law. *Tosafos* cites the *Yerushalmi* that explains the connection: "A farmer has Emunah in the Almighty and plants." Our Sages scoured all the world's professions and found that farming is the one that most embodies Emunah. Why is the farmer the quintessential person of Emunah? Is it not possible for a farmer to be an atheist? Perhaps a soldier in the foxhole whose life hangs on a thread, or someone who is immersed in the spiritual world, like an assiduous Torah scholar, would be a more appropriate archetype of Emunah?! Yet, the Talmud sees the planting farmer as the epitome of Emunah.

What is the connection between agricultural work and Emunah?

Intellectual Emunah vs. Instinctive Emunah

It seems that Emunah exists on two fronts. The basic Emunah is cognitive acceptance of the notion that the Almighty exists, everything is dependent upon Him, He is not dependent on anything else, and that

---

4   *Yeshayahu* 33:6.
5   *Shabbos* 31a.

He created, continually sustains, and supervises the world. This is an abstract idea that resides in man's intellectual spheres. We can call this "intellectual Emunah."

To be clear, though we may describe this level of Emunah as "basic," that is not to imply that it is *easy* to achieve. By dint of innate human nature, we face an uphill battle in developing *any* sort of relationship with our Creator. Our physical senses—the default tools that we use to interface with the world—are incapable of relating to God. "God sees but is unseen."[6] Humans are physically incapable of conceptualizing God on a sensory level. Worse yet, the absence of God from our physical purview tolerates doubts to His existence. To believe in God, we have to accept an invisible reality that we cannot interact with sensorially, and whose essence we can never quite fully grasp. Indeed, simply establishing faith in God in our minds is a challenge.

Still, mere cognitive acceptance of this invisible fact is only the beginning of the Emunah process; the end objective is for Emunah to become an *instinctive* reality. While indeed the body's instincts are precluded from Emunah—and so long as man considers it his essence, instinctive Emunah is impossible—through Mitzvos he can shift his identity from body to Soul and by extension upgrade his instincts from bodily, animalistic ones to the angelic instincts of the Soul. That would restore the Soul (the candle of God) to its primacy atop his consciousness and become the de facto interface with the world, thus transforming him into a Tzaddik who *lives* with Emunah.

Such Emunah is not an isolated intellectual, theoretical affirmation; rather, it governs his entire mindset and outlook. His thoughts, speech and behavior, pursuits, priorities, and agenda would all be shaped by Emunah. The basic, intellectual Emunah is not negligible or insignificant, but it's also just the first step. Once Emunah is firmly ensconced in the mind, the next step is for it to be drawn into *life*. This advanced Emunah that permeates the person's reality—instinctive Emunah—is the goal of all Mitzvos.

---

6   *Berachos* 10a.

Emunah and Cognitive Dissonance

A lot can go wrong if Emunah remains in the mind alone. The Talmud shares an astonishing perspective on why some Jews in antiquity worshipped pagan idols:

> *Rav Yehuda said in the name of Rav: The Jews always knew that idolatry had no substance, and they only worshipped idolatry to permit for themselves illicit immorality in public.*[7]

When the Jews of yesteryear were prostrating themselves before figurines of wood and stone, it was not based on a theological conviction of the truth of those deities, but rather was employed as a means to permit promiscuity.

This assertion seems strange. What is the connection between their desire to engage in immorality and their decision to adopt idolatry? *Rashi* explains that their *underlying* motivation was lust for licentiousness, but such activities are incompatible with a professed belief in God and Torah. Thus, the only way to achieve their true objective was to adopt alternatives, namely idolatry.

Choosing to have Emunah or to follow the foreign gods is not a decision that occurs in a vacuum. The Talmud acknowledges that if the sole factor was theological or intellectual, the Jews of yore would not have embraced idolatry, and instead would have remained faithful to the Emunah of their ancestors. It was only because of the cognitive dissonance stemming from their intellectual Emunah clashing with their promiscuous proclivities that caused them to abandon their Emunah.

This demonstrates the deficiency of cognitive Emunah alone. If the rest of the person's self, their behavior and outlook—i.e., their *life*—are not aligned with the Emunah of their head, it is subject to being upended and supplanted by whatever their behaviors and desires compel them. Beliefs not anchored by behaviors are notoriously fickle.

The Jewish idolaters initially had intellectual Emunah but ultimately rejected God as a means to permit promiscuity. The best way to remedy

---

7   *Sanhedrin* 63b.

their heresy would be to address the core of the problem—their Yetzer Hara that propelled them to promiscuity. By dismantling their Yetzer Hara for promiscuity, the heresy that had previously hinged upon it will immediately collapse, and the advanced instinctive Emunah—when the intellectual Emunah is unopposed by any conflicting behavior or perspectives—would result.

Emunah and the Soul

The verse, "A Tzaddik **lives** with Emunah," refers to the *advanced,* instinctive Emunah, where what began as an abstract, intellectual precept now permeates every aspect of his life. A Tzaddik does not suffice with rudimentary, intellectual Emunah, but *lives* and behaves with instinctive Emunah. Such a person has evicted the Yetzer Hara's foreign rule from within him and has reinstated the Almighty as his sole internal Power. The rudimentary Emunah of the mind is indeed much easier to fulfill; *Rambam* counts only three distinct Mitzvos related to it. Translating that into instinctive Emunah is the objective of Mitzvos in general.

In the previous chapters, we learned how Mitzvos transform man's identity into being Soul-like, and here we see that they convert theoretical Emunah into instinctive Emunah. These are two sides of one coin: *Emunah is the instinct of the Soul.* The Soul is called the "flame of God"[8] and the "candle of God."[9] Instinctively, without being tinkered with, calibrated or programmed, the Soul is a fiery torch of Emunah. The senses of the *body* are engineered to repudiate Emunah, but like the analogy of the sailor aboard the ship who knows the captain and relies upon him totally, the senses of the Soul harbor Emunah instinctively. If you were to isolate the Soul without any other inhibiting factors, total Emunah would be the reality that governs it.

The Soul's instinctive Emunah is displayed in the pre-birth narrative cited in the *Midrash Tanchuma* (*Pekudei* 3): God instructs an angel to extract a certain Soul from the Heavenly chamber of Souls, and when the Soul is ushered before Him, it immediately kneels and bows before

---

8   *Shir Hashirim* 8:6.
9   *Mishlei* 20:27.

the Almighty in total submission. *Without instruction*, the Soul knows to submit itself before God. In the same way that it innately knows Torah, the Soul before the introduction of the Yetzer Hara instinctively operates with Emunah. A Tzaddik who lives with Emunah is not creating a new identity that has hitherto not existed; a Tzaddik is someone who fulfilled the pre-birth instruction to preserve the purity of the Soul and eliminate the influence of the Yetzer Hara, and thereby restored the Soul's prominence and its latent Emunah to the way it was before the introduction of its adversaries.

The only way for a man to *live* with Emunah is by transforming himself into being more Soul-like and thereby shifting his perspective and instincts to those of the Soul. Mitzvos convert man into a person who identifies as his Soul, and a man who *lives* with Emunah is a man who now sees the world through Soulful lenses.

Chapter 11 Takeaways

- There are two types of Emunah: intellectual Emunah and instinctive Emunah.
- Instinctive Emunah is when the person sees the world as his Soul does and lives accordingly.
- The goal of Torah is to have instinctive Emunah.

Faith of the Farmer

an's identity can fall anywhere between being a totally pure Soul whose stature is loftier than angels (if he observes all 613 Mitzvos perfectly), and being someone whose Soul was destroyed and has become spiritually indistinguishable from an animal (if he capitulates to the Yetzer Hara and neglects all 613 Mitzvos). Mirroring the fluctuations of man's body-to-Soul ratio are the changes in his mindset: In every area of life, the body and the Soul—man's inherent angel and beast—see things differently. Their outlook, interests, aspirations, concerns, and instincts are different, and frankly, opposing. The Tzaddik who progresses toward becoming more Soul-like will begin to use his Soul to interface with the world and begin to exhibit the Soul's attitudes. With each Mitzvah, he becomes more like an angel and less like an animal, and everything in his world adjusts to his new identity. He will begin to *naturally* desire Mitzvos, and indeed lose interest in earth-based pleasures,[1] and his priorities and values will move to be in line with those of his Soul. This person is well on his way to become a Tzaddik who *lives* with Emunah.

---

1   *Rambam*, commentary on Mishnah, *Sanhedrin*, chap. 10, likens this to a king that is no longer desirous of playing with a ball as he was accustomed to in his youth.

The Vehicle of Life

The conflict of the Yetzer Hara and Soul jockeying for control of man's identity is comparable to a ride in a vehicle with two potential drivers, each with a different destination in mind and each struggling for control of the wheel. In our life, the Soul or the Yetzer Hara can be the "driver" of the "vehicle," i.e., the body. If the Soul is behind the wheel, it would be singularly focused on getting to Olam Haba and will use the body to help it get there. At birth when the Yetzer Hara is introduced, the Soul is submerged into the deepest recesses of man's innards; at that point, its influence is comparable to a potential driver languishing in the vehicle's trunk, and the Yetzer Hara commandeers the vehicle of life and it calls the shots. Under its command, the body itself and its world becomes the goal, and the Soul and its destination are ignored. Under such conditions, man only senses the instincts of his body, and the instinctive Emunah of the Soul is unobtainable. However, through Torah and Mitzvos man can increase the influence that the Soul has on his life's journey, and maybe even succeed in wresting control from the Yetzer Hara and installing the Soul as the guide and decision-maker of his life. To the degree that the Soul is influencing man's vehicle of life, its instincts, namely instinctive Emunah, are present within him.

When our Sages contrast a man who has complete Emunah with someone whose Emunah is limited, they are referring to the instinctive Emunah found naturally in the Soul. Surely Noach fulfilled the requirements for the basic Emunah, and, as the only person labeled by the Torah as a Tzaddik, lived with instinctive Emunah as well. But the Torah found that even his Emunah was not complete. Yes, he committed his life to doing God's Will, but there was still something missing: Total instinctive Emunah means to live *completely* as a Soul. It is to be governed by the Soul's perspectives *to the exclusion of all other perspectives*. Complete Emunah is when the Soul is the *only* driver of the vehicle. The Torah testifies that Noach entered the Ark "because of the waters of the flood." God's instruction was not the sole motivating factor. Visible weather still mattered, independent of the invisible God. There was a smidgen of hesitation to enter the Ark due to a forecast that called for sunny skies. The Almighty's instruction held water in Noach's eyes, but he did not enter the Ark until the earth around him held water too. Whatever legitimacy Noach ascribed to the meteorological conditions detracted from his complete Emunah.

The same can be said regarding the man who only has food for today and asks, "What will I eat tomorrow?" If the Soul is the only internal influencer and the Yetzer Hara was completely banished, the certainty that God will provide food for tomorrow will be unquestionable. Merely saying, "What will I eat tomorrow?" shows that God is not the only instinctive reality; empty cupboards and maxed-out credit cards matter too. If God is not the sole reality in a person's life, that demonstrates that the Soul's takeover of the person is not complete, and that is sufficient for them to be characterized as having limited Emunah.

Agricultural Miracle

Our Sages found an exact parallel to instinctive Emunah in the farmer. Consider a person planting an apple tree. He places an inedible seed in a hole, covers it with inedible soil, waters the area, and waits. Underground, the seed begins to rot, decompose, and decay. Dug up by an untrained eye, the conclusion would surely be that the inedible seed decaying in inedible soil would never yield fruit-bearing trees. The farmer himself is incapable of articulating exactly how planting works. Yet he plants. *He lives his life guided by an invisible and inexplicable reality.* The farmer has "instinctive Emunah" in the miracle of agriculture. He never wonders, "will it work this time?" In his mind, it is an unquestionable reality.

It is not just the farmer who takes the miracle of agriculture for granted: All life forms would die if the miracle of agriculture stopped, yet there are no doomsday-conferences to grapple with such a possibility. Our certainty in it always existing is total; questioning its continuity and reliability would be risible.

Instinctive Emunah refers to the Tzaddik's recognition of the invisible reality of God in the same way that the farmer relates to the miracle of agriculture. It is not a cognitive acceptance of a fuzzy, abstract idea; it is not ceremonial or ritualistic "faith"; instinctive Emunah is the way a Tzaddik lives. To lie awake at night and ponder (or worry) if this invisible reality is true would be as preposterous as worrying about the end of agriculture. *Living* with Emunah is only possible if man uses the Soul to interface with the world.

Basic, intellectual Emunah is a fixed, standalone Mitzvah that a person will or will not accomplish; it's black and white.

In the realm of instinctive Emunah—in the realm of being a Tzaddik—many different levels exist. For every degree that a person increases the volume of Soul in their identity, they commensurately inch closer to complete, instinctive Emunah. A person of "limited Emunah" lives with his Soul's perspective alongside other competing ones. His Soul has *some* say—it has some share of the steering wheel—but its dominion over him is not complete and thus his Emunah is limited. Complete Emunah is when the Soul is the only one behind the wheel.

Thou Shall Not Covet Wings of a Bird

The goal of all 613 Mitzvos is to bridge the gap between intellectual and instinctive Emunah. To illustrate this transformation, let us examine the Ten Commandments, a condensed synopsis of all of Torah.[2] The first commandment instructs a person to accept the existence and dominion of God. This refers to the beginning of man's journey—rudimentary, intellectual Emunah. The last of the Ten Commandments, "Do not covet," is a manifestation of living with *instinctive* Emunah. Thus, a continuum exists from the beginning to the end of the Ten Commandments that mirrors the transformation from basic to instinctive Emunah.

This insight (that to covet the things of others is a lack of Emunah) is found in the commentary of the *Ibn Ezra*.[3] He notes that many people wonder how is it an achievable Mitzvah to not even *desire* the nice things of others. Not to *act* upon those desires is surely within our free will, but to be commanded to not even desire other people's things seems unreasonable.

---

2   See *Rashi, Shemos* 24:12.
3   *Ibn Ezra, Shemos* 20:13.

Ibn Ezra begins his answer with a parable of a peasant of sound mind who realizes that he is at the very bottom of the social strata. When he sees a rich, powerful, and beautiful princess, he recognizes that she is completely out of his league; she's beyond his wildest fantasies—there is no conceivable scenario where he can marry her—and consequently *he does not even desire her*. Similarly, adds *Ibn Ezra*, a sane person does not desire to sprout wings from his forearms and soar like an eagle, knowing that it is an entirely unobtainable fantasy. Likewise, because God chose to give nice things to someone else, and not to me, the only way I can obtain them is if I can override God's intentions, which is obviously impossible and *even more unobtainable than the princess is for the peasant*, and therefore healthy, rational people will not even covet them.

Desire and lust are not blind; they are limited to the sphere of the potentially achievable. Things that are so plainly inaccessible, like growing wings and flying, are *not even desired to begin with*. *Ibn Ezra* acknowledges that some disturbed people do desire to fly like a bird because they imagine that it is indeed obtainable. That precisely parallels someone who desires what the Almighty decided belongs to his neighbor. Because God's dominion and oversight do not mold his purview, the man who covets what was divinely apportioned to his neighbor erroneously assumes that it is attainable. In *Ibn Ezra*'s parlance, such a person is disconnected from reality, akin to those who believe that growing wings and flying is feasible. This delusion is caused by the Yetzer Hara obfuscating God and forming for them a worldview wherein they identify as a body. At its core, to covet the things of your neighbor is a lack of instinctive Emunah.

Indeed, while seeing the world through the colored lenses of the Yetzer Hara and the body, it is surely unreasonable to expect us to not covet; the prohibition against coveting is an instruction to evict the Yetzer Hara from the driver's seat of the vehicle of life and supplant it with the Soul. With the Soul behind the wheel, he will naturally cease desiring what he now realizes is unattainable. For a person whose Soul controls his viewpoint and lives with instinctive Emunah, the decree of the Almighty holds sway over him and his desires in the same way that the limitations of biology preclude him from coveting wings to fly.

God's decisions form his immutable and inflexible reality, and desires that conflict with His Will are for the deranged.

When the Torah commands a person to not covet his neighbor's house, ox, wife, etc., it is commanding him to change the prism through which he views the world and adopt the viewpoint of his Soul that inherently recognizes that those goodies are wholly inaccessible. Thus, the last of the Ten Commandments is the ultimate culmination of the goal of all the Mitzvos: to be a Tzaddik who *lives* with instinctive Emunah; to ascertain that his Soul becomes a greater share of his identity and begins to assert its influence over his instincts. Each Mitzvah propels man a bit closer to this goal. In the next chapter, we will examine several examples of great Tzaddikim who adopted their Soul's mindset and thus exhibited instinctive Emunah.

Chapter 12 Takeaways

- The conflict of life is who is controlling the body: Is the Yetzer Hara commandeering the body to weaponize it to sin, or is the Soul in charge and utilizing the body to achieve its spiritual agenda?
- A man of complete instinctive Emunah is someone who interfaces with the world solely as a Soul to the exclusion of any other factors.

Rungs of Righteousness

*I*n a Talmudic episode in tractate *Gittin*, we get a window into the worldview of someone who has adopted his Soul's perspectives and instincts. The Talmud presents an extensive and dramatic account of the Roman siege of Jerusalem, and the ensuing destruction of the Temple and sacking of the city. While the mighty Roman army encircled Jerusalem's impregnable walls, a civil war between various Jewish factions brewed within. One faction sought outright war with the Romans and sabotaged the city's food and fuel storages in order to force the hand of the more pacifist sects to war. But this ploy backfired—resulting in mass hunger and devastation. Amidst these deplorable conditions, the venerated sage, Rabbi Yochanan Ben Zakkai, feigned his death and was smuggled outside of the city alive in a coffin. Once outside the city walls, he entered the Roman camp and greeted the Roman general overseeing the siege, Vespasian, by saying, "Peace be unto you, O king!" Vespasian responded harshly, saying that it is treasonous to call anyone "king" besides the Emperor, and threatened to summarily execute him. Rabbi Yochanan Ben Zakkai responded that Vespasian will surely be king, for it states in Scripture that "Lebanon" (a euphemism for the Temple) will fall in the hands of the mighty (i.e., a king).[1] As they were talking, a messenger arrived from Rome, telling Vespasian that the Emperor had died and that he was selected to replace him. Duly

---

1   *Yeshayahu* 10:34.

impressed with Rabbi Yochanan Ben Zakkai's clairvoyance, he granted him several wishes before heading off to Rome and handing off the siege to be finished by his son, Titus.[2]

This interesting story is worthy of analysis on several fronts, but I want to share the powerful observation of my grandfather, Rabbi Shlomo Wolbe, zt"l, drawn from Rabbi Yochanan Ben Zakkai's greeting of Vespasian, when he innocently addressed him as "king." One would surmise that Vespasian was *dressed* as a general, yet the great Sage *saw a king, not a general.* For sure, his physical eyeballs saw a general—perhaps identified with specialized insignia, or a certain number of stars on his uniform—and sent a message to his brain: "This is a general." But his instincts were not controlled by his body, but rather by his Soul. The Soul sees the world through the perspective of Torah, and thus when it sees the man on the brink of destroying the Temple, it filters this through the prism of Torah and it sees a king, as the verse states, "Lebanon will fall in the hands of the mighty." Rabbi Yochanan's Soul held a greater share of the control of the steering wheel than his Yetzer Hara. The Soul assumes the Torah to be more real than whatever messages physical eyeballs are conveying and thus he simply called it as he saw it, "Peace be unto you, O king!"

Gradients of Greatness

There is another Talmudic anecdote of Rabbi Yochanan Ben Zakkai that underscores this point: While on his deathbed, a cadre of students paid him a visit, and when he saw them, he started to cry. When queried, Rabbi Yochanan explained:

> *If I was about to be judged by a human king, whose power is limited (his reign is temporary; his anger and punishment are temporary; and he can be bribed with money or cajoled with words), I would nevertheless be crying in fear; now that I am heading into judgment before the Almighty, whose power is unlimited (His reign will never end; His anger and punishment*

---

2   *Gittin* 56a–b.

are permanent; and He cannot be bribed with money or cajoled with words), and I am not sure that I will prevail in judgment, and I should not cry in fear?![3]

Again, we see how the influence of his Soul superseded his Yetzer Hara, who deludes man into identifying as a body, an entity that is fearful of a human king but not of God. Rabbi Yochanan Ben Zakkai was *more* fearful of God than a human king because his Soul's reality trumped his Yetzer Hara in formulating his mindset.

It is important to note that Rabbi Yochanan Ben Zakkai conceded that he indeed *would* be fearful of a human king, but not *as* fearful as he was of God. Even when the Soul is the primary driver of the agenda, the Yetzer Hara's influence, albeit diminished, can yet be present. Perhaps Rabbi Yochanan demoted it to the back seat, or the trunk, but it was still present.

The deathbed narrative of Rabbi Yochanan Ben Zakkai continues. The students asked him for a blessing, and he capitulated, saying:

> *"May it be God's will that your fear of Heaven equal your fear of flesh and blood." They were surprised by this blessing: "And no more [Ought we not fear God more than man]?!" Rabbi Yochanan responded: "If only [you should fear God as much as other people], for man sins in hiding and hopes that no person sees him, but knows that God sees, yet ignores Him."*

This dialogue reveals some more important insights: Initially, the students did not appreciate Rabbi Yochanan's blessing. In their view, it seemed like a *downgrade* to be told that they should fear God only as much as they fear man. God warrants *more* fear than man! In his qualification, Rabbi Yochanan substantiated his point by noting that a Yetzer Hara–dominated person may be *theoretically aware* of God's Omniscience—i.e., he may have intellectual Emunah—but will still look to and fro before sinning. A person who sins comfortably before God but not before other people *fears man more than he fears God*,

---

3   *Berachos* 28b.

even if he stridently protests—or theoretically believes—otherwise. His blessing was that they should *personify* their fear of God; that the reality and palpability of God's Omniscience become as real to them as the existence of other people.

Rabbi Yochanan Ben Zakkai blessed his students that they achieve the level where they identify *as much as a Soul as a body*. It is indeed a great blessing to be able to achieve parity between the two.

Rabbi Yochanan Ben Zakkai himself was on a higher level: His fear of God *eclipsed* his fear of man. He managed to commandeer the steering wheel away from his Yetzer Hara and give it back to his Soul. His spiritual reality *supplanted* his physical reality. His students were instructed to aim for one notch lower: to transform their identity so that their Soul becomes as much a factor as their body; to elevate their spiritual reality to parity with the physical; to be as fearful of God as they were of man. Perhaps that would be like a vehicle equipped with dual-control steering wheels, one for the Yetzer Hara and one for the Soul, each contributing equally to determining the person's worldview.

Insanity of Sin

Transforming the spiritual realm of the Soul into being as real as the physical realm of the body is a very lofty benchmark of greatness, worthy of the giants of the Talmud. This recognition of how they saw the world sheds light on some of their otherwise inexplicable teachings. For example, the Talmud in *Sotah* states:

> *Reish Lakish said: A person only sins if a spirit of insanity enters him.*[4]

By conventional standards of mental health, this statement does not ring true. Many people who would not be classified as pathologically insane do indeed sin. However, in light of our understanding of the Talmud and its Sages' Soulful outlook, this statement is sound: To sin is to capitulate to the Yetzer Hara's agenda in a way that negatively affects the Soul; a sinner is brazenly rebuffing the expressed commandment of

---

4   *Sotah* 3a.

the Almighty who sees, is aware of everything, and will exact judgment from sinners. To the Sages of the Talmud who adopted the Soul's perspective, *sin is deliberate self-harm,* and can only be explained by temporary insanity.

Suppose a driver is stopped at a red light and sees a police car in the rear-view mirror. It would be crazy for him to barrel through the red light under such conditions. The consequences of running the red light are so real and tangible that no rational person would do it. That is precisely how the Sages perceived sin: Their Soul was in the driver's seat of their life's journey, and they were keenly aware of the watchful eye of God, His hearing ear, and the fact that all our deeds are inscribed in a Heavenly ledger for posterity. To sin when the consequences are so tangible can only be the product of temporary insanity.

Today, the degree that we can adopt our Soul's perspectives and instincts is capped. Since the Temple was destroyed, the spiritual capacities shrunk and men of Emunah—qualified as one who has bread in his basket for today and does not say, "What will I eat tomorrow"—ceased. Someone who has food for today but none for tomorrow and is totally at ease is a person to whom the reality that God is a loving Father is more palpable than an empty cupboard. That is the level that Rabbi Yochanan Ben Zakkai achieved, and the Talmud states that such levels are *not* achievable after the destruction of the Temple.

Post-destruction, we must obey the dictum:

If there is no flour, there cannot be Torah.[5]

In order to have peace of mind to engage in Torah, one must have both *bread* for today, and *flour* for tomorrow's bread. Knowing that, Rabbi Yochanan Ben Zakkai did not encourage his students to strive to be like him, and certainly it is beyond us today. But it seems that the stature of his students—where the physical and spiritual worlds are equally real; where the Soul influences as much of his weltanschauung as his Yetzer Hara does—is still accessible, and we can aspire to achieve it.

---

5   *Avos* 3:17.

Lobbying the President

Perhaps a yardstick to chart our progress can be prayer. For the Soul, prayer is to commune with the King of kings, Creator of heaven and earth; it is meaningful, powerful, and awesome. For the body, prayer is meaningless word-babbling. Wherever man's prayer falls between those extremes is indicative of how much the Soul and its instincts are operating within him.

Our diminished spiritual acuity notwithstanding, in contemporary times it is still possible for people to have instinctive Emunah, to make their spiritual world real, and to pray with joy and trepidation as they would if they were talking to a human king. While ill during his last months, my grandfather was in constant pain and discomfort, and needed nightly attending; every night a different grandchild would remain with him to attend and assist him in various ways until *Shacharis* at 7:00 a.m. Halfway through my shift one night, my grandfather woke up and asked me if it was time for *Shacharis*. I responded that it was only 3:00 a.m., and he went back to sleep. Half an hour later, this repeated itself: He awoke and asked if it was time to pray, and again I encouraged him to go back to sleep. At 4:00 a.m., he awoke again, and—with the eagerness of a child the night before a trip to an amusement park—insisted on getting up and dressed and preparing for *Shacharis*. I helped him to get dressed and ready (a painful and laborious process given his conditions), and he sat on his foyer bench with his hands resting on his knees, fully dressed in his rabbinic frock coat and hat, patiently waiting until it was time to pray. To him, the spiritual realm was real. For people whose Soul occupies a robust portion of their identity, prayer is a transcendental experience worthy of anticipating, not a religious ritual to get over and be done with.

The Final Puzzle Piece

The previous chapters demonstrated how Mitzvos were given to man to purge the Yetzer Hara from within him and train himself to identify as a Soul. That renders him into a Tzaddik who lives with instinctive Emunah. When the prophet Chavakuk whittled down all 613 Mitzvos into the short verse, "And a Tzaddik lives with Emunah," he showed us how a person who heeds the pre-birth instruction lives. Emunah, a pure Soul, and a suppressed Yetzer Hara are all different aspects of the same internal transformation brought about by Mitzvos.

When Hillel was asked to encapsulate all the Mitzvos, he invoked a different approach, and informed the conversion candidate that it is contained in the Mitzvah of loving your fellow as yourself. In the next two chapters, we will explore this Mitzvah and see how that fits into this paradigm.

Chapter 13 Takeaways

- Instinctive Emunah was the hallmark of the great Sages of yore, and it was manifested in their behavior and outlook.
- Throughout history, the degree of instinctive Emunah that is accessible to us has been capped, but we can still become Tzaddikim who live with instinctive Emunah, albeit incomplete instinctive Emunah.

CHAPTER 14

The Love Formula

*T*he Torah's most famous Mitzvah is perhaps its most difficult one to fulfill. We read in *Vayikra*:

You shall not take revenge, and you shall not bear a grudge against your countrymen; you shall love your fellow as yourself—I am Hashem.[1]

Most Mitzvos are confined to *actions*: don tefillin on your head and arm, affix a mezuzah on your doorposts, observe the laws of Shabbos, study Torah, etc. The Mitzvah to love other people is unique because it directs us to have an *emotion*. We are commanded to *feel* a certain way; not merely to *behave* a certain way. In contrast to the prevailing assumption that loving another person is just by chance ("falling in love"), the Torah believes that commanding Jews to love their fellow Jew as themselves is feasible. Demanding it from all Jews is not—in the Torah's view—an unreasonable expectation. How is this Mitzvah done?

As Yourself

Scripture is clear that the commandment is not adequately fulfilled unless one loves his fellow "as yourself." What is meant by the words "as ourselves"? It is unlikely to mean that we must love our fellow to the same *degree* that we love ourselves. After all, the Talmud rules that

---

1   *Vayikra* 19:18.

a person's own life supersedes the life of his fellow.[2] If my life takes precedence over someone else's, how could it be that I have to love him as much as I love myself?

Rabbi Nosson Tzvi Finkel (the Alter of Slabodka) interpreted the words "as yourself" to mean that I must love my fellow for the same *reasons* why I love myself. Healthy people love themselves not because they were *commanded* to do so, rather because they are physiologically and emotionally wired to look out for their own betterment. When the Torah instructs to love your fellow as yourself, it's not a measurement of the *quantitative* amount of love, rather of the *quality* of the love. If I love him solely because there's a Mitzvah to love him—if I clench my nose and love him against my inclinations—*I have not fulfilled the Mitzvah.* I need to love him *as I love myself.* Just as self-love is not a religious box to check, I must also love my fellow emotionally and not as a means of doing a Mitzvah. This exacerbates our problem: How do we flip a switch and achieve an emotion of love toward another person?

The juxtaposition of this Mitzvah to the two preceding ones also warrants investigation. What is the connection between loving your fellow as yourself and not taking revenge nor bearing a grudge? Beyond the fulfillment of the Mitzvah, the Sages maintain that it incorporates all of Torah. How can this one Mitzvah include all of Torah? What about all the Torah sections that relate to man's relationship with God? Lastly, how does this not conflict with the other teachings purporting to encapsulate all of Torah and Mitzvos, namely, instinctive Emunah, purification of the soul, and defeating the Yetzer Hara?

Repeatable Formula

To begin, let us attempt to understand the Mitzvah itself. Implicit in the instruction to love our fellow as ourselves is an assumption that a *repeatable formula* to do this exists. Discovering this formula will be doubly beneficial. Aside from enabling us to fulfill this critical Mitzvah, it would be a boon for our personal relationships. It is no secret that modern society struggles mightily in areas of love and relationships.

---

2 *Bava Metzia* 62a.

One not need be a marital therapist to recognize that far too many people who commit to love their spouses "till death does them part" renege upon their pledge. Given that people view the acquisition of love as a matter of chance—something that you "fall" into—it should surprise no one that it can get lost by chance as well. The Torah teaches that love is a repeatable formula, and those armed with that knowledge can fulfill both this Mitzvah and be confident that their love will not spontaneously erode.

Before we unveil the love formula, we can already deduce that it requires *us* to change. If you encounter another person who has sterling character and is delightful in every way, loving him is not very hard. If we can find a method to improve *other* people until they too have scintillating character, this Mitzvah would be a cinch. But the only people we can truly change for the better are ourselves. Hence when the Torah obligates us to love our fellow, it is telling us that we need to change something about *ourselves* that will cause us to love our fellow *despite his flaws*. What is this formula?

Definition of Love

Rabbi Noach Weinberg would frequently say that the Torah defines love as "the emotional pleasure one gets when he recognizes the virtues of another person and identifies that person with those virtues."

We find a corroborating source for this definition by looking at the first instance in the Torah wherein someone loves someone else. In *Bereishis*, we read:

> *And Yitzchak brought [Rivkah] to the tent of his mother, Sarah, and he married [Rivkah], and she was to him for a wife, and he loved her, and he was consoled regarding his mother.*[3]

The verse describes the marriage and budding love of Yitzchak and Rivkah, and it finds the need to mention Yitzchak's mother, Sarah, twice. Why must we be told that Yitzchak brought Rivkah into *Sarah's* tent, and that she provided him consolation following *Sarah's* passing?

---

3   *Bereishis* 24:67.

Rashi explains that due to Sarah's piety, steady miracles were present in her tent: an ever-present cloud hovered over it; her Shabbos candles remained lit for a week from Friday night until the following Friday; and there was abundant blessing in her challah dough. These miracles ceased when Sarah died, and when Rivkah entered the tent of Sarah, they resumed. The "tent of Sarah" is vital to the story because it is the *reason* for the events that followed: "And Yitzchak brought her to the tent of his mother Sarah, and he married her, and she was to him for a wife"—and the miracles returned, and consequently—*"and he loved her, and he was consoled regarding his mother."* The reason why Yitzchak loved Rivkah was because he recognized her resplendent character, righteousness, and piety akin to those of Sarah, and identified her with those virtues.

Eclectic Character Repertoire

This opens the door for a repeatable formula to foster an emotional love toward every person. Everyone has some admirable qualities, behaviors, and character traits. The Mishnah acknowledges this by teaching:

> *Who is truly wise? He who learns from every person.*[4]

If you want to be truly wise, you must integrate all the possible good characteristics into your behavior. How is it done? By learning from every person. Every person you encounter has been endowed with character traits worthy of emulation. The Mishnah counsels us to pinpoint the admirable traits of the people that we come across, find the areas that they excel in, and work on adopting those qualities. A person who follows this directive will overhaul his entire character until he becomes truly wise.

Alongside admirable qualities, every person also has characteristics that are less than stellar. A perfect person doesn't exist because a life bereft of *pursuit* of greatness would be meaningless. Thus, all humans—ourselves and other people—harbor a repertoire of good

---

4   *Avos* 4:1.

and bad character traits. Everyone is partly flawed and partly virtuous. The determining factor of love is which of these we choose to focus on and associate the person with: If we choose to recognize the *virtue* found in another person and identify them with their *qualities*, then we will invariably love them. If, instead, we dwell on their bad character and label them as such, we will not love them. The Torah commandment to love our fellow as ourselves is an instruction to reform the way *we* judge and evaluate people.

We are predisposed to easily notice another person's bad character and behavior and to immediately affix upon them that label; noticing the good in others requires effort. If we would be honest with ourselves, we will recognize that we also are a basket of deplorable and admirable character traits and behaviors. Yet we still love ourselves because we overlook our negative character and focus on the positive elements of our personality, and view ourselves as generally being good.

In the commandment to love others *as yourself*, the Torah is instructing us to be as charitable to others as we are to ourselves. The Torah is not commanding us to seek out objectively lovable people, rather to train ourselves to be on the prowl for the *good* in others, and provide them the same allowances for their misdeeds and bad character that we give ourselves, and automatically they will become worthy of love and admiration in our eyes. Indeed, it's possible to love (almost) everyone, provided that we are willing to change the lenses through which we judge others.

Rabbi Yeruchem Levovitz would compare a person with character flaws to a treasure chest full of gold and diamonds that also has a wormy, putrid fruit in it. Though the stench may be nauseating and we would surely not open the chest without gloves and a nose plug, we'd recognize its value, and would certainly not discard or disregard it. Even if it was a box full of rotten fruit with only a single diamond in it, the good would outweigh the bad in our eyes and we would cherish it. The Torah is instructing us to focus on the diamonds inherent in the people we meet, instead of being fixated on the shameful elements of their persona. Every person is a mixed bag. We love ourselves because we innately pay attention to the diamonds within us; in the Mitzvah to love others as ourselves we are commanded to do the same for everyone else. Integrating this love formula into our life will result in an *emotional* love of others, not due to an obligation to love them, but rather in the same way—and employing the same methodology—as we love ourselves.

We still, however, need to understand the verse as a whole. What is the connection between the earlier commandment to not take revenge nor bear a grudge and the Mitzvah of loving others? Also, how is this Mitzvah representative of Mitzvos at large, and how does it relate to the concepts addressed earlier, namely, instinctive Emunah, resisting the Yetzer Hara, and preserving and enlarging the purity of our Soul? To understand how these ideas intersect, we must probe the Mitzvah of loving your fellow as yourself a bit deeper.

Chapter 14 Takeaways

- A repeatable formula to emotionally love your fellow as yourself exists.
- Every person has a collection of good and bad character traits, and by focusing on another person's good characteristics, invariably you will love them.

CHAPTER 15

The Cocoon
of Selfishness

*T*he words of Scripture, "You shall love your fellow as yourself,"
appear hyperbolic. It seems impossible to literally love others as
much as I love myself. After all, each person is a distinct entity from
other people; we all sense our own pain and pleasure and not those of
our fellow. Given these presuppositions, we must seek nonliteral interpretations of the verse.

However, in a passage in Rabbi Moshe Cordovero's magisterial work
Tomer Devorah, we find that our presuppositions may be mistaken:

*All of Israel are blood relatives because their Souls are
united...Therefore, a person should seek and take joy in the
betterment of his fellow and let his fellow's honor be as dear as
his own, because his fellow is [in truth] literally [a part of] him.
For this reason, we are commanded, "You shall love your fellow
as yourself." [Ideally] a person ought to naturally desire success of his fellow and not speak of his fellow's shame, and not
desire...his fellow's shame, pain, and deterioration, and [his
fellow's pain] should pain him as if he was literally experiencing*

the same pain, and [he should take joy in his fellow's success as
if he literally was experiencing] the same success.[1]

We erroneously assume that there are immutable divisions separating one person from another. In the *Tomer Devorah*, we learn that each
person is only independent of his fellow man due to the existence of
the body and the Yetzer Hara encouraging man to identify as it. On the
Soul level, we are all united and we literally are parts of one whole. If we
could strip everything else away and expose just the Soul, it would be
clear that we are in reality one entity.

The Talmud teaches us that while awaiting to be matched with bodies,
all untethered Souls are stored in a Heavenly chamber, called "*Guf.*"[2]
Guf is also the Hebrew word for "body." In this peculiar tidbit—that the
name of the Heavenly vessel that harbors all unpaired Souls is called
"*Guf*"—our Sages are revealing to us a critical insight: From the stand-
point of the Soul, there need not be divisions between one Soul and
another. Souls can coexist with each other in one Heavenly "body"; it is
only the *physical* body that creates divisions between people.

This idea breathes new meaning into the Mitzvah of loving your fellow
as yourself. It's not a commandment to love him *despite* the divisions
between you two; rather it is to love him *precisely because* in your true
existence those divisions do not exist.

The Errant Butcher Knife

The Talmud employs this line of thinking to explain the beginning of
the verse: "You shall not take revenge, and you shall not bear a grudge
against your countrymen." It compares revenge to a butcher hacking
away at a slab of meat who mistakenly cut his left hand with a knife
wielded by his right. Surely it would be preposterous for the wounded
hand to exact revenge by lunging for the knife and slashing the per-
petrating one. Because we all are different parts of the same whole, to
pursue vengeance against our fellow man is equally asinine.[3]

---

1   *Ramak, Tomer Devorah*, chap. 1.
2   *Yevamos* 62a, 63b.
3   *Yerushalmi, Nedarim* 9:4.

Accordingly, the verse maintains a logical flow: It begins by establishing that two Jews are part of the same entity—like the right and left hands of a single person—when it warns against taking revenge. Then the verse declares, "You shall love your fellow as yourself." This is a natural extension of the same principle: If we are part of the same being, then surely we should naturally love each other quite literally as we love ourselves, pursue each other's betterment, and suffer with each other's pain for the same reason.

We only view ourselves as being different entities than our fellow because the Yetzer Hara influences us to identify as our body. If we were able to isolate our Soul, and see how it operates sans body and Yetzer Hara, we would *not* find divisions between two Souls. On this deep level, the Mitzvah of loving your fellow as yourself is not an isolated instruction to love other people, rather, it is a commandment to transform yourself back into operating as a pure Soul that does not have barriers separating it from others.

It is now clear how Emunah and loving your fellow as yourself can both be the objective of all of Torah. Both are byproducts of a pure Soul, and to achieve both you must break through the same opposition, namely the Yetzer Hara that causes division, both between man and his Creator and between man and his fellow.

The Genesis of the Yetzer Hara

The Yetzer Hara's endemic divisiveness is evident at the very beginning of its influence over man. Immediately after Adam and Chavah consumed the forbidden fruit in the Garden of Eden, and invited the Yetzer Hara within them, they realized that they were naked.[4] Prior to the sin, the Yetzer Hara (the Serpent) was entirely external. Their identity was that of an unsullied Soul freed from the Yetzer Hara's nefarious influence. Thus, they saw the world as their Soul does: The body was a mere fleshy cover to service them (their Souls). Just as we are unashamed if our cardigan is uncovered, it did not bother Adam and Chavah that their bodies were unclothed. With the consumption

---

4   *Bereishis* 3:7.

of the poison, their outlook was flipped on its head: Their body became their essence, and the Soul no longer reigned supreme. They adopted the Yetzer Hara's fiction that *you are the cover*, and were immediately concerned with its welfare, and became aware of their nakedness.

This new worldview was evident in the ensuing events (verses 8–10): They heard the sound of God and tried to hide. The Soul would never entertain the notion that ducking behind a tree would enable one to hide from God. But thanks to the Yetzer Hara, Adam and Chavah identified as bodies and saw the world through its prism. In the body's worldview, no one and nothing can see past physical obstructions. In short, the first manifestation of the Yetzer Hara in Adam and Chavah was that they identified as a body, and no longer as a Soul.

The next verses show how a person who is controlled by the Yetzer Hara behaves. In verse 11, God confronted Adam and asked if he ate from the tree. Instead of fessing up, Adam deflected culpability and implicated Chavah by saying, "The woman that You gave me gave me the fruit and I ate."[5] Prior to the advent of the Yetzer Hara, they were "one flesh";[6] after the sin Adam saw her as a different—and guilty—entity. In addition, *Rashi* points out that, in an act of egregious ingratitude, Adam subtly blamed God too—the woman that *You* gave me gave me the fruit and I ate. In his new and twisted view, he was all-righteous and others—Chavah and even the Almighty—were guilty.

By severing man from his Soul, the Yetzer Hara removes both God and other people from his purview. This is the root cause of all bad interpersonal character and man's estrangement from God. Absent the Yetzer Hara, the Soul alone, with its total subservience to God, constitutes a person's identity. The Talmud informs us that the signet of God is "truth."[7] With the Almighty guiding a person's compass, truth will always triumph. Truth mandates that man recognize and acknowledge his flaws and failures, and also the good character and behavior of others. Had Adam been governed by truth, he would have admitted

---

5   Ibid. v. 12.
6   Ibid. 2:24.
7   *Sanhedrin* 64a.

his guilt and acknowledged God's gift to him in the form of Chavah. Due to his sin, however, Adam was under the spell of the false god, the Yetzer Hara. The false god's signet is falsehood. Its presence distorts and clouds the truth, and falsehoods of all types are the order of the day. Adam *was* guilty, but his response to the accusations was a product of the falsehood of his newly acquired Yetzer Hara, and therefore he did not see his own evil, nor the good of others.[8]

By making man identify as a body and not as a Soul, the Yetzer Hara is also responsible for the disparity between man and other people. Due to it, man tends to love himself, and not others; to judge only himself favorably; to feel only his own pain and pleasure but not those of others; to notice his own virtue and not his flaws, while in others he sees the bad and not the good.

My grandfather would compare a person living under the influence of the Yetzer Hara to one incarcerated alone in a windowless room. All he has in his world is himself. The Almighty and other people do not exist in his sphere.

The Yetzer Hara tarnishes both man's ideal relationship with God (Emunah), and his ideal relationship with others (recognizing that they are parts of the same whole and loving them). By combating and undoing the Yetzer Hara, man is removing the barriers between both, and with each small crack in the wall, he deepens his relationship with

---

8   Adam's punishment for bringing the Yetzer Hara upon himself was that the earth will be difficult to cultivate, and he will have to sustain himself with the sweat of his brow. How does the punishment fit the crime?

My grandfather explained that Adam reaped exactly what he sowed. By ingesting the "poison" of the Yetzer Hara, Adam obviated the need for God by creating an alternative. As a consequence, the Almighty created the conditions where repudiation of God is feasible. Before the sin, Adam needn't labor at all to sustain himself. Fruit grew effortlessly, and even the barks of trees were edible. Under such conditions, rejection of God is an impossibility. Adam chose to embrace the possibility for the alternative when he invited the foreign god of falsehood into his world. As punishment, God commanded that thenceforth man's sustenance will be the product of his toil and sweat. This fostered an environment where the illusions of the Yetzer Hara gain credence. When the food only comes after intensive labors on the part of the person, he can be deluded that he—and not God—created this produce. Thus, the punishment is a direct byproduct of the sin. Adam chose to allow the fiction of alternatives to God, and his request was granted.

his Creator and with his peers. Each Mitzvah chisels a small hole in the concrete cocoon of selfishness of the Yetzer Hara and brings man one step closer to being a Soul, to Emunah, and loving his fellow as himself.

Natural Kindness

What does it look like when someone breaks free of the influence of the Yetzer Hara? For one, kindness comes naturally. An example of this can be found in *Bereishis* when Eliezer was scouting out a potential spouse for Yitzchak and he devised a test to determine the eligibility of the prospective girl. He would approach a candidate and ask her for water to drink. The girl who exhibits superlative kindness and responds by offering water to his camels as well is worthy of joining the dynasty of kindness of Avraham.[9] According to this test, the attribute of kindness is expressed only if the candidate perceives and addresses the *unstated needs* of the recipient. Rivkah was not asked to deliver water to the camels, and thus her volunteering to do that demonstrated her kindness.

This may strike us as odd:

- Had Rivkah given water to Eliezer alone, she would not have displayed the requisite kindness worthy of joining Avraham's family. Why specifically must the kindness be of the variety of recognition and volunteering to fulfill the *unspecified* needs of another?

- Another point to ponder is how indeed Rivkah sensed that Eliezer had other needs that he failed to mention?

- Also, Eliezer is apparently not concerned about her religious beliefs. Though she comes from a family and a society of idolaters, and were she to have such proclivities she would certainly be incompatible with Yitzchak, Eliezer did not incorporate that into his test. How can he know for sure that she is aligned with the Abrahamic theological ideals?

The answer to all these questions is that kindness of this sort lies in the person's reframing of self to identify as a Soul. In that state,

---

9   *Bereishis* 24:14.

a person senses the needs of others as easily and as viscerally as their own. Rivkah's fulfillment of the *unprompted* kindness showed that she *naturally* sensed what Eliezer needed without being directed toward it. Once Eliezer knew that she had dismantled the barriers of the Yetzer Hara with respect to other people, she necessarily did not have barriers separating her from the Almighty.

I witnessed a giant of Torah and Mussar preparing a cup of coffee for himself, and he asked others if they wanted some as well. Afterwards he confided in me that it is no great act of kindness to offer coffee to someone else when you are making one for yourself. Selfless kindness is when someone experiences what another person is going through and can predict their needs without being told about them, and without it being aroused to them as an extension of what the giver is personally experiencing.

The Jewish Definition of Greatness

This newfound perspective that Souls are united, and that the division of people stems from the body and the Yetzer Hara, sheds light on the Torah's articulation of human greatness. In Talmudic shorthand, a great person is an "*Adam Gadol*" or "*Gavra Rabbah*"—literally, a "large" man. Associating greatness with size is appropriate because the great person is someone who reorients his identity to be that of his Soul and thereby expands his identity to include others. When we are commanded to love others, we are being told to become greater, more expansive people, and to include others within our expanded identity. It is an instruction to recapture our identity as a Soul that we had in utero, and to chisel away at the walls of selfishness erected by the body and reinforced by the Yetzer Hara.

Babies are completely selfish. The control of the Yetzer Hara upon them is fierce and they are consumed by their own personal interests with nary a fleeting concern about others. They never wake up in the middle of the night to console or feed their needy parents. No one else is included within their identity.

The objective of Torah and Mitzvos is to undo the selfishness smothered upon man at birth. A person's greatness is measured in direct proportion to the degree that he successfully recreates the conditions that existed prior to being ensconced in the cocoon of selfishness of the Yetzer Hara. The greater a person becomes the more people exist under the canopy of his expanded identity and the "larger" he becomes.

This goal is aided greatly by marriage. The Torah describes an unmarried slave as one who "comes with the edge of his clothing."[10] Why does it use such a bizarre euphemism to describe a bachelor? *Rashi* answers that the world of a single person ends where their clothing ends. Their identity is limited to themselves. The essence of marriage is the expansion of identity to incorporate another person within you. When Adam and Chavah were first married, Adam exclaimed, "This time it is bone of my bones and flesh from my flesh."[11] Adam recognized that Chavah *was a part of him.* His identity expanded to include her too. In the following verse, the Torah guides us to do the same: "Therefore a man shall leave his father and mother and shall cleave to his wife and they shall be one flesh." Perhaps this is why the marriage of Adam and Chavah is invoked during the *Sheva Berachos* when the bride and groom are blessed to be "gladdened as [Adam and Chavah] were in the Garden of Eden." In the Garden, they had morphed into a single expanded identity.

This is also why acclimation of marriage is difficult. The only way to create a new merged identity is to break out of the previous one. To cleave to your wife and become one flesh, you must leave your father and mother, i.e., the identity that you have had since birth. As such, marriage mirrors the transformation toward achieving greatness. It demands abandoning the small identity and creating a larger one. The Talmud teaches that, "a man without a wife is not a man."[12] Without marriage which compels the painful but worthwhile expansion of self, man is not a man of greatness.

When the convert asked Hillel to distill the objective of Torah into one sentence, he told him, "Do not unto others what you do not wish done to you. This is all of Torah, the rest is commentary. Go study!" The

---

10   *Shemos* 21:4.
11   *Bereishis* 2:23.
12   *Yevamos* 63a.

goal of Torah and Mitzvos is to foil the Yetzer Hara and restore the Soul to its previous prominence. Battling the Yetzer Hara, safeguarding the purity of the Soul, acquiring Emunah, and loving your fellow as yourself are but different dimensions and aspects of the same process.

Chapter 15 Takeaways

- On the level of the Soul, all of Israel are truly a single, indivisible entity; it is only when the body is weaponized by the Yetzer Hara that we believe we are different entities.
- The Yetzer Hara is a force that breeds division between man and his Creator and between man and his fellow.
- Combating the Yetzer Hara automatically fosters instinctive Emunah and emotional love of one's fellow man.
- Man has an individual identity that includes his body alone, and to the degree that he transforms his identity into being Soul-like, he has a collective identity that includes others as well.
- The greater the man, the more people are included in his collective identity and the "larger" he is.

Summary of Parts One and Two

*T*he ideological framework for understanding how Torah and Mitzvos transform man is now complete.

A Soul is the epitome of holiness and purity. The pre-birth instruction places its purity on the same pedestal as the purity of the Almighty and His angels. Unlike the body, which is on a collision course with a destiny of worms and maggots, the Soul is man's true and eternal essence; it will outlive his stint in this world.

However, it is dumped into a war zone when it enters the world. "At the entrance sin crouches." Due to the Yetzer Hara that is forced upon man at that time, the Soul is placed into a situation where its purity is compromised. No longer is it driving the vehicle of life; now it is like a sailor flailing about in a raging sea of sin; the Soul is removed from above the person's head and buried in his inner chambers. The Yetzer Hara is the force engineered and committed to kill the Soul. It seeks to infect the Soul and corrupt it from within. It drapes the world around man with seemingly irresistible appeal. The world that ought to be used to fuel a journey toward Olam Haba is transformed into a destination; man's attention is diverted to the corridor and begins to ignore his Soul and to cease ensuring that it makes its way home. This is likely to result in a vicious, spiraling cycle of man placing his Soul on the fast lane toward destruction. For the wicked who don't take the necessary

113

steps to mitigate that catastrophe, even while their body is alive, their Soul is already dead and rotting inside them. The instant that the Soul is brought into this world, it is in great danger indeed.

But all is not lost. The Almighty communicated to us the exact instructions needed to preserve the life and purity of our Soul, and save it from being ravaged by the Yetzer Hara. The "captain" threw us a lifeline to grab and be saved from death. The Mitzvos awaken the dormant Soul within us. They are both the nourishment to infuse our Soul with life and vitality and the medicine to combat the Yetzer Hara's harmful venom. The more we connect with our Soul the further we move up the lifeline and the closer we get to God.

Our Sages hinted at the overall goal of Mitzvos in several places, each seemingly different. But in truth, they are only showing different dimensions of a pure Soul. Emunah is the instincts of a pure Soul. A person who lives with that perspective has successfully navigated the labyrinthine dangers of the Yetzer Hara and restored his Soul to its original prominence as a head-mounted beacon guiding his life. Starting from birth, the Yetzer Hara sits securely in the driver's seat of the vehicle of life; Emunah is the mindset of man when the keys have been transferred back to the Soul.

Such a person will also love his fellow as himself. A pure Soul does not exhibit a border separating it from other Souls just as it is not distant from God. When man tears down the walls of the Yetzer Hara cloistering him alone, he innately recognizes that in fact, on the Soul level, he is not distinct from his fellow man. Man's Emunah with respect to his relationship with his Creator is interpersonally manifested in loving his fellow as himself. Both are characteristics of a person who has secured a pure Soul, and both are accomplished by winning the war with the Yetzer Hara.

This three-pronged life objective is also hinted to in *Avos*:

> *Shimon the Tzaddik said: Upon three things the world stands: On Torah, avodah (worshipping God), and loving-kindness.*[13]

---

13   *Avos* 1:2.

The commentaries explain that Shimon Hatzaddik is delineating the three aspects of life's objective:

1. Man himself is made perfect through "Torah" (bearing a pure Soul free of a Yetzer Hara).
2. His ideal relationship with God is "avodah" (Emunah).
3. "Loving-kindness" corresponds to the ideal interpersonal relationship ("Love your fellow as yourself").[14]

When describing the state of a fetus in utero, the Talmud comments that those days are the best ones of his life. Before the arrival of the Yetzer Hara, the Soul is in an idealized situation. It is like the sailor who is still aboard the ship; the Soul has complete command of the vehicle of life. Emunah and loving others are completely natural.

Torah and Mitzvos were given to us to facilitate the return to that idyllic existence. They are the tools to navigate the Yetzer Hara's obstacles blockading the Soul's journey home. Thus, success in this world hinges upon man's struggle with the Yetzer Hara. The heroic warrior who successfully repulses, negates, and even dismantles his enemy is one who uncovers his pure Soul and achieves perfection in time for entry into the palace at the end of the corridor.

In Part II, we demonstrated how Torah and Mitzvos in general counteract the Yetzer Hara by empowering and nurturing the Soul.

In Part III, we will shift our focus to the sources that outline the tactical and strategic elements of direct conflict with the enemy.

---

14   Rabbeinu Yonah, *Avos* ad loc.

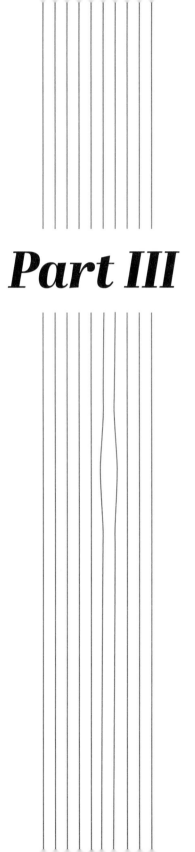

Part III

The Art of War
with the Yetzer Hara

*T*he Yetzer Hara is a malicious, relentless, and lifelong enemy. The Midrash states:

> *When people meet and spend an hour together, invariably they become friends. The Yetzer Hara is with man since birth, and accompanies him his entire life, nevertheless if it sees an opportunity to make him falter at age twenty, or forty, or seventy, or eighty, it will bring him down. Is there a worse enemy than this?![1]*

Even if it fails 100 times in its quest to usher the spiritual demise of man, the Yetzer Hara still schemes of new ways to trip him up. Unlike other enemies who surrender to the superior opponent, the Yetzer Hara never gives up. Lifelong companionship doesn't sway its determination to make man succumb.

Man's life objective—and the reason why we were given Torah—is to overcome and defeat this enemy. In the ensuing chapters, we will explore several Talmudic teachings that can guide our efforts in this most critical war. By following their time-tested battle plans, we can

---

1   *Midrash Tehillim* 34.

be triumphant in preserving and enhancing the purity of our Soul, and thereby move closer to God.

The Winning Strategy

The Talmud contains a vast repository of suggestions to avoid sinning. Though on the surface each appears to be a distinct approach to resisting temptation, we will discover that all their tactics stem from one core strategy that can be applied in many different ways. To explain this core strategy, we will be guided by a profound teaching of my great-grandfather, the illustrious spiritual dean of the Slabodka Yeshiva, Rabbi Avraham Grodzinski.[2]

He begins with a question: Before Adam's sin in the Garden of Eden, he did not harbor a Yetzer Hara, and the only force encouraging sin was the Serpent. Adam's sin itself is thus evidence that sin is feasible even without the influence of the Yetzer Hara. If the Yetzer Hara is not needed for sin to happen, what role does it play in effectuating sin?

Put another way, what is the difference between pre-sin choices that are uninfluenced by the Yetzer Hara and post-sin choices that are?

For our purposes, the answer to this question will help us isolate the effect that the Yetzer Hara has on choices and will enable us to construct an appropriate response.

Rabbi Grodzinski answers by establishing a fundamental principle: There are two kinds of choices of sin—logical choices and lustful choices. The Yetzer Hara does not *create* choices of sin that otherwise would not exist, but rather it *alters the nature of the choice from being logical to being lustful*.

Even before the sin and the concomitant insertion of the Yetzer Hara, Adam had the ability to choose sin, but that choice was of the logical variety; he had as much lustful desire to sin as we do to jump into a fire.[3] Adam's decision was not only logical, it was calculated. He knew perfectly well that committing the sin would lead to mankind becoming subject to the Yetzer Hara, and did so willfully in order to raise

---

2   *Toras Avraham*, p. 60.
3   *Nefesh Hachaim* 1:6.

the stakes of life. Thenceforth, mankind will have to overcome a more capable antagonist, and being triumphant in those lustful choices will be even more meaningful because of the principle that "to the degree of difficulty is the degree of the reward."[4] By making successful conquest of the formidable Yetzer Hara a precondition to accomplishing our task, Adam made it more difficult and thereby raised the potential rewards that we can earn.

Eradicating the Yetzer Hara for Idolatry

The Talmud gives a fascinating account of the contrast between logical and lustful choices; between the rational appeal of sins and how they are framed by the Yetzer Hara. It tells of the Men of the Great Assembly, a congregation of 120 Sages, which also included several of the later prophets among their ranks, who prayed to rid the world of the Yetzer Hara for idolatry. They petitioned God by saying:

> *This is what destroyed the Temple, and burned the Sanctuary, and killed the Tzaddikim, and exiled the nation, and it is still dancing among us! We don't want it nor its reward!*

After three days of fasting and intensive prayer, the Almighty acceded to their petition and delivered to them the Yetzer Hara of idolatry, which they promptly neutralized.

The narrative continues: Emboldened by their success, the Men of the Great Assembly figured to tackle the Yetzer Hara for sexual immorality while they are at it, and after their petition, that Yetzer Hara was neutralized as well. But three days later, even the chickens had stopped procreating and no new eggs were being produced. They recognized that the Yetzer Hara for immorality serves a vital role in ensuring the world's perpetuation. Ultimately, they struck a happy medium by ending the Yetzer Hara for immorality with one's immediate relatives.[5]

The Men of the Great Assembly knew that Adam's sin changed the nature of the choices of sin from being logical to being lustful. They also

---

4   *Avos* 5:23.

5   *Sanhedrin* 64a.

understood that he made a calculated gambit to augment the meaning of life by making the choices more difficult and thus increasing the Divine reward for overcoming them. But they said, no thanks, "we neither want it nor its reward." These Sages sought to undo the outcome of Adam's sin with respect to idolatry—to remove the lustful component of prostrating to statues—and they succeeded. Defanged of its lust, rejecting explicit idolatry is now supremely easy. We are even inclined to ridicule idolaters of yore who were foolish enough to bow down before man-made pagan deities! Thanks to the intercession of the Men of the Great Assembly, we cannot fathom the lustful appeal for idolatry and can only assess it logically.[6] The same is true with respect to immorality with relatives. Both sins are still possible after this change, but the Yetzer Hara no longer adds a lustful dimension atop those choices. Now we can logically evaluate the benefits and drawbacks of these sins in the exact same way that Adam was able to evaluate and weigh the options of his sin before he committed it.

If we could remove the Yetzer Hara's lustful framing for all choices of sin, they would all have the same appeal as genuflecting to figurines of wood and stone, and, bereft of their tantalizing appeal, victory would almost be assured.

This groundbreaking insight underlies all the tactics of battling the Yetzer Hara. Logically, the Yetzer Hara's positions are bankrupt. Its power lies only in its ability to distort the logical choices and redirect them to the lustful case for sin. If man accepts the Yetzer Hara's framing of the choice, the only way to win is to muster up the intestinal fortitude to resist its onslaught. But we don't need to fight the enemy on its terms. If we manage to extract the substance from the sizzle and restore the choices to the pre-sin variety where it is only a logical equation, we gain a decisive advantage over the enemy and can easily overcome it. Thus, the real objective is not in *responding* to the Yetzer Hara's choice, but *reframing* it logically. By evaluating the pros and cons

---

6   See ibid. 102b, regarding Rav Ashi and Menashe, King of Judah.

of both options in a cool-headed fashion, the Yetzer Hara gets excised from the choice—and invariably sins will be rejected.

Illogical "Needs"

An example of this perspective is found in a statement in the Talmud cited in chapter 5:

> *There is a small organ in a person—if he satiates it, it is hungry; if he starves it, it is satiated.[7]*

The hungry organ at the center of man's war with the Yetzer Hara does not operate as would be expected. Ostensibly, when a hungry entity is fed, the hunger is relieved, whereas with this particular organ, the way to satiate it is by *not* capitulating to its professed "needs." "Feeding" it will result in the opposite occurring; instead of satiation, further desire will ensue. Capitulation to this sort of hunger will backlash and spur further hunger, not satiation.

This is illustrative of our understanding of the Yetzer Hara. When viewed logically, its professed "needs" are not really needs at all. If they were, submission would quench the desires. This reality, however, is hard to recognize amidst swirling lust. The tactics for combating this force are oriented around highlighting the logical choice and shrinking the lustful one.

Avos offers this as general advice for avoiding sin:

> *Calculate the benefits of a Mitzvah with its loss, and the benefit of a sin with its loss.[8]*

The Yetzer Hara adds a lustful component to our choices that muddles our ability to evaluate the options logically. The way to counteract that is by restoring the logical variables to the decision-making process. If someone had to graph out the pros and cons of sinning on a spreadsheet—if they made a cost-benefit-analysis of their behavior—and

---

7   *Sanhedrin* 107a.

8   *Avos* 2:1.

made the decision based upon the data, logic would direct him to the proper choice. Let's see some examples of how this is done.

Avoid the Stimuli

Our Sages deconstructed the methodology of the Yetzer Hara:

> *The eyes and heart are traitors against the body by facilitating it to sin: the eye sees, the heart desires, and the body sins.*[9]

Sins depend upon *external stimuli*. The eyes are the portals of the Yetzer Hara through which its distortions can enter and begin the progression that will lead to sin. If we allow the Yetzer Hara to gain a beachhead in our hearts through our eyes, it will likely lead into an actual sin. Hence, the Talmud encourages us to avoid venues or situations that will begin a process that may culminate in sin.[10] The "needs" of the Yetzer Hara are not real and thus are not internally and physiologically motivated. We are encouraged to nip it in the bud—to curtail the Yetzer Hara in the nascent stages of its progression and not allow it to get the ball rolling.

The Talmud extends this a step further in saying that the *primary* battle with the Yetzer Hara occurs before the opportunity for the sin itself arises, i.e., when the person chooses whether to allow the Yetzer Hara a foothold.[11] In that source, the Talmud lauds someone who refrains from ogling at immodest displays, and in qualifying that teaching, the Talmud notes that if a person could have chosen an alternative route and sidestepped the immodest display yet chose not to, he is a sinner *whether he ogled or not*. The conflict with the Yetzer Hara is at the earliest juncture in the progression leading to sin. Once a comparatively minor concession is offered to the Yetzer Hara, the die is cast and the ultimate sin is almost inevitable. Lustful choices are hard to resist and we'd best avoid them.

---

9   Quoted by *Rashi, Bamidbar* 15:39.
10   *Avodah Zarah* 20b; *Bava Basra* 57b.
11   *Bava Basra* 57b.

Denigrate the Yetzer Hara

We find a second tactic along these lines. The Talmud in several places encourages a person to denigrate and belittle his Yetzer Hara.[12] When asked how he resisted temptation when confronted by imagery that could potentially trigger the Yetzer Hara for immorality, one of the giants of the Talmud responded that they appear to him as a gaggle of dancing and chirping roosters. The tantalizing offerings of the Yetzer Hara are truly nothing more than deceptive smoke and mirrors. One way to combat it is to expose it for what it is and thereby reducing its seductions to being pathetic and laughable.

Forgetting to Sin

A third approach is found in *Avos*:

> *Rabban Gamliel the son of Rabbi Yehudah Hanassi says: Combining Torah study with labor is commendable, because toiling in both causes a person to forget sin.*[13]

Boredom is fertile breeding grounds for sin. As such, a person who is busy with the study of Torah (and other pursuits) is less prone to sin.

A careful reading of the statement reveals a fantastic insight: By keeping busy, man *forgets* to sin. The urge to sin is something that a person needs to be reminded of. The actions that the Yetzer Hara peddles are neither *natural nor inevitable* occurrences that are bound to happen. For the Yetzer Hara's agenda to be placed before a person, it needs to artificially elbow its way into his purview. But if that person is preoccupied with *whatever*—Torah study and even other things—the Yetzer Hara cannot grab his attention and remind him to sin. Boredom provides an opening for the Yetzer Hara to encroach upon the person with its distortionary fantasies, and is thus a segue to sin. When busy, man evaluates the choices of the Yetzer Hara logically leading to good outcomes.

---

12   *Berachos* 20a; *Bava Basra* 109b; *Gittin* 57a.
13   *Avos* 2:2.

Delay Tactics

A fourth suggestion for restoring logical choices in the face of the Yetzer Hara is found in a strange-sounding episode in the Talmud:

> *Rabbi Tzadok was propositioned by a Roman noblewoman, and he told her, "My heart is weak and I do not have stamina, is there something to eat?" She responded that there was some non-kosher food. He said, "What difference does it make? Someone who does this (immorality) eats this (non-kosher)." She lit the oven and placed the non-kosher meat in it, and Rabbi Tzadok leapt into the fiery oven. Surprised, she asked for an explanation for his behavior. He told her, "Someone who behaves like this, gets cast into a furnace (Gehinnom) like this." She responds, "Had I known that you were so opposed to sin, I would not have propositioned you in the first place."*[14]

The commentators grapple with this story. What was the meaning of Rabbi Tzadok's apparent initial acquiescence to sin and to consume the non-kosher food, and what prompted his change of heart?

Ben Yehoyada writes that this episode is teaching another way to avoid sinning. Rabbi Tzadok never actually entertained acceding to her seductions, rather he used a *delay tactic* to resist the sin. The external Yetzer Hara distorts the world around us and blurs the lines between lust and logic. It gets a man's heart pulsating and creates the seemingly irresistible allure of sin. Its lust, however, is vulnerable. The artificial drive to sin starts with a fever pitch but begins to dissipate immediately like a punctured balloon. If a person can delay the full force of its efforts for a little bit, cooler heads can prevail. Rabbi Tzadok understood that the impulse to sin will be quieted if a few minutes elapse and the logical choice will be restored, so he concocted an excuse to delay any decision until then. By doing that, the shelf life of the Yetzer Hara expired, and when the person is "sobered up" from the haze, its suggestions can be properly assessed and dismissed. Thus, after the delay he made

---

14 *Kiddushin* 40a.

the correct decision that it is preferable to die in martyrdom than to capitulate, and he promptly climbed into the flames.

All told, we have brought four tactics from our Sages to combat and resist the Yetzer Hara:

- To avoid encounters with it
- To belittle and denigrate it
- To be too busy to engage with it
- To delay until its force wanes before confronting it directly

The root of these tactics is one: To avoid the lustful choices of the Yetzer Hara and restore the logical choices. These are important battlefield tactics in this lifelong war, and there are other similar suggestions offered by our Sages. However, as demonstrated previously, the Yetzer Hara operates on two planes: The external Yetzer Hara uses the power of renewal to entice sin, and the internal Yetzer Hara acts as a mutinous foreign god that overpowers and compels sin from within. The suggestions surveyed in this chapter are primarily oriented at resisting the external Yetzer Hara. Even more critical is our struggle to uproot and evict the internal Yetzer Hara—the foreign god—from within us. In the forthcoming chapters, we will examine a landmark teaching in the Talmud that contains the secrets to doing that.

Chapter 16 Takeaways

- The Yetzer Hara effectuates sin by altering a choice to sin from being a logical choice to being a lustful choice.
- The many tactics offered to resist sin are different ways to restore the choice to the logical case for sin, and without temptation resisting sin is easy.

Vanquishing the Villain

*I*f we are serious in our quest to eradicate the Yetzer Hara, the foreign god, from within us, we must go beyond tactics to wrestle with the threat and seek solutions to be victorious over it. Our guide is a concise teaching in the Talmud:

> *Rabbi Levi bar Chama said in the name of Rabbi Shimon Ben Lakish:*
>
> *A person should continuously agitate the Yetzer Tov (good inclination) upon the Yetzer Hara.*
>
> *If he defeats it, good; if not, he should study Torah.*
>
> *If he defeats it, good; if not, he should recite the Shema.*
>
> *If he defeats it, good; if not, he should remind himself of the Day of Death.*[1]

In the previous chapter, we scoured some battlefield tactics for engaging with the enemy successfully. These four methods (#1—Agitating it with the Yetzer Tov; #2—Studying Torah; #3—Reciting the *Shema*; #4—Reminding him of the Day of Death) may help us win the war.

---

1   *Berachos* 5a.

Fulfilling the Pre-Birth Instruction

A careful reading of this citation hints at the larger objective of man to become more Soul-like. As we saw, in the pre-birth instruction, the fetus is told:

> *You must know that the Holy One, blessed is He, is pure; His angels are pure; and the Soul that He placed within you is pure. If you safeguard its purity, good. If not, behold I will take it from you.*

It is quite interesting that both the pre-birth instruction and the present Talmudic piece that outlines how to defeat the Yetzer Hara use the same format: The pre-birth instruction is an exhortation to safeguard the purity of his Soul, and it adds: "If you safeguard its purity, good (*mutav*). If not..." The Talmud's offering on defeating the Yetzer Hara adds similar addenda: "If he defeats it, good (*mutav*); if not..."[2]

The overlapping word usage is not coincidental. The threat to the purity of the Soul is precisely the Yetzer Hara, and therefore the pre-birth instruction to preserve the purity of the Soul is another way of saying, "defeat your Yetzer Hara." The litmus test if someone safeguarded their Soul's purity is if he successfully eliminated the threat to it. As such, it is imperative to understand these four methods to defeat our foe, how they work, and how can we utilize them.

Before we dig in, there are some important questions to keep in mind:

- Are these four methods to achieve one goal, or are there four different levels of defeating the Yetzer Hara?
- Another matter to consider is the required sequencing: First you agitate the Yetzer Tov upon the Yetzer Hara. If that doesn't defeat it, study Torah. If that does not work, you move on to the next step, and so on. From the text it seems that skipping an earlier step would preclude a later one from achieving its aim. Only Torah study that is *first preceded by an earlier agitation of the Yetzer Tov upon the Yetzer Hara* will work; only a recitation

---

of *Shema* that is preceded by Torah study will work, etc. In our probing of each step, we will attempt to understand how it counteracts the Yetzer Hara, and why it is reliant on the preceding method(s) to succeed.

The First Method

The first approach to defeat the Yetzer Hara is to agitate the Yetzer Tov upon it. What precisely this entails is not immediately evident. *Rashi* explains this as an instruction to wage war with the Yetzer Hara. Elsewhere, *Rashi* elaborates:

> *If the Yetzer Hara says, "Go sin!" it is insufficient to withhold from the sin; rather he should go and do a Mitzvah.*[3]

The *raison d'être* of the Yetzer Hara is to propel man to identify as a body and exhibit that with sin, and to ignore the Soul and its needs. This first and best approach to defeating it is to wage total war against it using our Yetzer Tov who promotes the Mitzvos desirous of the Soul. We should agitate the Yetzer Tov upon the Yetzer Hara by not only refraining from heeding its counsel, but deliberately choosing the opposite and embracing Mitzvos.

The importance of using Mitzvos to stifle and frustrate the Yetzer Hara is demonstrated in an interesting law: The Talmud teaches that although the Mitzvah of unloading cargo and relieving the burden from another person's animal generally takes precedence over the Mitzvah of helping another load his animal, when choosing between unloading the animal of his *friend* and loading the animal of his *enemy*, he should opt for the latter.[4] In this instance, he is required to first load the animal of the person he hates. Why should he help his enemy load the cargo, even if the needs of the animal of his friend are more urgent?

The Talmud explains its rationale: "To subdue the Yetzer Hara." The overarching goal of Mitzvos is to weaken the murderous grip that the Yetzer Hara has upon man. If two Mitzvah opportunities are present,

3   *Sanhedrin* 111b, s.v. u'*misgaber*.
4   *Bava Metzia* 32b.

the option that best repels the Yetzer Hara should be selected. Helping an enemy load the cargo on his animal is a more difficult Mitzvah than helping a friend unload cargo from his animal because it is doubly opposed by the Yetzer Hara: aside from its standard opposition to any Mitzvah, the Yetzer Hara does not want to see enemies reconcile. In the war with the Yetzer Hara, more progress will be made by choosing to help the enemy, and therefore that option should be selected.

Opposing the Yetzer Hara was always at the forefront of the agenda of great Jews. As a young man, the legendary spiritual dean of Mir Yeshiva, Rabbi Yeruchem Levovitz, would levy a monetary penalty on himself if he failed to oppose its whims a minimum of five times every day. Rabbi Yisrael Salanter, a cigarette smoker, once awakened with a strong urge to smoke but he did not have any cigarettes, and the only shop open at that hour was a great distance away. The founder of the Mussar Movement was torn by the dilemma of competing desires; he was tired and wanted to go back to sleep, and he was craving a smoke that was only accessible with great effort. As a Mussar master, he recognized that there were two Yetzer Hara–fueled desires at play: one encouraging laziness (roll over and sleep); the other pleasure-seeking (walk the distance to buy cigarettes). Either option amounted to capitulation to and further entrenchment of the Yetzer Hara. So, Rabbi Salanter devised a third option: He woke up and made the trek to the shop, and thereby opposed and weakened the Yetzer Hara-fueled laziness. When he arrived at the shop, he opted to forgo the cigarettes, thus countering the pleasure-seeking Yetzer Hara, and returned home. This is the outlook of someone who utilizes his Yetzer Tov to wage total war on his Yetzer Hara.

Death by Agitation

To agitate the Yetzer Tov on the Yetzer Hara means to fight a comprehensive and continuous war to marshal the intellect of the Soul over the lust promoted by the Yetzer Hara. The first method to defeat the Yetzer Hara is to continuously and deliberately reject, disobey, deny, resist, oppose, stifle, and combat it in every arena of its influence.

This process can result in its defeat. Every victorious battle empowers the Soul and is a chink in the armor of the Yetzer Hara. Each success results in the Yetzer Hara being continually weakened and diminished, and perhaps after a lifetime of fighting back, the Yetzer Hara will be eliminated entirely and man will be freed from its tentacles.

The Talmud concedes, however, that not everyone will be able to finish the job using this method: "If he defeats it, good, if not he should study Torah." Even if a person's skirmishes with the Yetzer Hara do not bring about total victory, the lessons of self-control and resisting the Yetzer Hara learned in this method will be invaluable down the road in method #2: Torah study.

Chapter 17 Takeaways

- If someone wants to uproot the internal Yetzer Hara, there is a specific sequence of four actions that will achieve that aim.
- The first method to defeat the Yetzer Hara is to wage total war against it.

Elixir of Life

*T*he next method to defeat the Yetzer Hara is Torah study. This notion is echoed in the Talmud.[1] In the latter source, the Talmud furnishes an analogy:

> *"And you shall place [the words of Torah upon your heart]."*[2]
> *[The Hebrew word for "And you shall place" (V'samtem) can also be read as "a perfect antidote" (sam tam); Torah is compared to an elixir of life.] This is analogous to a man who struck his son, causing a grave wound upon which he placed a bandage. [The father] said to him, "My son, so long as this bandage is on your wound you can eat and drink whatever you desire (even things that are apt to cause the wound to worsen), and bathe in hot or cold [water] without concern. But if you remove the bandage, behold, boils will fester." So too, the Holy One, blessed is He, said to Israel, "My sons, I created the Yetzer Hara and I created the Torah as an antidote. If you study Torah, you will not be subject to it, but if you do not study Torah, you will surely be subject to it, as it is stated, 'At the entrance sin crouches.' Additionally, all the machinations of the Yetzer Hara are to spur you to sin, but if you wish, study Torah and you will rule over it."*

---

1   *Sotah* 21a; *Kiddushin* 30b.
2   *Devarim* 11:18.

This analogy is similar to the Midrashic depiction referenced above in chapter 9 in which man is likened to a drowning sailor who can only be saved by grabbing on to the lifeline thrown to him by the captain of the ship. Both analogies acknowledge that by foisting the Yetzer Hara upon man, the Almighty placed his Soul in mortal danger, a predicament that can only be remedied by Torah study and Mitzvos.

How does Torah study function as a magic elixir against the Yetzer Hara? Also, we have posited that the four methods of defeating the Yetzer Hara must follow the required sequence. Why would Torah study prove ineffective at defeating the Yetzer Hara if it was not preceded by the first method of agitating the Yetzer Hara with the Yetzer Tov? *Rambam* will be our guide in answering both questions.

Thoughts of the Heart

At the end of the Laws of Forbidden Relationships, *Rambam* writes:

> *Thoughts of Yetzer Hara exist only in a heart devoid of wisdom.*[3]

In this short statement, *Rambam* demonstrates the structure of how Torah study counteracts the Yetzer Hara. In order for it to influence man, the Yetzer Hara must occupy the "thoughts of his heart." Man's heart, however, has room for only one kind of thought. By default, the Yetzer Hara fills that vacuum. But it is possible to evict those thoughts and replace them with thoughts of Torah. If man's heart is replete with thoughts of Torah, the Yetzer Hara will have no real estate in his heart to peddle thoughts of sin.

Laying out the structure of how Torah study counteracts the Yetzer Hara does not yet give us the complete picture. To gain a deep understanding on the matter, we must answer several fundamental questions:

- Why are thoughts of Torah and thoughts of the Yetzer Hara such opposites that they cannot coexist in the same heart?
- How indeed does man fill his heart with thoughts of Torah?

---

3   *Rambam*, Laws of Forbidden Relationships, 22:21.

• *Rambam's* formulation is also intriguing: Why does he identify the *heart* as the seat of thoughts? Is not the mind—the *brain*—where thoughts happen? Evidently, there are thoughts of the heart that are different than thoughts of the mind. What's the difference, and why will only Torah thoughts of the *heart* banish the Yetzer Hara?

Love of God and Knowledge of God

To find answers, we must examine the Mitzvah of loving God and *Rambam's* teachings relating to it. The Torah commands us to love God, "with all our heart, with all our Soul, and with all our resources."[4] Upon initial reflection, this Mitzvah does not appear to be doable. We have a hard time conceptualizing and defining God. Moreover, given that by design we are precluded from grasping God's Essence and thus contemplating it is futile and likely to distance man from Him, we are not allowed to enunciate the Name that refers to God's Essence. How can we be required to develop a comprehensive *emotional* love—"with all our heart, with all our Soul, and with all our resources"—for an Entity that we cannot even fully comprehend, and whose Name is therefore ineffable?

To compound this question, in the introduction to the *Sefer Hachinuch*, we learn that the Mitzvah of loving God is one of the six constant Mitzvos that apply at all times. Loving God is not an isolated activity that we *do*, rather it is a *constant state of being*; it is who we *are*. It does not seem achievable if we actively tried, yet it has to become second-nature so that it is continuously and effortlessly present. How do we develop a comprehensive emotional love of God that is present all the time?

In the *Book of Mitzvos*, *Rambam* shows the way:

> *The third Mitzvah is that we were commanded to love God. This is achieved by thinking and ruminating on His Mitzvos, His Torah, and His handiwork, until we grasp Him, and with grasping Him we will experience the greatest pleasure. That*

---

4   *Devarim* 6:5.

is the requisite love [of God.] In the words of Sifre: The verse instructs, "And you shall love Hashem your God," but I do not know how to love God? The [next] verse therefore continues, "And these words that I command you today shall be upon your heart." Through [placing the words of Torah upon your heart], you recognize and know He who spoke and the world was created.[5]

Our question—how can we love God when we cannot conceptualize Him—troubled the *Sifre* too. In the answer, we see that the way to love God is to *understand* Him, to grasp Him. *Once you recognize and know God, you will invariably love Him.* But how can we understand something that we are inherently precluded from understanding?

The *Sifre* reveals the workaround for this dilemma: *The Torah acts as a proxy for God.* It is His Mind, it is indivisible from Him, and to the degree that we understand Torah we understand God, and consequently we love Him. Hence the juxtaposition of the verses to love God and to have God's Torah upon your heart. Via the latter we can fulfill the former. When the words of Torah are upon your heart, you will have knowledge and understanding of God in your heart, and automatically you will love Him.

Foiling the Foreign god

Let's go back to our original subject of how Torah study foils the Yetzer Hara. *Rambam* taught us that "thoughts of Yetzer Hara exist only in a heart devoid of wisdom." Now we know why Torah and the Yetzer Hara are opposites. Torah is not a mere discipline of study; it is a proxy for understanding God. The degree of his immersion in Torah determines a person's level of knowledge and consequent love of God. Torah is therefore incompatible with the foreign god, the Yetzer Hara. At its core, the war with the Yetzer Hara is about who wields control over a person: Is it God who conveys His Will via the Torah and Mitzvos, or is his master the foreign god who seeks to usurp the Almighty's throne

---

5   *Rambam, Book of Mitzvos 3.*

and to compel man to follow its orders; to be its slave; to pursue bodily temptations; to treat this world as man's eternal home and to forget that it is merely a corridor to prepare for Olam Haba? Torah study affixes God in man's heart, which immediately results in him loving God and evicting the foreign god from within.

However, not just any kind of Torah study engenders knowledge and consequently love of God and eviction of the Yetzer Hara; only when the words of Torah "are upon your *heart*" does it lead to love of God. Only when your *heart* is full of thoughts of Torah is there no leftover room for the Yetzer Hara to squat. What is the distinction between thoughts of the mind and thoughts of the heart, and why will only thoughts of the heart evoke these desired results?

From *Rambam*'s words, we find the answer: Active, directed, and focused thoughts that are commissioned by choice are thoughts of the mind. A person *chooses* to think with their brain. *The thoughts of the heart are the undirected thoughts.* They are the thoughts that he reverts back to when he is not thinking about anything in particular. Thoughts of the heart are not the product of what a person chooses, but *a reflection of who he is*. If a person thinks thoughts of Torah when there isn't a Torah book open before him—when he has not made a conscious choice to study Torah yet his thoughts meander to Torah—then Torah occupies the thoughts of his heart, and that will yield love of God and banishment of the foreign god from his heart.

Rambam invokes this requirement when describing the process to achieve love of God: "This is achieved by *thinking* and *ruminating* on His Mitzvos, His Torah, and His handiwork, until we grasp Him." Actively thinking Torah thoughts is insufficient to bring about love of God. To love God, a person needs to think about Torah and go to the next step of ruminating and contemplating those thoughts *at all times*. The heightened connection between man and the Almighty's Torah—when Torah occupies the thoughts of his heart—results in love of God. This love of God is not an isolated emotion, rather it is a fixed state of being. The person and his heart have changed, and the love of God brought about by this change is constant, fulfilling the requirement that the Mitzvah of loving God be ever-present.

By examining the thoughts of man's heart, we can also find out who is his master. By default, the Yetzer Hara controls our heart, and therefore all the undirected thoughts are guided by it, and as a result we neither know nor love the Almighty. But through the process of converting the thoughts of our heart to those of Torah, our heart becomes occupied with Torah and consequently knowledge and love of God, and the Yetzer Hara gets scraped clean from within it, and the person achieves the great coveted victory over the enemy.[6]

Rabbi Akiva's Torah Study Modality

The kind of Torah study that results in transformation of heart was manifested by Rabbi Akiva. Our Sages tell his backstory: At the age of forty, he was a totally ignorant shepherd who harbored hostility to those who studied Torah. One day, while tending to his flock, he had an epiphany that prompted him to completely commit himself to Torah study: He was standing near a well and noticed an unusual cylindrical

---

6   Besides Torah, *Rambam* enumerates God's Mitzvos and handiwork as items to ruminate upon and thereby love God. Mitzvos are the Almighty's commands, and His handiwork refers to the world that He created and the miracles of nature. The Almighty's presence is embedded in each of these three, and through all three of them it is possible to access an understanding, awe, and love of our Creator. Perhaps, for that reason, *Rambam* does not say at the end of *Issurei Biah* that there are no thoughts of Yetzer Hara only in a heart devoid of Torah, rather in a heart devoid of wisdom. There are three kinds of thoughts that accomplish that goal, not exclusively Torah.

However, the Mishnah (*Avos* 3:7) teaches us that Torah study is the best of the three:

Rabbi Shimon says: If someone is walking along the way and studying Torah, and stops studying and remarks, "how lovely is the tree, how lovely is this field," behold he is liable with his life.

It is well-documented that refraining from Torah study is viewed very harshly by our Sages. What is Rabbi Shimon's point by noting that if he stops and comments on how lovely the foliage is that he is liable with his life? Perhaps he is invoking the principle that we can also conceive an understanding of our Creator via marveling at His world. The person who he is addressing is not mindlessly stopping to study Torah in order to talk about shrubbery; rather, because he passes by vibrant examples of the Almighty's stunning world, he decides to utilize the opportunity to ruminate upon the Almighty's handiwork in order to deepen his relationship with the Creator and to love God. Rabbi Shimon teaches that this person is making a grave miscalculation. Indeed, it is possible to love God via His handiwork—the wonderful and breathtaking world that He created for us—but an even better and more effective way to love God is through His Torah. Someone who settles for the mediocre way of connecting to God is "liable with his life."

hole bored into a rock. Upon inquiry, he learned that a steady drip of water aimed at that exact spot had, after many years, bore the hole into the rock. Immediately he applied a lesson to himself by saying, "if soft water can penetrate a hard rock, Torah that is hard can surely penetrate my heart which is soft." With conviction and determination, Rabbi Akiva immersed himself in Torah study and eventually became the foremost scholar of his age.[7]

Beyond being a motivational lesson that it is never too late to study Torah on the highest level, this teaching demonstrates the mechanics of *how* Rabbi Akiva studied Torah: It penetrated into his heart and fundamentally changed it. Elsewhere, the Yetzer Hara is compared to a stone heart.[8] With consistent and committed Torah study dripping upon man's stone heart, the Torah itself can penetrate and force the foreign god to abdicate its usurped throne.

Torah or Mitzvos?

The Talmud records a debate conducted by several Sages who were hiding out in an attic in order to escape Roman persecution. The question was posed: Which is greater: Torah study or Mitzvos which require actions?

Initially Rabbi Tarfon argued that Mitzvos are greater. In the end, a consensus coalesces behind Rabbi Akiva that:

> *Torah study is greater because Torah study leads to actions of Mitzvos.*[9]

There are several key problems with this citation:

- First, how can it be asserted that Torah study necessarily engenders actions of Mitzvos? Is it not possible to study Torah and not be a person of impeccable behavior?

---

7   *Avos d'Rabi Nosson* 6:2.
8   *Sukkah* 52a.
9   *Kiddushin* 40b.

- Second, the conclusion obviates the argument: If Torah study includes actions of Mitzvos as well, certainly it is greater, and who can possibly argue to the contrary?
- Third, the Talmud elsewhere seems to arrive at the opposite conclusion: "Rava was accustomed to say, 'The objective of Torah study is repentance and good deeds.'"[10] This implies that Mitzvos are greater than Torah study. Was Rava unaware that this question was already settled centuries earlier when the Sages in the attic concluded that Torah study is greater than Mitzvos?

The debate in the attic was not abstract; it was a halachic one. If someone must choose between Torah study and Mitzvos and can only do one of them, which is preferable? All the participants of that debate were in agreement that the *goal* of Torah and Mitzvos is to create a perfect person who does Mitzvos, as Rava maintained in his aphorism, and thus Rabbi Tarfon argued initially that Mitzvos are a better choice. Rabbi Akiva responded that if we were judging these activities *in isolation*, Mitzvos which achieve the goal are greater. But actions don't live in a vacuum. In Rabbi Akiva's view, Torah study necessarily mandates actions of Mitzvos, and therefore the collective benefit of Torah study tips the scale in its favor.

Rabbi Akiva was the appropriate figure to teach us that there is a kind of Torah study that fundamentally changes the person. Through the dripping of Torah upon it, the stone heart of the Yetzer Hara is remediated and automatically the person's behavior changes. The only reason why a person would consider not doing Mitzvos is due to the Yetzer Hara within him that suppresses his identity as a Soul. Torah study of the kind that Rabbi Akiva was accustomed to necessarily causes actions of Mitzvos because it changes the inner workings of the causes of actions; it chips away at the stone heart of the Yetzer Hara that inhibits actions of Mitzvos from being natural and preferable to begin with. Torah study *of this variety* is indeed a perfect antidote for the Yetzer Hara.

---

10 *Berachos* 17a.

But does any generic Torah study rebuff the Yetzer Hara? In a stunning statement, the Talmud shows that the answer is a resounding "no":

> *If he is meritorious, his Torah study is an elixir of life; if he is not meritorious, it is a potion of death.*[11]

Torah study is a perfect panacea against the Yetzer Hara *provided that certain conditions are met.* There is in fact a form of Torah study that is harmful, and instead of infusing a person with life, it is poisonous and deadly. Suppose a person studies Torah for the sake of receiving honor or plaudits, or to use the accrued knowledge to flaunt and lord over others, or to bend the Torah to conform to a preexisting view and not vice versa. Such Torah study accelerates rather than retards the Yetzer Hara's agenda. It is, therefore, a potion of death because it promotes the Yetzer Hara's goal to cause the Soul's demise.

Now we see why the Talmud says that the method of defeating the Yetzer Hara via Torah study is predicated on the preceding one—agitating it with the Yetzer Tov. The Yetzer Hara and Torah are only polar opposites when the Torah study is pitted against the Yetzer Hara's interests. If a person studies Torah in a way that the Yetzer Hara is desirous of, it is delighted to assist him in imbibing the potion of death. *The only way to use Torah study to defeat the Yetzer Hara is if the Torah study is against the Yetzer Hara's wishes.* The Yetzer Hara creates all sorts of challenges and obstacles to stop man from studying or, at a minimum, to divert the study into the kind that advances its agenda. To study Torah in a way that it replaces the foreign god with the knowledge and love of the Almighty, a person must have already acquired ample self-control and discipline by resisting all the Yetzer Hara's maneuvers as outlined by the first method of defeating the Yetzer Hara. This kind of Torah study will surely result in a total Torah takeover of his heart and evict the Yetzer Hara from squatting there.

---

11 *Yoma* 72b.

The Talmud acknowledges that this may not finish the deal. In the next chapter, we will attempt to follow the Talmud's next prescription: "If he defeats it, good; if not, he should recite the *Shema*."

Chapter 18 Takeaways

- We cannot foster an emotional love for God by thinking about theology; instead, we must ruminate upon His marvelous creations, such as His Torah.
- Torah study affixes God in man's heart and thereby removes the foreign god from squatting there.
- When study of Torah fills man's heart, when his undirected thoughts are of Torah, he will automatically develop a love of God, and there will be no room for thoughts of Yetzer Hara in his heart.
- Torah study of this variety transforms the person entirely, cleanses the Yetzer Hara from within him, and perfects all of his character.

The Shema

T he third way to defeat the Yetzer Hara is by reciting the *Shema*, the twice-daily recited prayer composed of three Torah sections.[1] An example of the *Shema* being used for this purpose is found in the narrative of the reunion of Yaakov and his favorite son, Yosef, after decades of separation. In describing the joyous and emotional initial meeting, the verse states that Yosef cried, but it makes no mention of Yaakov reciprocating the sentiment.[2] Quoting from our Sages, *Rashi* comments that indeed only Yosef was crying on Yaakov's shoulder, but Yaakov was stoically reciting the *Shema*. The commentaries (e.g., *Maharal*) puzzle over this discrepancy: If it was the appropriate time for reciting the *Shema*, why was Yosef *not* reciting it too, and if it was not the time to say the *Shema*, why *was* Yaakov saying it?

My grandfather offered a fantastic explanation: Our Sages teach that just as a king's chariot is always ready for any journey at the king's whim, our forefathers—Avraham, Yitzchak, and Yaakov—were always ready for prophecy.[3] Prophecy is the state of man when all barriers between him and the Almighty—chief among them being the Yetzer Hara—are removed, and only the Almighty fills his heart. The forefathers were permanently in that state. In preparing for the reunion with

---

1   *Devarim* 6:5–9, 11:13–21; *Bamidbar* 15:37–41.
2   *Bereishis* 46:29.
3   *Bereishis Rabbah* 47:6.

Yosef, Yaakov was worried that the gush of love and emotion of the momentous occasion would make him lose focus of the Almighty and perhaps the Yetzer Hara would fill that void, leading him to momentarily lose the state of readiness for prophecy and consequently being permanently removed from God's "chariot." To forestall the potential diminishing of his spiritual readiness, he recited the *Shema* and ensured that the Yetzer Hara would gain no foothold in his heart.

Still, some questions remain:

- How indeed does saying the *Shema* counter the Yetzer Hara?
- Also, is recital of *Shema* alone enough to uproot the Yetzer Hara from within?
- Thirdly, why does it not seem to work for us? We recite the *Shema* twice daily, yet for most it is a habitual exercise with little meaning. Why is that so?

Pledge of Allegiance to God

It is not hard to see how the *Shema* stands in opposition to the Yetzer Hara. The Talmud classifies the *Shema* as "accepting the yoke of the Kingdom of Heaven."[4] It is a declaration that the Almighty is One: Nothing else has independent existence, and everything else only exists because, and insofar as, He wills it to. By declaring the *Shema*, a person accepts that the Almighty is his Master to the exclusion of all other masters. The Yetzer Hara is the *foreign* god because it creates the illusion that entities outside God have inherent value. Adherents of the Yetzer Hara, as all humans are by default, bear *its* yoke. They are subject to the whims of this phony master and obey its directives unquestioningly. The objective of Torah and Mitzvos is to shed the yoke of this fallacious god and become faithful subjects of the Almighty, Creator of heaven and earth. The *Shema* is the pledge of allegiance to God, declarations in direct opposition to the Yetzer Hara and its rogue dominion.

---

4   *Berachos* 13a.

Realistic Shema and Aspirational Shema

The *Shema*, therefore, holds divergent meanings depending on who says it:

- For people who have successfully ridded themselves of the Yetzer Hara, declaring that God is One is a *conveyance of their existing reality*.
- For those in earlier stages of growth, the *Shema* is *aspirational*: they hope to purify themselves by purging the Yetzer Hara from within them and actually exhibiting that there is no power other than the Almighty. For those people, the *Shema* is a tool aiding in the process of becoming a person who embodies that ideal.

We find sources for both kinds of recitation of the *Shema*. The Talmud relates that on Yaakov's deathbed, the Divine Presence departed from him, and he worried that perhaps, like his grandfather Avraham with Yishmael and his father Yitzchak with Esav, one of his children had strayed from the way of God. In unison, his sons assuaged his fear by saying the *Shema*, indicating that just as Yaakov himself, they were totally subservient to the Almighty.[5] In this instance, reciting the *Shema* was a reflection of their *existing* mindset.

The *Shema* can also help a person to *acquire* that mindset. *Rambam* advises that the first step in the journey to achieve the life objective is to concentrate during the recitation of the *Shema*, an exercise that should be a primary emphasis of a person's spiritual agenda for *many years*. As such, the *Shema* headlines both the beginning of a path to purity and its conclusion.[6]

Rambam's guidance to spend *years* plumbing the depths of a few Torah paragraphs may raise eyebrows. Even the most intricate and nuanced ideas do not need years until they are properly understood. It seems that the hard work that *Rambam* is describing is not about *understanding the ideas of the Shema*, rather about *integrating and internalizing*

---

5   *Pesachim* 56a.
6   *Rambam, Guide to the Perplexed* 3:51.

them. It is not enough to *say or intellectually believe* that Hashem is One; we have to make that idea true within us by employing all the available measures to eradicate the foreign god from within us. That indeed is a multi-year journey.

Given that a person's involvement with the *Shema* spans many years, for our purposes we must address the following question: At which point along this continuum does our Talmudic teaching that *Shema* enables the defeat of the Yetzer Hara apply?

It seems that the power of the declaration of the *Shema* is in exact proportion to the degree that someone has worked on integrating the concepts of the *Shema* into his heart. The *Shema* is a transcendental confrontation with the powerful reality that nothing in the world has any meaning except the Creator—provided that this notion is congruent with the person's reality. The further along the journey of making himself compatible with the notion that God is One, the more evocative his recitation of the *Shema* is. If his recitation of *Shema* is rote lip service alone, i.e., if it does not stir up a powerful awakening, that indicates that within his heart that Yetzer Hara still rules supreme.

Rabbi Akiva's Recitation of the Shema

To demonstrate how evocative the *Shema* can be for someone who has dedicated a lifetime internalizing its messages, let us examine the striking episode of the martyrdom of Rabbi Akiva as chronicled in the Talmud. The Roman authorities had decreed that study of Torah was prohibited on pain of death, but Rabbi Akiva refused to comply and defiantly gathered crowds and taught them Torah. An onlooker inquired why he was not afraid of any repercussions, and Rabbi Akiva responded that Torah for Jews is like water for fish: Only while immersed in it can we truly have life. Though the harsh Roman decree promises to execute those who study Torah, without it we are surely dead.

In short course, Rabbi Akiva was arrested and tortured in a gruesome and barbaric manner. As the Romans were flaying his skin with iron combs, Rabbi Akiva was reciting the *Shema*. When his students asked him to explain why he was reciting the *Shema*, Rabbi Akiva responded:

My entire life I was distressed by reading the words of the Shema that command us to love God "with all our Soul," which teach that we must be willing to give up our life for God, saying, "When will this opportunity come so that I may fulfill it?" Now that the opportunity arrived, should I not fulfill it?![7]

The narrative continues that as Rabbi Akiva elongated the enunciation of the last word of the first verse of the *Shema*—*echad*—his Soul departed his body and a Heavenly voice declared:

Praiseworthy is Rabbi Akiva that his Soul departed with the word echad. Concurrently, the ministering angels said to the Almighty, "This is Torah and this is its reward?!"

The narrative concludes with a second Heavenly voice which boomed, "Praiseworthy are you Rabbi Akiva, for you are invited to the life of Olam Haba."

This Talmudic narrative is intriguing for many reasons, not the least of which is grappling with the theodical problems inherent in such terrible things befalling the great Rabbi Akiva. But for now, I want to examine two points:

- First, Rabbi Akiva told his students that for all his days, he bemoaned the fact that he never had an opportunity to die for God in martyrdom. Every time he recited the *Shema* and *verbally* pledged to give his life for God, he yearned for the chance to *actualize* that commitment, and was greatly distressed by the lack of such an opportunity. Halachah mandates that a Jew forfeit his life to sanctify God's Name under certain circumstances, but we hope to never have to face that dilemma. Ideally, we would prefer to never be confronted with those situations and need to die. Rabbi Akiva was dejected at the opportunity to die for God *not* arising. What is the explanation of Rabbi Akiva being anxious to die for God on a daily basis?

---

7   *Berachos* 61b.

- A second matter to puzzle over is the precise words the angels use to express their incredulity at the sight of Rabbi Akiva's grisly death—"This is Torah and this is its reward?!" While it is certainly shocking that the Almighty allowed Rabbi Akiva to endure such suffering, in this particular episode his Torah greatness is not on display. Why then do they contrast "this is Torah"—as if his Torah mastery is before them—with "and this is its reward?!"

Interestingly, these exact words—"This is Torah and this is its reward?!"—appear elsewhere in the Talmud with respect to Rabbi Akiva's death. In that source, we are told that when Moshe ascended to Heaven to receive the Torah, he asked the Almighty why He needed to draw crownlets above the letters in the Torah scroll. The Almighty responded that in the future a great Sage named Rabbi Akiva will deduce many Torah laws from each jot and tittle above the letters. Moshe was then granted a prophetic vision of Rabbi Akiva's Torah prowess. After seeing his Torah greatness, Moshe was also shown his macabre execution by the Romans. Like the angels, he too asked, "This is Torah and this is its reward!?"[8] In Moshe's case, however, there was a juxtaposition of Rabbi Akiva's death and his superlative Torah greatness, and contrasting the two was appropriate. Here, the angels saw Rabbi Akiva reciting the *Shema*, and thereupon ask, "This is Torah..." as if Rabbi Akiva's Torah greatness was exhibited before them, even though it was not. While we can certainly answer that Rabbi Akiva's reputation preceded him, and his greatness in Torah was well-known to the angels, perhaps there is a specific reason why the angels referenced his Torah during his death.

Torah and the Shema

In the previous chapter, we learned how Rabbi Akiva's Torah bored into his heart and thereby supplanted the stone of the Yetzer Hara with love of God. Through Torah, Rabbi Akiva had expelled the Yetzer Hara and its influences, and transformed himself into a pure Soul and

---

8   *Menachos* 29a.

adopted its agenda as instinctive. In the Talmud's narrative about his death, we see the same quality exhibited. Torah is as vital for the Soul as oxygen is for the body. When Rabbi Akiva refused to abide by the Romans' decree against Torah study, he compared a Jew removed from Torah to a fish out of water because, as someone who identified with his Soul sensorially, *he literally felt that he needed Torah for his survival.* Abstinence from Torah was, for Rabbi Akiva, not an option.

When Rabbi Akiva recited the *Shema*, there was no disparity between what he said and how he lived. Declaring *"Hashem Echad,"* that God is the sole Power, was not a platitudinal saying; rather, it was a true reflection of the most basic reality that he had integrated into his life *through his Torah study.* For him, recitation of the *Shema* created such an awakening that he felt a strong urge to actualize it with the ultimate act of demonstration that the Almighty is One and that the Yetzer Hara's agenda is hogwash by forfeiting his life for God. When he said the first verse of the *Shema* every day, he was galvanized to die for God and was saddened when he could only *verbally commit* to doing so in the second verse, "and you shall love Hashem your God with all your hearts, with all your Soul..." The experience of saying the *Shema* was so powerful that merely verbally committing to give up his life for God was insufficient to satisfy Rabbi Akiva's intense acceptance of the yoke of Heaven; he yearned and awaited the day to finally be able to do it in practice.

When the angels saw his demise, they asked, "This is Torah and this is its reward?!" The way the angels processed this story, Rabbi Akiva's Torah was on display too. He invested a lifetime immersed in the previous method of defeating his Yetzer Hara—Torah study—that penetrated his Yetzer Hara as the steady water bores a hole through a rock. The Torah changed him internally, uprooted his Yetzer Hara from within him, and transformed him into a person who lived exclusively as a Soul and strove only for Olam Haba. *As a result of his assiduous Torah study and the transformation it effectuated*, his recitation of the *Shema* amounted to a transcendental acceptance of the yoke of Heaven, and prompted a daily bemoaning of the fact that he does not have an opportunity to actualize his submission to God in martyrdom. When he finally fulfilled this Mitzvah, while on the surface it looked like an act of *martyrdom*, the angels plumbed to its roots and they saw the culmination of Rabbi Akiva's Torah and aptly wondered, "This is Torah and this is its reward?!"

Provided that the preconditions of *integrating* the *ideas* of the *Shema* into the person's reality have been met, the *Shema* is an incredible tool for vanquishing the Yetzer Hara. Only after someone has filled his belly with the first two methods to defeat the Yetzer Hara—frustration of the Yetzer Hara and Torah study—will reciting *Shema* work to disrupt the Yetzer Hara. Yaakov completed this journey. Like Avraham and Yitzchak, he was totally free of submission to the Yetzer Hara,[9] and therefore was totally submitted to God, and had no inhibitors to being always ready for prophecy. Hence, his declaration of *Shema* was remarkably potent in ensconcing God as the only One that has any independent value. When he was about to meet Yosef, he was worried that this unexpected reunion would amount, for him, to a spiritual degradation of losing his status as being part of the "chariot" that is always primed for prophecy, and he unleashed this tool. Rabbi Akiva too: His valiant efforts to install the Almighty as his supreme internal Master resulted in daily craving for martyrdom when he said the *Shema*.

In short, the third method of defeating the Yetzer Hara must be preceded by the previous two because the feelings of submission to God evoked by the *Shema* are proportional to the earlier work of resisting the Yetzer Hara. That said, even for those of us who are not deeply moved by the *Shema*, concentration while saying it can go a long way toward making it a meaningful daily encounter with the Almighty's Omnipotence, and thereby propel us forward in our journey.

If reciting the *Shema* does not succeed in defeating the Yetzer Hara, the Talmud instructs us to proceed to the final method: to remember the Day of Death.

---

9   *Bava Basra* 16b.

Chapter 19 Takeaways

- The *Shema* prayer is a pledge of allegiance to God, to the exclusion of the foreign god.
- The more that reality is true within a person, the more powerfully evocative the person's recitation of the *Shema* will be.

Remember
the Day of Death

*T*he fourth and final method to vanquish the Yetzer Hara is remembering the Day of Death. That thinking about one's own
demise prevents sin is already established in the Mishnah:

> *Akavia Ben Mahalalel says: Visualize three things and you will
> not come to sin: know from where you came, to where you are
> going, and before Whom you are destined to give a reckoning
> and accounting. Know from where you came: from a putrid
> drop; to where you are going: to a place of dust, worms, and
> maggots; and before Whom you are destined to give a reckoning
> and accounting: before the King of kings, the Holy One, blessed
> is He.*[1]

When a person dwells on the shameful origins of his body, the tem-
porality of life in this world, and the pending reckoning before the
Almighty, he is less likely to sin.

We have postulated that these four methods follow a specific sequencing: The process must begin with agitating the Yetzer Tov upon
the Yetzer Hara; if that does not complete the job the next step is
Torah study; and then reciting the *Shema*; and finally if all those three

---

1   *Avos* 3:1.

do not succeed, remembering the Day of Death. The Talmud does not conclude, as by the previous three, how to proceed if remembering the Day of Death is ineffective. Evidently, this approach is guaranteed to succeed, provided that the three earlier methods were attempted. Why does thinking about the Day of Death counter the Yetzer Hara; how is it done; and why will it only work after the previous methods have been attempted?

Choose Your World

Life's central conflict is the choice of which world to prioritize: this one or Olam Haba. Our Sages train us to view this world as a corridor wherein we must prepare ourselves for Olam Haba. The Yetzer Hara instructs us to transform *this world* into the goal by encouraging the prioritization of the body and its physical world (sin).

But one thing is undeniable: Any act that favors this world has a definitive shelf life. On the Day of Death, when man crosses over from this world to the next, all investments of time and resources that he plowed into this world and into his body instantly become valueless. Consequently, the only way that the Yetzer Hara can con man into making choices optimized for the temporary world and neglecting the permanent one is if the fact that man's time here is fleeting and swiftly coming to an end is obscured. Man only sins if under the impression—consciously or otherwise—that this world is the only one that he has. The Yetzer Hara's power lies only in a fallacy that the Day of Death *will not arrive*. Thus, the Yetzer Hara's perspective implodes when the person remembers the Day of Death. With a stark reminder that what the Yetzer Hara is advocating is nothing short of a Ponzi scheme destined to collapse at the Day of Death, man will recalibrate which world he is living for and adjust his behavior accordingly.

The Nazir from the South

This approach is captured in a wonderful Talmudic story regarding a Nazir, someone who accepts a vow to abstain, typically for thirty days, from wine (and other grape derivatives), from coming into contact with impurity, and from hair cutting. At the conclusion of the thirty-day period, the Nazir would travel to Jerusalem and undergo a procedure that included the shaving of all of his hair. Should a Nazir accidentally become impure during the period of his vow, he must also travel to Jerusalem and offer a sacrifice before restarting his Nazirhood. In general, the Sages frowned upon people becoming Nazirim because they are creating unnecessary prohibitions and "what the Torah prohibited is sufficient." In this episode, we learn about a particular Nazir whose vow was lauded by Shimon the Righteous, the High Priest and greatest Sage of his time:

> *Shimon the Righteous said: I never partook in the offering of a Nazir who became defiled (out of disapproval of people accepting the Nazir vow), with one exception: Once, a good-looking Nazir with beautiful eyes and flowing locks came from the South. I asked him, "Why did you decide to destroy your beautiful hair [by becoming a Nazir who must shave his hair]?" He said, "I was a shepherd overseeing my father's flocks, and once, while filling water from a spring, I saw my handsome reflection in the water, and my Yetzer Hara pulsated and sought to destroy my world (by propelling me to utilize my looks to pursue a life of sin). I said to my Yetzer Hara," continued the Nazir, "'Wicked one! Why are you taking pride in a world that is not yours; in a body that will eventually be consumed by worms and maggots? I hereby pledge that I will cut off my hair for the sake of Heaven.'" Immediately, I (Shimon the Righteous) stood and kissed his head, and said, "My son, may there be more Nazirim like you in Israel."[2]*

The Nazir saw his handsome visage reflected in the water, which caused his Yetzer Hara to flare up and incite him to sin. He responded to the threat by spelling out its ludicrous implications: "Why are you taking pride in a world that is not yours; in a body that will eventually be consumed by worms and maggots?" The Yetzer Hara's proposal is to

---

2   *Nedarim* 9b.

cause man to value the world of the body as an *end*, and that is absurd because the body is clearly a *means*; its ultimate destiny is worms and maggots. The Nazir remembered the Day of Death and hence that this world is *not* his, rather it is a preparatory one to create the upcoming world *which is his*. This realization deflated his Yetzer Hara, and immediately the Nazir behaved accordingly by dedicating the same entity that spurred the sin—the hair—for a Mitzvah, i.e., as a means to achieving Olam Haba.

The Time-Travel Argument

Remembering the Day of Death can also provide a logical case for Mitzvos, irrespective of religiosity. Suppose someone was able to time-travel twenty years into the past. Once there, the profitable thing would be to buy stocks (make investments) guided by his foreknowledge of the future. It would be patently absurd for him to make long-term investments in companies that he knows will go bankrupt. A time-traveler would be the greatest investor because time travel affords the advantage of future knowledge.

With respect to choosing where to invest the resources of our life, we do indeed know the future: Our Day of Death will come and our body will be consumed by worms and maggots. For the purposes of making investments today, *we are like time-travelers*. When the Yetzer Hara tries to get us to invest in our body-centric existence and ignore our Soul, we know for sure that this is a long-term investment that is bound to crash to zero at the Day of Death. Even those who are dubious about the existence of Olam Haba have to admit that the mere *chance* of eternal dividends outweigh the assured crash of what the Yetzer Hara is peddling.

Vivid Awakening

To fully capture the power of remembering the Day of Death, a dose of visualization is needed. The Talmud does not state that a person should remember *that he will die*, rather he should remind himself of the *Day of Death*. The Mishnah also stresses that you must "visualize three things and you won't come to sin"; simply *knowing* them is insufficient to make it tangible. In addition, both the Mishnah and the Nazir add color to the idea that our life here is temporary by noting that man's body will soon be consumed by "worms and maggots." As a theoretical abstraction, everyone knows that their life as it is currently constituted will end. The vivid image of your lifeless body being lowered into a hole, covered with dirt and dust, and worms creeping through your casket to nibble and gnaw at your flesh is *confronting that reality in a way that inspires action.* "It is better to go visit a house of mourning than a house of feasting, for it is the end of every man, and the living will take it to heart."[3] While visiting a house of mourning, you do not discover a hitherto unknown fact that people die; rather it creates a strong, palpable reminder of the ephemerality of body-based life that has a sobering effect on the Yetzer Hara who is determined to make you act as if that was untrue.

Still, even remembering the Day of Death will only defeat the Yetzer Hara after the previous three methods were attempted. For someone who is already inclined to becoming a Tzaddik, musing on his mortality will push him across the finish line to defeat it.

For a Rasha, remembering the Day of Death *will likely yield the opposite outcome*: a frenzied rush to maximize bodily pleasures before time expires. The Chofetz Chaim noted that when Esav the Rasha confronted his own demise, he willingly signed off on the most lopsided transaction in history: forfeiting his firstborn birthright with all its eternal benefits to Yaakov in exchange for a bowl of red soup. His justification for this transaction: "Behold I am going to die, and what is the birthright for me?"[4] For Esav, remembering the Day of Death did *not* evoke a spiritual reawakening and a newfound appreciation of matters of the Soul. To the contrary, remembering that his days in this world are numbered made the spiritual birthright *less* valuable in Esav's eyes compared to the physical soup.

The Talmud guides us to remember the Day of Death after consistently frustrating the Yetzer Hara, studying Torah, and reciting the *Shema.* For someone who is already conditioned to have self-control, to love the Almighty, and to accept His dominion, remembering his own

---

3   *Koheles* 7:2.
4   *Bereishis* 25:32.

demise will stifle his Yetzer Hara. Such a person is already *intellectually* aware that this world is a corridor before Olam Haba, but is struggling with a formidable Yetzer Hara who strives to make that relegated to the theoretical realm alone. When he is confronted with his pending death, that theoretical notion becomes tangible, and his Yetzer Hara's fiction evaporates like a fleeting dream.

Chapter 20 Takeaways

- Visualizing one's Day of Death directly torpedoes the Yetzer Hara's modus operandi and will save someone from sin, provided that he has developed a taste for spiritual matters.
- For a person who is not on the path toward becoming a Tzaddik, thinking about their death will likely create the opposite effect.

CHAPTER 21

The Scope of Victory

*A*t the onset of our analysis of the four methods to defeating the Yetzer Hara, we asked if they are four different ways to arrive at the *same result*, or does each approach affect the Yetzer Hara in its own way, and if so what are the differences?

Upon studying how each method counters the Yetzer Hara, it seems incontrovertible that each of the four defeats the Yetzer Hara on a different dimension and scale. Let's analyze the evidence.

Disparity of Time of Engagement

For starters, each of the four methods involves some sort of engagement with the Yetzer Hara, but with each ensuing method the time of engagement *decreases*.

The first one states: "A person should *continuously* (*l'olam*, literally, *forever*) agitate his Yetzer Tov upon his Yetzer Hara." In order to succeed in defeating the Yetzer Hara by agitating it with the Yetzer Tov, a neverending, unrelenting, and uncompromising battle is needed.

The next method is Torah study. While the verse teaches that we must study Torah "by day and night,"[1] which would seem to imply that there is no downtime from it, the Talmud notes that it is not obligatory at all times.[2] There are even times when the study of Torah is *forbidden* (such

---

1   *Yehoshua* 1:8.
2   *Menachos* 99b.

as when in the restroom). When *Rambam* maps out a recommended daily schedule, he apportions three hours for working along with nine hours for Torah study.[3] By any standard, nine hours of Torah study daily is impressive, but it is still less than "continuously."

The third method is the recitation of the *Shema*, which under normal circumstances is only said twice daily. Yes, Yaakov deployed the *Shema* to forestall a threat of the Yetzer Hara at other times too, but for the most part it is limited to twice daily.

The final method—remembering the Day of Death—does not even have a designated time to be done, and it is only used as a way of preventing the clear and present danger of an immediate sin, as in the case of the Nazir from the South.

The disparity of time of engagement is not by chance. Our Sages have likened the Yetzer Hara to an enemy with whom we must wage war. As in warfare, being victorious in a skirmish does not guarantee success in a battle or a campaign, and certainly not in the whole war. The degree, duration, and intensity of the battle with the Yetzer Hara determine the scope of the ensuing triumph over it.

Method #4: Fending off Sin

Let us begin with the last method, remembering the Day of Death, which enables the narrowest scope of victory, and work our way back to the earlier, more comprehensive methods of defeating the enemy.

Remembering one's own demise is a highly effective tactic to repulse the Yetzer Hara's advances of *sin*. The Mishnah's words are precise: "Visualize three things and you won't *sin*: know from where you came…" Remembering the Day of Death prevents the Yetzer Hara from *completing* its actions; only the *sin* is stopped, not the force behind it. Of course, every victorious battle over the enemy weakens it and helps contribute toward its ultimate decimation, but after resisting one sin, another battle is sure to come. This method will not achieve total victory by *eliminating* or *neutralizing* the enemy, nor will it prevent future attacks.

---

3   *Rambam*, Laws of Torah Study 1:12.

Method #3: Avoiding the Battle

Defeating the Yetzer Hara by reciting the *Shema* expands the scope of the victory. Yaakov recited the *Shema* to *prevent* the Yetzer Hara from attacking. He sensed that his upcoming reunion with Yosef may be fertile grounds for him to momentarily forget his Creator, and he averted the danger by reciting the *Shema*. By accepting the yoke of Heaven, he sidestepped the battle entirely.

That said, even this method only provides a temporary cease-fire. Rabbi Akiva was inspired to die for God each day *while reciting the Shema*, but after he finished the *Shema* that desire quieted. When employed properly, reciting the *Shema* creates a temporary upswing of commitment to the Almighty that suppresses the possibility of sin for a short while. The *Shema* averts the attack of the Yetzer Hara, but after the inspiration dissipates the enemy lies in wait.

Method #2: Neutralizing the Yetzer Hara

Torah study provides an even greater victory over the Yetzer Hara. The Talmud teaches that the Torah is a *shield* against the Yetzer Hara.[4] Unlike the *Shema*, which will only prevent individual attacks, so long as the person is connected to Torah study, the Torah protects him with a blanket shield from the Yetzer Hara's incursions.

However, even in this method the Yetzer Hara is not *eliminated*. The Yetzer Hara is compared to a wound and Torah study to a bandage that covers it and provides protection from infection so long as it is not removed.[5] If the "bandage" would be removed, invariably the dormant "boils" of the Yetzer Hara will erupt. Torah study does not eliminate the Yetzer Hara, it only *suppresses it from surfacing*. Underneath the bandage, the wound still exists and the threat of it surfacing looms large. In fact, *Rashi* writes that while the Torah study shields its bearer from the Yetzer Hara, the Yetzer Hara is still active, not in enticing sin but

---

4   *Sotah* 21a.
5   *Kiddushin* 30b.

in trying to undermine and destabilize that shield itself by trying to disrupt the Torah study.[6]

Method #1: Eliminating the Enemy

The best form of victory over the Yetzer Hara is when it is no longer a threat. If someone is successful in implementing the first method brought by the Talmud—agitating the Yetzer Hara with the Yetzer Tov—by utilizing all the various tools, including those of the subsequent methods, to continuously fight and resist the enemy, over time his Yetzer Hara will weaken until it is eliminated entirely.

The Talmud shows the two ways that this could play out:

> *Avraham converted his Yetzer Hara into being good, but King David was unable to do that and instead killed it.*[7]

Avraham managed to convert the force designed to make man sin into a Mitzvah-seeking Yetzer Tov. He transformed his erstwhile enemy into an ally! David had to struggle with the Yetzer Hara, and achieved the next best option: total decimation of the enemy. After they were done, David harbored only a Yetzer Tov, an unopposed Soul, but Avraham converted his Yetzer Hara into a second Yetzer Tov.

This raises an interesting question. Resisting the Yetzer Hara weakens it, and it is conceivable that David continuously starved his until it died. But Avraham took his Yetzer Hara and made it *good*. How was that done? By what means can a person reprogram the nature of the entity designed by the Almighty to push him to sin?

Even Greater than Altruism

An approach can be suggested from a seemingly inexplicable Talmudic teaching:

---

6   *Sotah* 21a, s.v. *v'adayin.*

7   *Yerushalmi, Berachos* 9:5.

> *Someone who pledged to give a sela (coin denomination) to charity in order that his son be healed or in order that he merit Olam Haba, behold he is a complete Tzaddik.*[8]

The Talmud arrives at the surprising conclusion that when a person gives charity with the express condition that in its merit he should garner a tangible benefit, it demonstrates that he is a complete Tzaddik. Subsequently, the Talmud qualifies this by noting that the giver's *true intent* was to give the charity, even if he does not receive his professed kickback; i.e., even if his son subsequently died from his illness, he still wanted to give that donation.

This teaching is problematic on two fronts:

- First, why is such a giver portrayed as a *complete* Tzaddik? Seemingly, the *altruistic* giver who gives charity out of the goodness of his heart with no strings attached is even greater. It would be understandable had the Talmud declared that *even if* someone gives charity with an expectation of getting something in return, he is doing a Mitzvah and is righteous. By labeling the non-altruistic giver as a *complete* Tzaddik, the Talmud implies that his Mitzvah is even greater than the altruistic giver. The opposite seems more appropriate.

- A second problem lies with the Talmud's assertion that his true desire was to give charity even if he failed to receive what he explicitly conditioned his donation upon. How does the Talmud know that he wanted to give the charity even if his child dies? How can we be certain that he holds altruistic intentions that *contradict his explicit statement at the time of the Mitzvah*?

I once heard an explanation for this Talmudic teaching from Rabbi Yosef Jacobs of Jerusalem, who argued that it is describing the highest form of opposing the Yetzer Hara. Even greater than resisting and warring with the Yetzer Hara is forcing it to desire the agenda of the Soul. The person in question genuinely wanted to obey his Soul and give charity. He was keenly aware, however, that he faced stiff resistance

---

8   *Bava Basra* 10b.

in doing this Mitzvah from the Yetzer Hara. The Yetzer Hara sees no tangible, earthly benefit from giving money to charity, and strongly opposes this Mitzvah. To counteract this resistance, the giver devised a scheme to leave the Yetzer Hara with no choice but to support the endeavors of the Soul. By adding an irresistible kickback-clause to the Mitzvah that the Yetzer Hara also wants, he handcuffed the Yetzer Hara into supporting the agenda of the Soul, and, with its resistance cleared, the Mitzvah was easily fulfilled.

The Talmud justly maintains that even if his son dies, his true intention was to give charity nonetheless. The condition that he placed upon the Mitzvah was not his ultimate intention—just the persuasion device used to compel his Yetzer Hara to support it. A person who combats his Yetzer Hara with such ingenuity is well on his way to defeating it entirely and becoming a complete Tzaddik.

This approach is the highest fulfillment of the Talmudic instruction that a person should always agitate their Yetzer Tov upon their Yetzer Hara. When a person links the Mitzvos to the interests of Yetzer Hara as well, the Yetzer Hara gets agitated and frustrated because its hands become tied and it is forced to root for the Mitzvos. As this continues to happen, the Yetzer Hara develops a taste for Mitzvos and begins to alter its preferences. Avraham skillfully and consistently employed this method until his Yetzer Hara was healed of its sinful proclivities and was transformed into being solely desirous of Mitzvos.

Regardless of whether through the Abrahamic or Davidic variety, defeating the Yetzer Hara via the first method of frustrating it with the Yetzer Tov results in the complete and permanent neutralization of the enemy. While it is unlikely that we could completely defeat our Yetzer Hara, hopefully we will deploy the wide array of tools and tactics delineated in Part III to engage with the enemy and resist its efforts to sully our Soul. The vise that the Yetzer Hara maintains over man is vast, and its power may seem insurmountable, but by being mindful of its deceptive schemes and by studying and practicing the methods to thwart it, we will begin to rack up wins against our mortal foe.

————————————————————————— **Chapter 21 Takeaways**

- The four methods to defeat the Yetzer Hara achieve different degrees of victory:
  - Remembering the Day of Death—a tactic to prevent sin.
  - Reciting the *Shema*—momentarily prevents the Yetzer Hara from operating within man.
  - Studying Torah—a blanket shield that suppresses but does not eliminate the Yetzer Hara.
  - Agitating the Yetzer Hara—this method can potentially result in the Yetzer Hara being eliminated entirely, either by it being "killed" or by it being converted into a second Yetzer Tov.

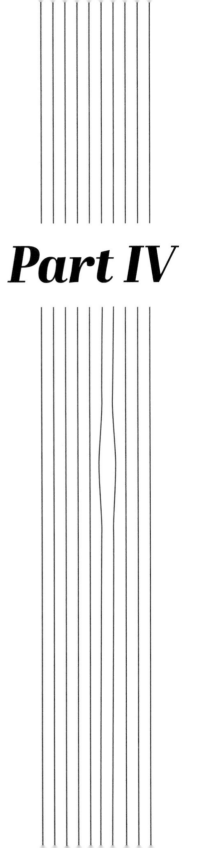

Part IV

The Values Hierarchy

T he study of how Torah and Mitzvos change a person would be incomplete if we did not survey the greatest paragons of Jewish history and deconstruct their ascent to greatness. Part IV will focus on the prophets of yore, with a particular emphasis on Avraham and Moshe. In this section, we will try to characterize the respective achievements of these spiritual giants, and see how their personas fit into what we have hitherto discovered regarding what Torah and Mitzvos do to man.

The Three Forefathers

Our Sages give us two interconnected teachings about the three fore-fathers of our nation, Avraham, Yitzchak, and Yaakov:

> The Rabbis taught: Three people were given a taste of Olam Haba in this world by the Holy One, blessed is He: Avraham, Yitzchak, and Yaakov…
>
> Three people were not subject to the control of the Yetzer Hara: Avraham, Yitzchak, and Yaakov.[1]

The triumvirate of Avraham, Yitzchak, Yaakov were unique on two accounts: They got to experience a flavor of the next world, Olam Haba, whilst residing in this world, and all three of them were freed from the clutches of the Yetzer Hara. The Talmud deduces both teachings

---

1   *Bava Basra* 16b–17a.

from the fact that the Torah uses the word *"kol,"* meaning "throughout all," by each of them, implying that the presence and the dominion of the Creator permeated them entirely. The mere existence of the Yetzer Hara within a person detracts from the Almighty's total dominion over him, even if its influence is minuscule. When we are told that the presence of God permeated Avraham, Yitzchak, and Yaakov *entirely*, invariably we know that the foreign god was eliminated from within them.

By this same line of reasoning the Talmud concludes that they were able to taste Olam Haba. Olam Haba refers to the spiritual world where the presence of the Almighty is pervasive and the Yetzer Hara is non-existent. For us, that world is the *next* world. By proactively ridding themselves of the foreign god, Avraham, Yitzchak, and Yaakov created the conditions of the next world despite being present here, and therefore got a flavor of what that world is like.

Battling and defeating the Yetzer Hara is our life objective. The Talmud teaches that only Avraham, Yitzchak, and Yaakov were *totally* victorious in that war. To understand the achievements of our three forefathers we must answer three questions:

- First, what is the extent of the Yetzer Hara's influence?
- Second, how did they manage to totally excise it?
- Third, what are the consequences of removing the Yetzer Hara entirely?

Let us analyze the sources that outline the processes that our forefathers—primarily Avraham—undertook to reach their greatness, and perhaps we can find answers to these questions.

Charting Avraham's Journey

Our Sages give a surprising statistic about Avraham's war on idolatry. It teaches that while our books of Mishnah and Talmud that cover the laws of idolatry contain five chapters, the book of the laws of idolatry that Avraham had consisted of four hundred chapters.[2] In other words,

---

2   *Avodah Zarah* 14b.

Avraham's laws of idolatry were eighty times more comprehensive than ours!

What was included within the parameters of idolatry for Avraham but not for us? We can piece together the answer with what we already know. Capitulation to the Yetzer Hara is synonymous with idolatry. The Yetzer Hara, after all, is the foreign *god*, and to whatever degree that it maintains control over man, God is not man's Master. In the five chapters of the laws of idolatry that exist in our version of the Talmud, battling the Yetzer Hara does not make an appearance. It is possible for us to fully abide by our laws of idolatry while the foreign god still has a foothold within us. Avraham expanded the boundaries of the laws of idolatry eightyfold to include all aspects of subjugation to the foreign god, and with herculean effort eradicated all vestiges of the foreign god from within him. Once freed from the clutches of the Yetzer Hara, Avraham tasted the spiritual sublimity of Olam Haba.

Why does the presence of the foreign god preclude man from tasting Olam Haba? My grandfather would explain the critical distinction between this world and Olam Haba with this Shabbos morning prayer:

> *There is no value as Your value, Hashem our God, in this world;*
> *and there is nothing besides You, our King, in Olam Haba.*

In this world, every person gets to decide what is important and what is not, and how important each thing is. Thus, every person has an internal totem pole of values in descending order from their most important value on downward. This internal hierarchy of values is the underlying determining factor of free-will choices: When forced to decide between two values on his totem pole, man unconsciously refers to his list and opts for the higher value. Every free-will choice is thus *merely a reflection of the pre-existing values hierarchy.* The key decisions happen when the person determines—not necessarily via conscious, rigorous, or cognitive deliberation—the allotment of spots on his values hierarchy and their assigned ranking. Once that is fixed, the choices that are made regarding them are already predetermined.

Is God one of the values on a person's totem pole? In this world that choice is up to man. *This capability is only possible in this world*, but in the clarity of Olam Haba—*there is no value besides God*. In Olam Haba, it is evident that God is not only the *top* value, He is the *only* value.

Whatever sits atop a given man's hierarchy is that person's supreme master. The Yetzer Hara deludes a person into assigning other entities that are not God as the highest value, resulting in him having a *foreign god*—some other thing that would supersede God if the person had to choose between the two. A sin is the result of man allowing the Yetzer Hara to populate his values hierarchy and even set his top value. Once those values are entrenched, decisions favoring them are assured. Accordingly, every sin reeks of the stench of idolatry as well.

Every Shabbos morning, Jews worldwide affirm that "there is no value as Your value Hashem our God, in this world." We strive to not only place God in our values hierarchy, but to make Him the *highest* value on our list. Certainly, our life is a high value, but if we are faced with a choice between two options—our life or God—we must choose God. In effect, every Shabbos morning we declare our intention to give up our life in martyrdom—should the opportunity arise.

What is the difference between our book on the laws of idolatry and Avraham's—between the laws of people who have never tasted Olam Haba and Avraham's who did? For us, the laws of idolatry convey that God ought to be the *top value* in our hierarchy. *Avraham tasted Olam Haba in this world*. In Olam Haba, there is *nothing besides the Almighty*. He did not suffice with making God the *top* value on his list, he aligned his values hierarchy with Olam Haba and made God the *sole* value on his list.

The Scope of the Yetzer Hara's Interference

In studying Avraham's tenacious scraping of the foreign god from within him, we learn that the Yetzer Hara's meddling into man's values hierarchy extends beyond trying to entice him to sin; it seeks to weaken the power and purity of Mitzvos too. A Mitzvah is the combination of its *action* and the *intention* of the person performing it at the time. Of course, the Yetzer Hara attempts to get the person to obey its directives and to sin, and to refrain from Mitzvos, but it also seeks to interfere into the *motivation of Mitzvos* that man does. The struggle with the Yetzer Hara does not end when a person achieves mastery over it in the realm of *actions*; even people who do Mitzvos exclusively will be prodded by their Yetzer Hara to perform Mitzvos with imperfect *motivations*.

Suppose a person performs a Mitzvah but his motivation is that others will laud him for it. There are two values at play: one righteous and one wicked; one of the Soul and one of the Yetzer Hara. His *action* is noble but his motivation is influenced by the Yetzer Hara. *An action of a Mitzvah motivated by sinful intentions is in itself a sin no less than an action of sin itself.* After all, in that action the person is *motivated by the foreign god*! As a practical matter, we are encouraged to perform actions of Mitzvos albeit with imperfect motivations, with the understanding that it is a necessary evil on our path to achieve totally perfect Mitzvos.[3] To be totally freed from the tentacles of the Yetzer Hara, however, one needs to cleanse not only their actions and deeds, but also their motivations for Mitzvos.

Avraham rendered the *entire* domain of the Yetzer Hara—values, actions, and motivations—as anathema and tantamount to idolatry and succeeded in extricating himself entirely from the clutches of his Yetzer Hara. For him, anything that was not service of God was as unconscionable as idolatry. When Avraham performed Mitzvos, they were free of any other motivation aside from doing the will of the Almighty. Avraham's values hierarchy was a perfect replica of Olam Haba despite him residing in this world.

Avraham's Ten Tests

What were the steps of Avraham's growth? The Mishnah teaches that Avraham was tested by the Almighty with ten increasingly difficult tests and was triumphant in all of them.[4] For us, tests are likely to be in the realm of *actions*—to follow the directives of God or those of the foreign

---

3   *Nazir* 23b.
4   *Avos* 5:3.

god. Avraham's arena of tests was to inspect his *total* commitment to God: values, actions, and even the motivations for his Mitzvos.

The first test was when Avraham had to choose between his life and God, and Avraham willingly chose to be cast into a fiery furnace and not repudiate his Emunah, thereby demonstrating that he valued God more than his own life. Later tests included instructions to commit horrifyingly *unkind* and *barbaric* acts, such as banishing his son, Yishmael, from his home, and killing his other son in the episode of the *Akeidas Yitzchak*. These tests were designed to discern if Avraham's kindness and morality were motivated solely by God, or if he was inclined to kindness and morality for any other reason. The answer is ascertained when *God* tells him to do egregiously *unkind* and *immoral* acts.

If there was any morsel of Avraham's kindness that originated in any source other than God, Avraham would seek to exercise it and act kindly with Yishmael and not send him away. By banishing Yishmael, Avraham demonstrated that his kindness was a result of the Godly motivation alone.

The test of *Akeidas Yitzchak* clarified Avraham's motivation behind refusal to commit the most heinous crime imaginable: murder of his own son. You do not need to be someone who is influenced by God to recognize that filicide is barbarically cruel and evil. Even people under the dominion of the foreign god tend to believe that. Avraham was someone who divested himself of any other priority in his life, leaving God as the singular value on his hierarchy and rendering everything else that is not related to God as idolatry. When God instructed him to murder his own son, he responded with the same eagerness and excitement as he performed all his acts,[5] thus demonstrating that obeying the will of God was his *only* motivation. His values hierarchy was cleansed of all the Yetzer Hara's nominations. His totem pole in this world was identical to Olam Haba wherein there is nothing besides the Almighty.

---

5   See *Rashi, Bereishis* 22:4.

How does a person who is not governed by his Yetzer Hara behave? What are the consequences of living with a Soul unrestrained by a foreign god? We will find out in the next chapter.

Chapter 22 Takeaways

- In this world, man creates a hierarchy of values, in descending order from the highest priority of his life.
- A choice between two options is a reflection of those two options' relative rankings on his internal hierarchy of values.
- In Olam Haba, God is only one value.
- Avraham tasted Olam Haba because he made his values hierarchy a replica of Olam Haba.

CHAPTER 23

The Stature of Avraham

W e began this book by dissecting Talmudic teachings regarding the state of the child pre-birth and the hallowed Instruction administered to him immediately prior to being born, which urged him to safeguard his Soul's purity and prevent it from becoming defiled by the Yetzer Hara that arrives at that moment. In telling that Avraham, Yitzchak, and Yaakov managed to defeat the Yetzer Hara entirely, the Talmud is also informing that their Souls reverted to being as unrestrained as all Souls are in utero before the introduction of the Yetzer Hara. Eliminating the Yetzer Hara has transformative consequences.

Torah

For one, the Talmud relates that the forefathers studied all of Torah and observed its Mitzvos, despite predating the giving of the Torah at Sinai by several centuries.[1] How did they access the Torah that was still chambered in Heaven? The Midrash offers two puzzling answers:

- According to the first, Avraham studied Torah from *himself*.
- The second posits that Avraham's two kidneys transformed into two Torah-spouting wellsprings.[2]

Both explanations raise questions: How can Avraham study Torah from himself? If he already had Torah to teach, why did he need to study it?

---

1   *Yoma* 28b.
2   *Tanchuma, Vayigash* 11.

And certainly, we must make sense of the nephrological origins of Avraham's Torah knowledge as posited by the second opinion.

In light of the discovery that the forefathers restored the spiritual makeup that existed before birth, the Midrash's answers are eminently logical. For nine months in his mother's womb, the fetus has a candle mounted on his head, meaning that the Soul is at the forefront of his consciousness. As a consequence of his unhindered Soul, the child in utero innately knows the entire Torah that is "baked into" every Soul. At birth, the Yetzer Hara arrives and supplants the Soul, which is consequently submerged into the innermost parts of his body as the verse states, "The candle of God is the Soul of man; searching the chambers of his innards."[3] From then on, the Soul is removed from the child's consciousness and thus the child forgets its Torah. But the Torah is still contained within the Soul that is now searching the chambers of his innards.

Avraham (and subsequently Yitzchak and Yaakov) removed the Yetzer Hara's influence and restored the Soul to its original perch on his head. As a result, he unearthed his Soul with all the Torah captured within it and rediscovered the intrauterine Torah that was only concealed due to the existence of the Yetzer Hara. As the first opinion in the Midrash teaches, Avraham studied Torah from himself, i.e., from the bastions of Torah contained in his (now exposed) Soul. The second opinion does not disagree. It also recognizes that this was the source of Avraham's Torah; it just conveys it with flair. After the Soul is demoted, it is languishing, together with all its Torah, in the deepest chambers of his innards. The Sages employed a euphemism for the deepest part of man's guts: his "kidneys." When Avraham removed the inhibitors of his Soul, the Torah contained in his "kidneys" sprang to the surface.

Avraham's re-discovery of his pre-birth Torah can be compared to a property owner who is aware of a massive crude-oil deposit eight thousand feet beneath his land. As the owner of the mineral rights, he technically owns a great deal of valuable oil, but if he wanted to fill up

---

3   *Mishlei* 20:27.

a barrel, that oil is effectively useless. Two miles beneath the surface, the oil is eager to gush forth; but for the moment, it is completely inaccessible and it garners him no benefit. In order to tap that veritable gold mine, he would need to undertake the laborious task of drilling a pipe through all the layers of sand and rock in order to create an escape route for the pressurized oil. That is an exact parallel of what Avraham did. Like all Soul-bearing humans, the Heavenly Torah existed within his Heavenly Soul, locked and buried in the innermost recesses of his body beneath the labyrinthine barrier of the Yetzer Hara. Avraham successfully dismantled the Yetzer Hara and consequently the Torah harbored in his newly unearthed Soul gushed forward.

Prophecy

Another consequence of an unrestrained Soul is prophecy. The Midrash informs us that the forefathers were the "chariot of God."[4] The commentaries explain that just as a king's chariot is always ready for him at a moment's notice, Avraham, Yitzchak, and Yaakov—unlike ordinary prophets who need to spiritually "tidy up" to get in the proper frame of mind for prophecy—were always ready for prophecy.[5]

What are the qualifications to be a prophet? Common perception views prophecy as a spiritual lottery, as if God randomly chooses to speak to someone. This is erroneous on two accounts:

- First, prophecy is not arbitrarily achieved; a self-proclaimed prophet who is not renowned for his piety is automatically considered a false prophet without taking into account the content of his alleged prophecy, and even if he fulfills other criteria of eligibility.[6]
- Second, becoming a prophet is not a reflection of a change from God's perspective, as if God choosing to speak to someone renders them a prophet; rather, it reflects a change on the part of the prophet by *rendering himself into a vessel capable of prophecy.*

---

4   *Bereishis Rabbah* 82:6.
5   *Seforno; Ramban.*
6   *Rambam,* Laws of the Foundations of Torah 7:7.

Put another way, prophecy is a unique status not because God ordinarily does not broadcast messages, rather because people are ordinarily incapable of *absorbing* God's messages. The existence of a radio signal beaming through the airwaves is imperceptible absent a receiver tuned to that frequency. The process of becoming a prophet is akin to creating and perfecting a radio receiver attuned to receive Godly messages. Prophecy is entirely meritocratic; there is no luck involved.

Another misconception regarding prophecy that must be dispelled is with respect to the "hardware" used to receive Godly communication. The human *body* is incapable of communication with God. In fact, the body is *engineered to resist* prophecy. Prophecy is communication between the prophet's *Soul* and God. If we could theoretically isolate our Soul from the other elements of our existence, it would immediately be capable of prophecy. In the pre-birth narrative told in the Midrash, the isolated Soul of a child in utero is in constant communication with God via angels.[7] The Talmud relates many similarities between the Soul of man and God, and communication between them is quite natural.[8] In truth, our *inability* to prophesy despite our inherent Soul is unusual.

Why are humans not prophets by default? Why indeed is our Soul unable to communicate with God after birth? The answer of course is that our Soul is not operating in isolation. Over the course of the development of man, the Soul is bound to entities that weaken its capacity for prophecy, namely, the body and the Yetzer Hara. The Soul is indeed a perfectly functional radio receiver with precisely attuned antennae to intercept the spiritual messages, but even a flawless receiver needs certain conditions to be able to pick up those signals. A radio's signal will lose reception underground, in a tunnel, or when surrounded by materials that block or repel the signal. Our Soul on its own would immediately have prophecy, but it operates in an environment that weakens and disrupts those signals. It is buried deep within the bowels of a signal-repelling body; it is cast into a staticky world, and it is

---

7   *Tanchuma, Pekudei* 3.
8   *Berachos* 10a; *Niddah* 30b.

disrupted by the opposing signals of the Yetzer Hara. These factors hamper the Soul's normal ability to access prophecy.

The pre-birth instruction exhorts us to resist the assault of the Yetzer Hara on the purity of our Soul—to *contain* the danger. These are guidelines to become a Tzaddik, but they would be insufficient to attain prophecy. For that, we must *roll-back and undo the network of inhibitors to our Soul.* A child in utero experiences prophecy because his Soul is free of the Yetzer Hara and if we succeed in dismantling the infrastructure of the Yetzer Hara and restoring the Soul back to a prominent position within us, our prophecy would immediately resume.

Rambam writes:

> One of the foundations of our religion is the knowledge that God communicates with people. Prophecy only rests on a great scholar; who is mighty in character; whose Yetzer Hara does not overpower him in any matter in the world, rather he always overpowers his Yetzer Hara with his willpower; and one who possesses exceedingly broad and correct knowledge.[9]

The only reason the Soul's antennae cannot access even the lower levels of prophecy is because of the disruptions of the Yetzer Hara; if man removes the disruptions, the normal, inherent prophetic capabilities of the Soul will immediately be restored. *Rambam* adds that there are many different levels of prophets. The strength of the prophetic signal that a prophet's Soul can absorb hinges on the extent that the prophet undid the disruptors to prophecy.[10] Avraham, Yitzchak, and Yaakov succeeded in dismantling the inhibitors to prophecy and consequently were always in the state of being ready for Divine communication.

Bris Milah

Avraham's grand achievement is symbolized in the first Mitzvah that he was instructed to do, the *bris milah* (circumcision). Avraham excised

---

9   *Rambam*, Laws of the Foundations of Torah 7:1.
10   Ibid. 7:2.

his Yetzer Hara and by doing that stripped away the barriers blockading his Soul, and restored it to its prominence in his consciousness.

Circumcision mirrors both aspects of this process. The Talmud lists seven names for the Yetzer Hara, and one of them is "uncircumcised."[11] Circumcision thus symbolizes the removal of the Yetzer Hara. But circumcision is also about revealing the "crown of God." Just as the Soul is unearthed when the Yetzer Hara—the proverbial foreskin—is removed, man has an organ that gives him creative and eternal capacities that is exposed when the barriers covering it are removed. Avraham was the first to dismantle the Yetzer Hara and thereby expose the Godly Soul within him. It is therefore appropriate that he merit the Mitzvah of circumcision that symbolizes this transformation.

Kindness and Emunah

Avraham's transformation is also evident in the way he is portrayed in the Torah. *Rambam* gives us Avraham's backstory: As a young, precocious child, he began to question, investigate, and ponder matters of theology by day and night. Though he was submerged in a sea of paganism, Avraham utilized his penetrating intellect to arrive at the truth that all the powers in the world are coalesced in a Single, Divine Power and He alone is worthy of worshipping. Upon development and honing of this principle, he undertook a mission to promulgate it throughout the world: He aggressively debated with pagans and overwhelmed them with the force of his logical arguments, and created a movement for adherents of monotheism. Avraham's dissemination of monotheism was not well-received by the idolworshipping leaders of his country who tried to kill him, but he was miraculously saved by God and continued to promote the belief in the One God for his entire life.[12]

If this biographical account was all you knew about Avraham, it would seem that his theological discoveries and triumphs—his Emunah—was his most outstanding attribute. Interestingly, the Torah presents him in a different light: He is not shown as the paragon of *Emunah*, rather

---

11   *Sukkah* 52a.
12   *Rambam*, Laws of Idolatry, chap. 1.

as the paragon of *kindness*. In one episode, we are told how Avraham personally extended superlative hospitality to three pagan travelers in the stifling heat, despite being ninety-nine years old and mere days removed from circumcision surgery. In a second, the Torah elaborates in fine detail his efforts to intercede on behalf of the sinners of Sodom and Gomorrah when informed that their end was near. Indeed, Avraham is forever identified with kindness in Scripture: "Give truth to Yaakov and kindness to Avraham."[13]

Why does the Torah choose to highlight Avraham's greatness in kindness more than his achievements in Emunah? Also, how did he manage to accomplish greatness in such disparate areas—to be the founder of monotheistic faith and the consummate exemplar of kindness?

Thanks to our journey thus far, the answer is clear: Emunah and superlative kindness are two sides of the same coin. Both are the characteristics of the Soul that can only surface if the Yetzer Hara is removed. Lack of Emunah is a result of the foreign god creating a barrier between man and his Creator. The same barrier that separates man from God walls him off from his fellow man in a cocoon of selfishness that leads to lack of kindness. To connect to God, you would need to remove the foreign god. Once Avraham broke through the shackles of the Yetzer Hara, he became a man of *kindness and Emunah* at once.

The indivisibility of man's relationship with God and his relationship with others is echoed in a bold statement in the Talmud:

> *Whoever studies Torah and does not act with kindness is akin to one who does not believe in God.*[14]

Though someone may study Torah—the only antidote for the Yetzer Hara—prodigiously, if that is not manifested in kindness it shows that the cocoon of selfishness of the Yetzer Hara still stands strong. His lack of kindness demonstrates that the foreign god is present within him and can aptly be classified as one who does not believe in God, his study of God's Torah notwithstanding.

---

13   *Michah* 7:20.
14   *Avodah Zarah* 17b.

Avraham's "Double Vision"

In the verse's depiction of Avraham's kindness, this point brought to life:

> And [Avraham] lifted his eyes, and he saw, and behold three men were standing before him, and he saw, and he ran toward them from the entrance of the tent, and he bowed to the ground.[15]

Rashi asks why the verb, "and he saw," appears twice in the verse? He answers that the first sight was the way everyone sees, while the second refers to *understanding*. Avraham did not just see the sight of three men; he understood that they were uneasy and did not want to bother him, and he sprang to action. Avraham had double-vision. Like everyone else, he saw the world from his own perspective. But unlike everyone else, *he also saw the world through the perspective of others*. Avraham removed the artificial distinction separating him from others, and as a result he was keenly aware of the needs and the outlook of other people too. When a person dismantles the Yetzer Hara that wants him cloistered up in his own world, the void is going to be filled with the Almighty and other people, with Emunah and with loving your fellow as yourself.

What about Moshe?

After reading the last two chapters regarding Avraham, Yitzchak, and Yaakov's total decimation of their Yetzer Hara and all that it spurred within them, one glaring question remains: What about Moshe? Absent from the discussion hitherto is any mention of the greatest man who ever lived. If the forefathers achieved the pinnacle of human achievement—if they rolled back the clock to a time in utero when the Yetzer Hara did not exist and got a taste of Olam Haba—what is left for Moshe? In the next three chapters, we will find out what can possibly eclipse total eradication of the Yetzer Hara.

---

15   *Bereishis* 18:2.

————————————————————————— **Chapter 23 Takeaways**

- By eliminating his Yetzer Hara, Avraham restored his spiritual state to the way things are in utero when the Soul is unaffected by a Yetzer Hara.
- Just as a Soul in utero experiences prophecy and innately knows all of Torah, by getting rid of the Yetzer Hara, Avraham unlocked the latent Torah harbored in his Soul, and became a great prophet.
- The Mitzvah of circumcision, which consists of removing the foreskin (one of the names of the Yetzer Hara) to expose the "crown," parallels Avraham's transformation.

The Greatest Man
Who Ever Lived

*I*n this chapter and the two that follow, we will present some of the Torah's portrayals of Moshe to construct a cohesive framework of his persona, and see how it dovetails with what we have discovered thus far.

Moshe's "Double Vision"

The first source to examine is the maiden episode of Moshe's adulthood:

> *It happened during those days that Moshe grew up and went out to his brethren, and he saw their suffering; and he saw an Egyptian man striking a Hebrew man of his brethren.*[1]

The introductory verse of Moshe as an adult contains an oddity that appears in only one other verse in the Torah—the repetition of the verb, "and he saw." As was highlighted in the previous chapter, Avraham is the only other individual regarding whom the Torah attributes this "double vision."

---

1   *Shemos* 2:11.

As was true with respect to Avraham, the sources ponder the meaning behind this repetition. The Midrash suggests two explanations for what Moshe saw:

> *What is meant by the words, "And he saw?" He would see their suffering and weep saying, "Woe onto me for you, if only I could die for you," for there is no work more strenuous than molding bricks. [Moshe] would shoulder the burdens and help each one of them.*
>
> *Rabbi Elazar the son of Rabbi Yosi from the Galilee says: He saw a large load on a frail person and a light load on a large person; a load intended for a man on a woman, and a load intended for a woman on a man; a load intended for an elderly person on a youngster, and a load intended for a young man on an elderly person. Moshe abandoned his stature, and went to alleviate their suffering under the guise of assisting Pharaoh. [Consequently,] the Holy One, blessed is He, said, "You set aside your matters and went to witness the plight of Israel and treated them like brothers, I, too, will set aside the lofty and lowly matters and talk to you."[2]*

According to the first explanation of the Midrash, Moshe saw the suffering of his brethren and chipped in as best he could to aid them with their hard work. The second explanation offered by the Midrash is that he witnessed the distinct suffering of each individual.

Let us analyze these two explanations, beginning with the latter. The Jewish People were enslaved and abused by their Egyptian over-lords with all manners of cruelty. In a particularly malicious form of torture, the Egyptians would deliberately assign people to tasks that they were uniquely ill-suited to perform: A small and frail person was given a heavy load; the strong person suited for that load was devilishly tormented in a different way. He was tasked with a frustratingly futile and light load—say the transportation of individual toothpicks—that

---

2   *Shemos Rabbah* 1:27.

under-utilized his capabilities, etc. Upon witnessing their suffering, Moshe saw what others didn't. Moshe did not see generic suffering, rather he *noticed the unique suffering of each individual*.

This is an admirable quality on two fronts:

- One, Moshe noticed even the comparatively *minor* pain of others. Obviously, the pain of a light load on a large person is less than the crushing burden of a large load on a frail person, yet, Moshe picked up on both.
- Two, Moshe was able to discern the *subtle specifics* of the suffering of others.

When confronted with the pain of others, people tend to either not perceive it at all, or to see suffering only in general terms. Moshe's superlative "vision" is thus manifested by noticing the major *and minor* pain of others, and the specific *details* of their suffering. The Midrash concludes that as a result of Moshe lowering his stature to notice the pain of others, God declared that He will descend from His Heavenly Abode and talk to Moshe. The transformational quality that catapulted Moshe to the highest level of prophecy was that he noticed the pain of others.

This raises several questions: First, how does this "vision" constitute a gateway to prophecy? *Rambam* outlines the qualifications of prophecy, and seeing the suffering of others is not enumerated.[3] Second, this Midrash indicates that the distinction between Moshe and everyone else was specifically in the area of seeing the pain of others. Only Moshe—not anyone else—noticed the pain of others in this manner. Why is that so? Why are people generally not inclined to notice the pain of others as Moshe did, and how indeed did Moshe achieve this?

The Midrash's first answer must likewise be pondered. Moshe saw the suffering of the people schlepping bricks and was aroused by their pain, and he lowered his shoulder to help them with this laborious task. This description does not seem to directly address the posed question of what Moshe *saw* that others did not. Quite the contrary: If, as the Midrash explicitly notes, there is no more strenuous task than

---

3   *Rambam*, Laws of the Foundations of Torah 7:1, quoted in the previous chapter.

brickmaking, one would imagine that you needn't any grand vision to perceive that; presumably it would be noticeable to all. Why is Moshe's perception of what they were going through deemed special?

Another question: What impact did Moshe imagine that assisting his brethren in molding and transporting bricks would have? The enslaved Jews numbered in the millions. As one man, Moshe could not possibly have alleviated the pain of more than perhaps a few dozen. His contribution was a mere drop in the bucket. It made no real dent in the plight of the nation and its multitudes of sufferers. Perhaps he ought to have conceived of a grand solution to the larger problem. Assisting slaves piecemeal is nice, of course, but does not appear to be a particularly significant accomplishment. Why is Moshe so lavishly lauded for manually assisting the Jewish slaves?

More Questions to Ponder

Other aspects of the Torah's portrayal of Moshe ought to be scrutinized:

- For one, the Torah testifies that, in addition to being the greatest prophet ever, Moshe was the humblest man on the face of the earth.[4] How did Moshe manage to reach the absolute pinnacle of these two, ostensibly disparate fields?[5]
- The Torah also attributes supernatural capabilities to Moshe. Several times the Torah stresses that for the forty-day duration of Moshe's ascent at Sinai—a journey done thrice—he neither ate bread nor drank water.[6] Ordinary humans cannot survive for that long without sustenance. How did Moshe survive, and what is the significance of this anecdote?
- Moshe's radiating countenance is also in need of an explanation. The verse tells that upon his descent from Sinai, his face shone

---

4   *Bamidbar* 12:3.
5   In truth, the Talmud (*Nedarim* 38a) links the two, saying that the Almighty only confers His Divine Presence on a mighty, rich, wise, and humble person. *Ruach Chaim* notes that really the only level of prophecy is humility, but a poor, feeble, and unwise person faces little resistance to humility. That said, there still needs to be an explanation for why the two are connected.
6   *Shemos* 34:28; *Devarim* 9:9, 9:18.

as bright as the sun.[7] From that point onward, Moshe had to wear a mask to avoid blinding the people. What is the meaning behind Moshe' luminous visage?

- A third supernatural quality of Moshe was his ability to time travel. The Talmud recounts the two times that Moshe traveled 1,400 years into the future to witness Rabbi Akiva—first as a guest in Rabbi Akiva's lecture hall, and second to witness Rabbi Akiva's grisly death.[8] What is the secret behind Moshe's transcendental ability to unbind himself from the constraints of time and space?

- The Midrash contains yet another teaching to be pondered: "Moshe is equal to all of Israel."[9] What does this puzzling statement mean? Also, technically this seems to be inaccurate. "All of Israel" would presumably include Moshe as well. How can Moshe on his own be equal to all of Israel, when the other side of the scale includes Moshe *plus the rest of the nation*?

Needless to say, the Torah's portrayal of Moshe is in need of an explanation. Let's search for answers.

Chapter 24 Takeaways

- The first episode of Moshe's life, where he commiserated with his brethren, set him along a path to becoming the greatest man who ever lived, but the particular details of the story warrant investigation.

- Moshe is also shown as someone who can survive forty days without food or water, who is the humblest of man, whose face was as bright as the sun, who was capable of time-travel, and who is "equal to all of Israel." What is the essence of Moshe's greatness?

---

7   *Shemos* 34:29, per *Bava Basra* 75a.
8   *Menachos* 29b.
9   *Devarim Rabbah* 11, quoted in *Rashi, Shemos* 18:1.

Angelic Man

*O*ur central thesis until this point has been that the Soul of man undergoes a grave demotion at birth due to the arrival of the Yetzer Hara. The objective of life is to harness Torah and Mitzvos to resist the Yetzer Hara and preserve the purity of the Soul, and perhaps even reverse the curse of birth by expelling the Yetzer Hara from within—as Avraham, Yitzchak, and Yaakov did when they reverted themselves back to the status of a fetus in utero. Accordingly, the situation in utero is ideal for the Soul. It innately knows Torah, sees from one end of the world to the other, is able to communicate with God via angels; indeed, the Talmud states plainly that the months of gestation are the apex of man's life, an idyllic utopia that is shattered at birth. The forefathers recaptured that status and thus reached the acme of human greatness.

Upon further examination, however, we learn that the arrival of the Yetzer Hara at birth is *not the first demotion that the Soul undergoes.* While the Soul seems totally pure and unrestrained prior to the advent of the Yetzer Hara, during the months preceding birth, the Soul is reeling from an earlier setback that occurred at *conception.* To understand the greatness of Moshe, we must research the state of the Soul *before* conception, before it had any bond with physicality and this temporary world.

The Isolated Soul

The primary source detailing what transpires to the Soul before conception is a fascinating and lengthy teaching in the Midrash regarding the process of a Soul's extraction from the Heavenly chamber called *"Guf"* in which all unassigned Souls are contained, and its insertion into the primordial biological matter that will comprise a body:

> The Holy One, blessed is He, tells the angel who oversees the Souls: "Bring Me this and this particular Soul whose appearance is such and such from Gan Eden"...When the Soul appears, it immediately kneels and bows before the King of kings, the Holy One, blessed is He. At that moment, the Holy One, blessed is He, says to the Soul: "Enter into this drop that is in the hands of Lailah, the angel who oversees conception." The Soul protests: "Master of the world, I am content in the world that I have resided in from the day that You created me. Why do You wish to insert me into this putrid drop? Behold, I am holy!" God responds to the Soul: "The world that I am inserting you into is preferable than the one in which you were residing, and I only created you in order to place you in this drop." Immediately, God forcibly inserts the Soul into the drop and the angel places him in his mother's womb, and two angels are summoned to guard against him leaving or being miscarried.[1]

The Midrash clearly indicates that the Soul is dissatisfied *long before* the Yetzer Hara arrives at birth. It stridently protests being inserted into the drop that will be the body, despite the fact that the Yetzer Hara is not yet present to challenge it. If the Yetzer Hara was the only disruptor of the Soul's equilibrium, the Soul should be entirely at ease and content so long as the Yetzer Hara does not threaten it. What is the cause of the Soul's earlier displeasure?

With a careful reading of the Soul's protest, we can find out what, precisely, are the sources of its discontent. It tells God:

---

1   *Tanchuma, Pekudei* 3.

> *Master of the world, I am content in the world that I have resided in from the day that You created me. Why do You wish to insert me into this putrid drop? Behold, I am holy!*

The Soul is displeased on two fronts:

- First, the Soul prefers the spiritual *world* to the physical *world*.
- Second, the Soul is revolted by the proposal to bind it to a putrid drop. The Soul is totally holy, and it is being asked to compromise its spiritual identity and to be fused with a physical component in order to create a merged identity—a human.

In His response, the Almighty addresses *both* concerns:

> *The world that I am inserting you into is preferable than the one in which you were residing, and I only created you in order to place you in this drop.*

Despite God's assurances, the Soul needs to be *inserted forcibly* into the nascent "body," and angels must be stationed to guard it from escaping. Though the Soul is *relatively* unencumbered in utero—it still has pole position over the combined identity of man—it is still smarting from being in an impure world and an impure body. If not for the angels standing guard to prevent that, the Soul would escape its bodily incarceration.

At birth, a final blow is dealt to the Soul when the Yetzer Hara is thrust upon it. The aforementioned Midrash records the Soul's aversion to this final degradation:

> *And the Soul does not want to leave [the womb] until [the angel] strikes him and extinguishes the candle that was lit upon his head and forcibly extracts him into the world. The baby immediately forgets all that he saw upon his exit and all that he knows.*

Though the Soul was displeased in utero, at least it was still the dominant influence over the child. At birth, the candle is functionally extinguished and is buried deep within the body, relegated to search out the chambers of his innards, and thenceforth the Yetzer Hara reigns.

All told, the Midrash reveals that the Soul is demoted twice:

- At conception, due to it being withdrawn from the spiritual world and placed in the physical world and in a body
- At birth, due to the arrival of the Yetzer Hara that militarizes the physical body and world to threaten the Soul's purity with sin[2]

The Ultimate Pinnacle of Human Greatness

The discovery that the Soul undergoes multiple demotions paves the way for a new class of greatness. Avraham, Yitzchak, and Yaakov were God's "chariot." They completely removed the impact of their Yetzer Hara and restored their Soul's status to the way it was before birth, and as a result they managed to get a *taste* of Olam Haba. But even the forefathers' Souls were harbored in physical bodies and existed in a physical world. They only *tasted* Olam Haba; they did not *live* in it. They were always *primed* for prophecy, but even they did not have completely unhindered prophecy due to the—albeit minor—signal disruptions to the clarity of the signal caused by their body and the temporary world.

Moshe was the greatest man who ever lived. *He managed to revert his Soul back to its status before any of the degradations were foisted upon it.* Unlike the forefathers who restored their Souls to its *pre-birth* state, Moshe reinstated the status of his Soul to the way it was *before conception*. Moshe completely dismantled the axis of evil foisted upon his Soul and restored it to its entirely uninhibited status as it existed when the Soul was harbored in the Heavenly "*Guf*." Of course, he too eliminated his Yetzer Hara, but he also purified his body entirely and transformed his environment into being a replica of Olam Haba.

---

2   Interestingly, on all accounts, God views it differently. He created the Soul in order to place it in this world and body, and the Midrash (*Bereishis Rabbah* 9:9) teaches that God views the Yetzer Hara as "exceedingly good." Our Soul is thrice devastated with the advent of factors that can potentially taint it, but the Almighty disagrees with that assessment. On a related note, the Talmud (*Eruvin* 13b) concludes that for mankind, the drawbacks of being created outweigh its benefits. For us, it would be preferable to not have been created, but the Almighty, obviously, does not concur.

Moshe's Prophecy

This is why Moshe was the greatest prophet ever. Moshe's spiritual "radio" was able to absorb the prophetic signals with no restrictions, whereas all the others still had some degree of negating effects, resulting in four qualitative differences delineated by *Rambam*:

> *All the prophets prophesied in dreams or visions, but Moshe prophesied while awake and alert…All the prophets prophesied via an angel—therefore they see through parables and riddles—but Moshe prophesied not via an angel, as it states, "Mouth to mouth I speak to him," and "And God spoke to Moshe face-to-face"…as if to say "without parables, rather he sees the matter clearly without riddles and without parables"…All the prophets are stricken, frightened, and exhilarated, but Moshe is…as a person speaks to his friend…All the prophets cannot prophesy whenever they wish, but Moshe is not like that; rather, whenever he desires, the holy spirit envelops him and prophecy rests upon him.*[3]

These substantive differences between Moshe and all other prophets stem from the disparity of their respective spiritual cleansing.

For all other prophets, the existence of a physical body interferes with the prophetic signals intended for the Soul. To achieve prophecy, the negative effects of the body must be mitigated by limiting prophecy to times when the body is asleep. Alternatively, the body must be bribed, placated, assuaged, or distracted by linking the Soulful prophecy with something that the body enjoys. For example, when Yitzchak sought prophecy to bless Esav, he asked for a delicious meat meal to throw a bone to the body and mute its protests; David HaMelech did the same with music. Even when prophecy powers through a recalcitrant body, the body suffers with weakness and convulsions.[4]

Another limitation to prophecy caused by the body is the inability to communicate with God directly. Elsewhere, *Rambam* enumerates

---

3   *Rambam*, Laws of Foundations of Torah 7:6.
4   Ibid. 7:2.

ten levels of angels: the highest and closest to God are called *"Chayos,"* and the lowest and closest to man are called *"Ishim,"* who intermediate between God and prophets.[5] Another general manifestation of body-bound prophecy is the need to batter through internal resistance. As such, prophecy was not a natural form of communication. It was an *occasional, atypical experience* that evoked in the prophet fear and exhilaration as one.

Moshe's prophecy differed greatly. While his initial foray into prophecy at the Burning Bush was of the lower degree—via an angel and marked with trepidation[6]—at Sinai he shed free of the last vestiges of physical body-hood. Thenceforth, he was akin to an angel, a pure Soul entirely free of any adversaries—as it was before conception. Tellingly, when the Midrash recounts the pre-conception narrative, the Soul is prophesying directly with the Almighty. However, once it is fused with a body and inserted into this world, its capacity is diminished and is only capable of prophecy via an angel.

In all of human history, only Moshe succeeded in achieving the highest level of pre-conception prophecy—to communicate directly with God without intermediaries, parables, or imagery. The Talmud comments that each prophet conveys the messages from God with his own style.[7] They are prophetically shown an image that they must interpret and articulate with their own formulizations. Moshe prophesied with the words, "This is the word of God." God's communication to him was verbal and scintillatingly clear. The prophecy did not need to filter through him and needed no interpretation or reformatting. He was but a funnel through which God communicated to the people; Moshe added none of his own stylistic embellishments or interpretations.

As solely a Soul, prophecy was Moshe's normal mode of communication, as one would converse with their friend. Quite the contrary, *Moshe's communication with people was unnatural.* Moshe re-established the Soul as his sole entity of existence. With the blinding light of his

5   Ibid. 2:7.
6   *Shemos* 3:2, 6.
7   *Sanhedrin* 89a.

Soul unleashed from its chambers, his face appeared sun-like and the Jewish People could not look at him. To speak to them, he was forced to mask his face.[8] In other words, *Moshe had to create an artificial body when communicating to the body-centric masses.* Prophecy with God became normal; interacting with humans ceased to be so.

Rambam concludes the list of distinctions between Moshe and all the other prophets:

> *All prophets, when prophecy ceased, they returned to their tents, meaning to the functions of their bodies—as the rest of the nation. Therefore, they do not depart from their wives. But Moshe our teacher did not return to his first tent; therefore, he separated from his wife forever, and from all things similar to it. His mind was tied to God, the splendor did not cease forever, the skin of his face glowed, and he became as holy as angels.*

All the other prophets achieved their heights *despite their opposing bodies.* They *temporarily* soared to great spiritual heights with prophecy, but when that concluded they re-entered this world as a returning spaceship hurtling back into earth's atmosphere. They resumed life as standard body-inhabiting humans, albeit holy ones who have undone their Yetzer Hara, each to their own level. Moshe did not return to his tent. Prophecy became his new normal. He became like an angel, a completely unfettered Soul who existed in Olam Haba here and to whom prophecy was natural.

Moshe' Deathbed Narrative

Moshe's stature as a Soul freed from any bodily restraints is also manifested in the Midrashic account of the run-up to his death. Initially, the Almighty sent a series of angels to extract Moshe's Soul, and Moshe fended them off. Ultimately, the Almighty Himself descended from the heavens to take his Soul and the following exchange is recorded:

---

8   *Shemos* 34:33.

*At that time, the Holy One, blessed is He, called out to the Soul
inside [Moshe's] body and said to it, "My daughter, I ordained
that you be placed in the body of Moshe for 120 years. Now is
your time to leave. Leave, do not delay." The Soul responded,
"Master of the world, I know that You are the God of all Souls;
the Souls of the living and the dead are in Your Hands; and You
created and formed me and placed me in the body of Moshe for
120 years. Now, is there a purer body in the world than Moshe's,
in whom no putrid spirit, nor worms and maggots appeared?[9]
Therefore, I love him and do not want to leave." The Holy One,
blessed is He, said to her, "Neshamah, leave, do not delay, and
I will bring you to the upper Heavenly Heavens, and I will place
you under My Throne of glory near the various angels." The
Soul responded, "Master of the world…please leave me in the
body of Moshe."[10]*

This narrative stands in stark contrast to the Soul's typical relationship with the body. Usually, it loathes its existence in this world and
in a body, and views death as *liberation*, and seeks to escape its bodily
confinement. Moshe succeeded in creating an environment where the
Soul *preferred* his body as the most hospitable of abodes. Moshe was,
as a veritable angel, unaffected by a physical body. Likewise, his Soul
felt no negative effects of this world because his existence here was
indistinguishable from Olam Haba. In this world, Moshe was an angel
walking among men.[11]

---

9   The term "worms and maggots" usually describes the conditions of the body in the grave,
     where worms and maggots gnaw away at the flesh of sinners. Interestingly, the Soul describ-
     ing a typical living person uses this term. It appears that the Soul views sins in this world
     as what they really are—worms and maggots. This explains the suffering of the Soul in this
     world. The other elements of man can get duped by the allure of sin, yet the Soul sees it for
     what it really is and is thus nauseated by sin, but cannot assert itself and stop the person
     from imbibing the maggots.

10   *Devarim Rabbah* 11:10.

11   For more sources, see the full text of the Midrash describing Moshe's death, where the
     Midrash plainly states that he became an angel of God whose countenance was akin to the
     sun; see also *Daas Tevunos* 70.

In the next chapter, we will expand the concept of Moshe as an angel, learn about the consequences of this distinction, and hopefully answer all the questions posed in the previous chapter satisfactorily.

Chapter 25 Takeaways

- Before the Soul is bound to the primordial body at conception, when it was still housed in the Heavenly *"Guf,"* it existed at the highest spiritual plane.
- While the forefathers restored their stature to the way Souls exist in utero, Moshe restored his Soul to the way it was before conception, and therefore his prophecy was qualitatively different than all others.

CHAPTER 26

The Stature of Moshe

At Sinai, Moshe ascended to Heaven where he spent forty days and nights with God and His angels. How did an earthling venture into that other, entirely spiritual world? The truth is that we all are *returning citizens* of that world. Our Soul came from there and is destined to return there. Indeed, if we could isolate our Soul from its contaminants, it would instantly be capable of living in the spiritual world. Moshe restored his Soul to its state before it was bound to any bodily influences, and therefore he was perfectly primed to exist in that world.

As a veritable angel, Moshe was able to coexist with other angels and argue with them as a peer. The Talmud relates:

> When Moshe ascended to Heaven, the angels said before the Holy One, blessed is He, "Master of the world, why is the child of a woman among us?" God said to them, "To receive the Torah." They said before Him, "A treasure that has been hidden for 974 generations prior to the creation of the world, and You seek to give it to flesh and blood?!"

The Talmud proceeds to tell how Moshe successfully rebutted the angels:

> [Moshe] said before Him, "Master of the world, the Torah that you are giving me, what does it say in it? 'I am Hashem

197

your God who took you out of the land of Egypt.'" He said to
[the angels], "Did you descend to Egypt? Were you enslaved to
Pharaoh? Why should the Torah be yours?..."[1]

As an equal, Moshe was capable of vigorously defending his position against the objections of the angels.

A nuanced reading of this exchange reveals that the angels themselves distinguish Moshe from other humans. When inquiring about his presence, they describe him as "the child of a woman," whereas when they incredulously question the notion of giving the Torah to people, they call the receivers "flesh and blood." The angels acknowledge that the only difference between Moshe and them was his *pedigree*—his mother was a woman; the people however were "flesh and blood," incomparable to angels due to their being influenced by bodily forces.

Understanding Moshe's makeup explains all the unusual characteristics and abilities ascribed to him. We asked how he survived for forty days and nights without food or water. To answer that question, we must examine the world in which he operated. The Talmud teaches:

> *Rav would often say: This world is dissimilar to Olam Haba: in*
> *Olam Haba, there is no eating, nor drinking, nor procreation,*
> *nor commerce, nor envy, nor hatred, nor competition; it is*
> *only Tzaddikim sitting with their crowns on their heads and*
> *enjoying the radiance of God.[2]*

This world is characterized by its inhabitants being Souls enshrouded by bodies. Bodies mandate that we eat and drink, etc. In Olam Haba, we are Souls unmolested by bodies and freed from its agenda. Despite being here, Moshe lived in that world and needed neither food nor water—nor sleep for that matter[3]—to subsist. As a purely spiritual being, a Soul, permanently residing in the Olam Haba dimension, Moshe was

---

1   *Shabbos* 88b.
2   *Berachos* 17a.
3   *See Shemos Rabbah* 47:7.

unbound by the physical constraints of this world, and was capable of visiting Rabbi Akiva who lived many centuries hence.

A Heavenly "Body"

Still, our understanding of what Moshe became is incomplete. The Midrashic account of his death demonstrates that he *still had a body that housed his Soul.* Angels do not have bodies at all. How can we reconcile Moshe being both angelic and harboring a body? It seems like those two options are mutually exclusive. The answer is that Moshe had a body, though his was only nominally similar to our bodies. Let's explain what that means.

As we have mentioned, before a Soul is inserted into a body, it is stored, along with all the other unbound Souls, in a Heavenly chamber called "*Guf.*" It is in that state when the Soul is at its zenith. It is unsullied by a body, by this world, and certainly it is untainted by a Yetzer Hara. It is in that "*Guf*" that the Soul is most pristinely pure. As we have noted, the Hebrew word for body is "*guf.*" The Soul is initially housed in the Heavenly *Guf,* along with perhaps billions of other Souls, and at conception is transferred into an earthly *guf.*

In truth, it is a bit surprising that the Heavenly chamber that harbors multitudes of Souls shares a name with an earthly body that holds a single Soul for its duration of life. What commonalities do they share, and what can we learn from this? It seems that we can deduce two critical insights:

- First, it highlights the primacy of Souls relative to bodies. A *guf* is only significant due to it being a vessel for a Soul. Despite the vast gulf separating the Heavenly *Guf,* a spiritual chamber full of Souls, and an earthly *guf,* a transient body destined to disintegrate after burial, both are equally defined *solely by what they contain.* From the Torah's perspective, the Soul's importance will outweigh its encasement regardless if it is a cache containing billions of Souls in the spiritual world, or a sin-inducing, earthbound body.
- There is a second transformative insight relating to the essence of earthly bodies that we touched upon in Chapter 15: An earthly

body inhibits the Soul and creates grounds for sin. But what specifically about the earthly encasement of our Soul causes these potential missteps? We can find the answer by contrasting the two disparate *gufs* that have held the Soul: The Heavenly *Guf* houses multitudes of Souls simultaneously, but an earthly *guf* can only contain one Soul.

In addition, whilst in the Heavenly *Guf*, the Soul is instinctively subservient to God as evident in the Midrashic account of the conduct of the Soul when the Almighty inserts it into the drop. Once it is transferred into an earthly one, however, the new entity loses this innate Emunah. This demonstrates the basic principle of earthly *gufs*: They create divisions between the Soul within it and other Souls, and between the Soul and God, a condition exacerbated multifold by the Yetzer Hara. Thus, once a Soul is placed in this new earthly container, its erstwhile deep bonds with other Souls and with God ceases.

Moshe's Metamorphosis

Moshe accomplished what no one else managed: He entirely shattered the walls of division of his body. Put in other words, Moshe *converted his earthly guf into a Heavenly Guf.* Moshe nominally had a body, but it bore none of the typical ill effects that bodies foist upon Souls. His body did not create any divisions between him and God, nor him and his fellow man. He undid all the demotions of his Soul, and succeeded in transforming his physical *guf* into an exact replica of the Heavenly *Guf*, the ideal abode for Souls. When Moshe's time to pass came, his Soul preferred remaining in the "*guf*" that Moshe created over his lifetime.

As such, Moshe's "*guf*" was capable of housing *more than a single Soul.* This fabulous insight illuminates the cryptic Midrash cited earlier that Moshe was "equal to all of Israel." *Moshe expanded himself to include not only his own Soul within himself, but the Souls of all the people of Israel.* If you could use a spiritual microscope to examine the contents of Moshe's "body," you would find an exact replica of all the Souls of the entire nation!

Moshe began his life with an earthly body harboring his Soul alone. His progression to greatness saw the transformation of his earthly body into a Heavenly one and his expansion of self to include others within his identity. The first verse of Moshe as an adult hints at this change:

> *It happened during those days that Moshe grew up (Va'yigdal Moshe) and went out to his brethren.*

The words *Va'yigdal Moshe* are typically translated in relation to age[4]—*Moshe grew up*—but the literal translation is *Moshe became larger*. Perhaps the words *"Va'yigdal Moshe"* are intimating his spiritual metamorphosis: He became spiritually larger by incorporating the Souls of others within his newly expanded identity. Ultimately, Moshe himself mirrored all of Israel in his collective identity.

Both Avraham and Moshe had "double vision." But Moshe had it at the beginning of his adult life and Avraham had it when he already achieved much of his greatness and was given the Mitzvah of *bris milah*. Our Sages tell us that Moshe was *born* circumcised,[5] i.e., Moshe accomplished the stature of Avraham at a much earlier stage. Avraham also expanded himself to include others. Scripture describes him as, "the great giant of men,"[6] a reference to his vastness. But Moshe was equal to all of Israel.

Feeling the Pain of Others

One way that a person's expanded self is manifested is with regard to experiencing pain. We are wired to feel our own pain, but not the pain of someone else. However, there are exceptions: when a person's child experiences pain, it hurts the parent too. The principle that we only feel our own pain still applies, but a child is part of his parent's collective identity. Bearing a child expands a person to include that child within the parent.

Moshe expanded himself to include all of Israel within him. As a result, he literally "felt" their pain as if it were his own. The coming-of-age verse continues that he went out and saw the suffering of his brethren. The Midrash cited earlier questions what did Moshe specifically see, and

---

4   See *Rashi* ad loc.
5   *Midrash Tanchuma* 58:5.
6   *Yehoshua* 14:15.

answers that Moshe saw the people bearing the burden of brickwork and assisted them all. We wondered earlier how Moshe can possibly make any tangible impact on the plight of the nation by helping one slave at a time. We also asked how the Midrash answers its own question. The question was what did Moshe *see*, and the answer seems to extend beyond what he *saw* when it relates what he *did*, namely assisted everyone that he could with their labor. How does that answer the question?

With our newfound knowledge of Moshe's transformation, we can now answer both questions: The way Moshe acted in response to encountering his brethren's pain demonstrates what he saw that others did not see. Moshe did not see their pain as an *outsider*; if so, a more comprehensive solution for the crisis of national enslavement would be appropriate. Moshe saw their pain in a way that resulted in instinctive attempts to alleviate it, and, consequently, he began assisting the laborers with their work. As a "larger" person who incorporated his brethren within him, Moshe was racked with their pain, and, although all the pain cannot be instantly subdued, he instinctively proceeded to remedy it as best he could.

Moshe's humility is also a reflection of this characteristic. Hubris is a byproduct of the divisiveness of our earthly body. The separation of man and his fellow allows for one to lord over the other. Absent an earthly body, haughtiness of one over another, and competition in general, is as preposterous as one arm feeling superior to the other arm. In a *"guf"* that encompassed multitudes of Souls, *Moshe's own Soul captured an infinitesimally insignificant portion*. Of his expanded self, his own Soul accounted for a mere six-hundred-thousandth or .00016% of his total self. Thus, Moshe twin superlative achievements—being both the greatest prophet and the humblest person—both stem from the same transformation of self. Moshe dismantled his earthly body and unearthed his Soul's total power, thus achieving the highest levels of prophecy, and thereby including all of Israel within him, and correspondingly shrinking his own self, and achieving the highest level of humility.

A Replica of Adam Pre-Sin

The esoteric sources that elaborate on these topics tell us that prior to his sin, Adam was an amalgam of all of the Jewish Souls. When Adam sinned, however, he acquired a Yetzer Hara and his expansive Soul was divided into a large number of smaller ones. Initially, that same expansive Soul was incorporated within the triumvirate of Avraham, Yitzchak, and Yaakov. Subsequently, it branched out to the twelve tribes, and the seventy Souls that descended to Egypt, and at Sinai, the number of smaller Souls that cumulatively equaled Adam's Soul pre-sin was six hundred thousand.[7]

Like the forefathers, Moshe evicted the Yetzer Hara from within him, but Moshe went a step further and expanded his body to house all six hundred thousand Souls of the Jewish nation, and thereby refashioned himself into an exact spiritual replica of Adam pre-sin.

Our Marching Orders

"Never again did a prophet arise in Israel like Moshe, who knew God face to face."[8] No one will ever rival Moshe's stature. There will never be another person who exists on the Olam Haba dimension in his lifetime. What is feasible for us is to purify ourselves to the degree that we become a Tzaddik worthy of Olam Haba after our passing.

Olam Haba is not only our destination; it is also our origin. Our Soul hails from the Heavenly *Guf* in the spiritual world. In that state, it was like Moshe and Adam pre-sin, free of any scintilla of impurity. We begin our life in this world as Adam right after the sin, booted from the spiritual world, bound and subjected to a physical identity, and condemned to contend with the Yetzer Hara. In this world, our Soul is in grave danger of losing its purity and dying. Torah and Mitzvos are the tools to navigate our Soul's journey home. If we emerge from this world as a Tzaddik, we too will merit regaining access to Olam Haba.

What is Olam Haba? How can we guarantee that our Soul will be readmitted?

In Part V, we will examine the world that our Soul calls home.

---

7   See *Shaar Hagilgulim* 11.

8   *Devarim* 34:10.

- Moshe transformed himself into being like an angel and was able to interact with angels in Heaven as a peer.
- Moshe did have a body, but it was akin to the "*Guf*" that harbors Souls before they are placed into bodies.
- Just as a single Heavenly "*Guf*" can house billions of Souls, Moshe transformed himself into a replica of Adam pre-sin and was able to incorporate all of Israel within his collective identity.

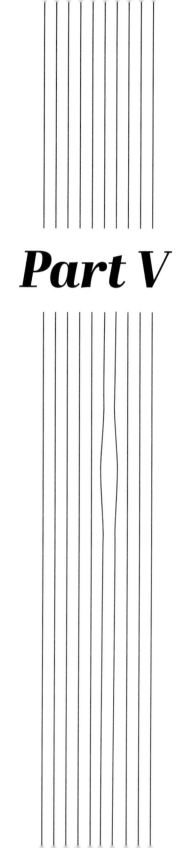

Part V

Spiritual Pleasure and Olam Haba

*I believe with perfect faith that the Creator, blessed
is He, rewards those who observe His commandments
and punishes those who transgress them.*

T his declaration, the eleventh of the thirteen core principles of
Jewish belief codified by *Rambam*, states a basic premise that the
Almighty rewards those who observe Torah and Mitzvos and punishes
those who do not. What is the nature of that reward? In his Commentary
on the Mishnah, *Rambam* dedicates a sweeping, authoritative treatise
to answering that question.

He begins by delineating five commonly held positions on the matter:

- Some believe that the ultimate reward for Mitzvos is a post-
  mortem Paradise.
- A second group says it's the security and hegemony of the days
  of Mashiach.
- A third argues that it's the Resurrection of the dead.
- A fourth opines that it is having a good life, prosperity, health,
  etc., in this world.

- A fifth group lumps all of these together and says that the reward for Mitzvos is Paradise, plus the days of Messiah and Resurrection, coupled with a happy and prosperous life in this world.

While each group offers Scriptural evidence to support their claim, *Rambam* concludes that these rewards are incidental to the ultimate reward for Mitzvos, which is the Soul's eternal pleasure in Olam Haba.[9]

This principle is echoed by *Ramchal* in the first chapter of *Mesilas Yesharim*:

> *Behold, our Sages instructed us that man was created for the sole purpose of experiencing the pleasure of God and enjoying His Divine Presence, which is the true pleasure and the greatest delight of all the possible delights. The venue for this delight is, in truth, in Olam Haba, which was created with the necessary preparation for this, and the means to achieve this ultimate goal are the Mitzvos, which are only fulfillable in this world.*

When two of the greatest authorities on Torah philosophy write unequivocally that the ultimate reward for Mitzvos is spiritual pleasure in Olam Haba, it encourages us to probe the nature of Olam Haba and the spiritual pleasure native to it. Finding clear answers is hard, however, because Olam Haba is one of the most enigmatic ideas in Jewish philosophy. In fact, much of our Sages' teachings on the subject revolve around its impenetrability. For example, the Talmud portrays Olam Haba as a vastly different world than ours:

> *Rav would often say: Olam Haba is unlike this world. In Olam Haba there is no eating, drinking, procreation, commerce, envy, hatred, or competition, rather it consists of Tzaddikim sitting with crowns on their heads and enjoying the Divine Presence.*[10]

---

9   *Rambam*, introduction to chap. 10 of *Sanhedrin*.
10   *Berachos* 34b.

In our current world, we eat, drink, procreate, engage in commerce, and must contend with unrefined character. None of that is found in Olam Haba. As people currently situated in this world, it is unsurprising that matters relating to the next world are difficult to comprehend. We are not alone in our lack of understanding of Olam Haba:

> *Rabbi Chiya Bar Abba said in the name of Rabbi Yochanan: All the prophets only prophesied regarding the days of Messiah, but regarding Olam Haba the verse states, "An eye cannot see it, only God can."*[11]

If the prophets cannot conceptualize Olam Haba, we certainly cannot plumb its depths. However, recognizing *why* we are precluded from fully comprehending it will go a long way in helping us delve into the subject.

The Tools to Absorb Spiritual Pleasure

When highlighting the incomprehensibility of Olam Haba in his treatise, *Rambam* adds a revealing comparison:

> *You must know that just as a blind person cannot fathom colors, and the deaf cannot grasp the sound of noises, and the eunuch cannot grasp carnal desire, so too bodies cannot grasp spiritual pleasures.*

The body is inherently precluded from absorbing spiritual pleasures. Just as a blind person cannot understand what color is—without experience, no amount of explanation can articulate "green"—so too, a body cannot comprehend Soulful pleasures. Seeing from your elbow is as plausible as sensing spiritual pleasure with your body. Just as the blind, deaf, and eunuchs don't have the physiology—the very anatomy—needed to experience what they are lacking, the body lacks the hardware needed to grasp spiritual pleasure and Olam Haba.

Given what we have discovered hitherto, we can now chart a path to understanding—and even partaking in—the spiritual pleasure of Olam

---

11   *Berachos* 17b, quoting *Yeshayahu* 64:3.

Haba. Man is not pigeonholed to exist only as a body. Via Mitzvos, man can choose to shift his identity to being more Soul-like. Olam Haba is a world of pleasure for the Soul, and as a body that notion is incomprehensible. But spiritual pleasure is as palpable to the Soul as physical pleasure is to the body. To the extent that we become Soul-like, we acquire a taste for spiritual pleasures.

Rambam himself spells this out:

> *In this bodily world, the pleasures of the spiritual world are unknown. [By default,] we only have the physical and sensory pleasures of eating, drinking, and copulation, and everything that is beyond those is for us non-existent; we do not recognize it, and we will not grasp it upon initial thought, only after great contemplation."*

Rambam's words are unambiguous that spiritual pleasure is indeed accessible—after much contemplation. Spiritual pleasure is beyond us as long as we are body-centric. But our spiritual Soul is perfectly calibrated to experience spiritual pleasures. If we work assiduously to identify more as our Soul and to start feeling what it feels, we will understand spiritual pleasure.

The Difference between Spiritual Pleasure Here and in Olam Haba

Rambam's notion that it is conceivable to experience Olam Haba-type pleasures in this world should give one pause. He certainly knew the Talmudic teaching that even the prophets could not perceive Olam Haba, yet he leaves the door open for simple people like us to perceive spiritual pleasure in this world. Clearly, there is a crucial distinction between the spiritual pleasure of the Soul that is, with hard work, accessible here, and Olam Haba itself that even the great prophets are locked out of.

Ramchal reveals the distinction when he details the two defining characteristics of spiritual pleasure in Olam Haba:

> *Behold, our Sages instructed us that man was created for the sole purpose of having the pleasure of God and enjoying His*

Divine Presence, which is the true pleasure and the greatest delight of all the possible delights. The venue for this delight is in truth in Olam Haba, which was created with the necessary preparation for this.

In qualifying spiritual pleasure, *Ramchal* notes that it is the *truest pleasure* and the *greatest delight*. It supersedes any other pleasure both qualitatively and quantitatively. Qualitatively, spiritual pleasure is a different *type* of pleasure, a *true* one that is incomparable to physical pleasures. It is also the *greatest* delight. The *magnitude* of spiritual pleasure supersedes any physical pleasure.

Is it possible to experience the spiritual pleasure of Olam Haba here?

It depends. The first defining aspect of Olam Haba pleasure, that only it is the *true pleasure* as opposed to physical pleasure—the *qualitative* element of Olam Haba pleasures—*is* accessible here. The second defining characteristic of Olam Haba, the fact that it is the *greatest delight*—a pleasure of unmatched magnitude—that is the exclusive domain of Olam Haba. Quantitatively, the Mishnah calculates that one moment of spiritual pleasure in Olam Haba outweighs the collective sum of all feasible physical pleasures of this world.[12] The *scope* of Olam Haba is beyond the purview of prophets, but with dedicated work of training ourselves to harmonize with our Soul, we can have an inkling and an understanding of spiritual pleasure even in this world.

My grandfather drew this fundamental distinction from *Ramchal's* usage of two different Hebrew words to describe spiritual pleasure: "*taanug*" (pleasure) and "*idun*" (delight). More specifically, when *Ramchal* highlights the *qualitative* supremacy of spiritual pleasure, he uses the word *taanug* ("which is the true pleasure"), and when mentioning the *quantitative* quality of spiritual pleasure in Olam Haba he uses the term *idun* ("the greatest delight of all the possible delights"). Yet when he informs us that the *location* where this pleasure is conveyed is in Olam Haba, he only references *idun* ("The venue for this *delight* is in truth in Olam Haba, which was created with the necessary preparation

---

12   *Avos* 4:17.

for this."). By not saying that Olam Haba is the place of "delight" *and* "pleasure," *Ramchal* demonstrates that the venue for "pleasure" is not limited to Olam Haba; it can also be experienced here, though the full-blown version of that pleasure is only found in Olam Haba.

The bottom line is that the reward for Mitzvos is the spiritual pleasure and delight of basking in God's Presence in Olam Haba. That pleasure is experienced only by the Soul and not by the body. When the body is stripped off, the Soul can fully partake in spiritual pleasure without dilutions. That degree of spiritual pleasure is incomprehensible to anyone who is still hindered by vestiges of the influence of the Yetzer Hara and the body. Even prophets cannot comprehend that world. That said, Avraham, Yitzchak, and Yaakov destroyed their Yetzer Hara and therefore got a *taste* of Olam Haba, and Moshe who upgraded his body into a replica of the Heavenly "*Guf*" *lived* in that world. We, too, can catch a hint of a scent of that world: To the degree that we manually minimize the influence of the Yetzer Hara who deludes us into identifying as our body, we can experience some of the pleasures of Olam Haba here.[13]

In the next chapter, we will try to deepen our understanding of spiritual pleasure and Olam Haba by examining a particularly cryptic Talmudic teaching.

Chapter 27 Takeaways

- Olam Haba is the world wherein God rewards the Tzaddikim for their Torah and Mitzvos.
- The pleasure of Olam Haba is spiritual, and spiritual pleasure is only experienced by the Soul; to the degree that we transform our identity to be more Soul-like, we can experience a little bit of spiritual pleasure.

---

13   See *Rambam, Book of Mitzvos* 3, for exact instructions how to do it.

Surveying Olam Haba

A lthough the prophets, and certainly regular people, cannot fully grasp Olam Haba, the Talmud lists three items that exist in our world that have overlapping qualities with Olam Haba:

> *Three things are a measure of Olam Haba: Shabbos, the sun, and "tashmish" (a word that can mean either marital relations or relieving oneself). Which "tashmish"? It cannot refer to marital relations ("tashmish ha'mitah") because that weakens a person; rather it must be referring to relieving oneself ("tashmish nikavim").*[1]

The Sages scoured the entire world to find things that share commonalities with Olam Haba, and they found Shabbos, the sun, and an ambiguous word, *"tashmish,"* that the Talmud ultimately understands to mean going to the restroom.

In what ways are these items similar to Olam Haba? The last one is particularly strange for two reasons:

- First, how is going to the bathroom in any way connected to Olam Haba?
- Second, the Talmud could have avoided this circuitous rigmarole by saying simply *"tashmish nikavim"* (relieving oneself). Why did the Talmud choose to initially employ an ambiguous term that it

---

1   *Berachos* 57b.

must later clarify? It appears that the Talmud is making a point of explicitly highlighting that marital relations do *not* qualify. What can we deduce from the emphasis that *tashmish nikavim* is similar to Olam Haba but *tashmish ha'mitah* does not?

Let us explore these three items one by one and see if we can discover what attributes they share with Olam Haba.

Shabbos

Shabbos is likened to Olam Haba elsewhere in the vast sea of the Talmud:

> *Whoever toils before Shabbos will eat on Shabbos; whoever did not toil before Shabbos, from what will they eat on Shabbos?!*[2]

Obviously, the Talmud is not offering good housekeeping tips; rather, it is conveying a deep insight into the relationship between this world and the next. This world is akin to the weekday when work and preparation is possible, and Olam Haba is like Shabbos when work is no longer possible. If you want to eat food on Shabbos, the requisite preparation must be already done prior. Similarly, Olam Haba is the world of enjoyment of the product of the hectic preparation done in this world.

A profound insight emerges from this comparison: We tend to erroneously assume that Olam Haba amounts to a prize granted to those who observe Mitzvos in the same way that a child who excels in his studies is awarded a lollipop. Our Sages paint a different picture. When you make food before Shabbos, *you consume that very same food* on Shabbos. It's not an unrelated reward. When we engage in the activities that bring us to Olam Haba—i.e., Mitzvos—we are creating the "food" that we will consume in Olam Haba. The action you do and the reward that it spawns are the same. No one would argue that my *reward* for making Shabbos food is eating Shabbos food. The output is the direct consequence of the input. Mitzvos create the spiritual entities that benefit their doer in Olam Haba.[3]

---

2   *Avodah Zarah* 3a.

3   See *Rambam*'s comment to *Avos* 1:3.

A Taste of Heaven

An additional idea of how Shabbos relates to Olam Haba can be proposed. The Talmud proclaims:

> *Rabbi Shimon Ben Lakish said: The Holy One, blessed is He, places an extra Soul into man on Shabbos eve, and at the conclusion of Shabbos they remove it from him.*[4]

Simply understood, the Talmud is telling us that during the week we have *one Soul and one body*, but for the duration of Shabbos every person is granted an additional Soul, bringing the total to *two Souls and one body*. By extension, perhaps we can postulate that death is more complicated on Shabbos because two Souls need to be extracted instead of one. That seems odd.

If the words of the Talmud sound strange, the problems with this citation are compounded by *Rashi's* commentary. He explains that the extra Soul allows for "expansiveness of heart to rest and be joyous and be opened wide and eat and drink and not vomit." The Soul is interested in the *spiritual* realm and *spiritual* pleasure. If a person is given the extra Soul on Shabbos, that would lend itself to the person being more *spiritually* inclined on Shabbos. Yet *Rashi* explains that the extra Soul allows for uninhibited immersion in *physical* pleasures on Shabbos. What can we make of this bizarre teaching?

Perhaps we can suggest an explanation for this strange sounding teaching that will also provide us with another way Shabbos overlaps with Olam Haba. A Mitzvah is *an activity of a Soul performed by the body.* The 613 Mitzvos are a complete list of the Soul's agenda. For a body-centric person, many Mitzvos seem meaningless. Such a person starves his Soul of its necessary nourishment, but because he only senses the needs of his body, he is blissfully unaware of his Soul's torment. A person can neglect their Soul for their entire lifetime and never sense its acute agony. For the Soul, Mitzvos fulfill innate needs. But to the degree that we do not identify with it, we feel awkward doing them.

---

4   *Beitzah* 16a.

The roles are reversed in Olam Haba. In Olam Haba, the body's agenda doesn't matter (there is no eating, drinking, etc.); all that matters is the Soul's agenda. For those dominated by the body's identity that is difficult to imagine. To the body, Mitzvos feel unnatural and out of character; the spiritual realm seems foreign.

There is one Mitzvah that bucks the trend: Shabbos. On Shabbos, we dress in our finest clothes, spend quality time with family, partake in delicious meals and fine alcohol, and naps and marital relations are encouraged. The Mitzvos of Shabbos are not just food for the Soul *that do not resonate with the body*; Shabbos is the one thing that both the Soul and the body can get behind.

On Shabbos, man is given an extra Soul. This does not mean that on Shabbos man has two Souls and a single body. On Shabbos, *the body itself becomes like a Soul* because on that day, it too is desirous of Mitzvos. This is not to suggest that the body on Shabbos begins seeking spiritual pursuits; rather, the Mitzvos of Shabbos tantalize and excite the body as well as the Soul. Normally the pursuit of physical indulgences reviles the Soul. On Shabbos, those same physical pleasures are Mitzvos and the body and Soul join together in pursuit of a common agenda. On Shabbos, we have two Souls and harbor no entity that feels awkward doing Mitzvos.

Shabbos is a measure of Olam Haba. To understand what it's like to be in Olam Haba and what it's like to feel totally at home pursuing a Mitzvah, we must examine the Mitzvos of Shabbos that resonate with our body as well as our Soul. That experience mirrors what our Soul feels when we shake the lulav, study Torah, or don Tefillin, and is a smidgen of the spiritual serenity that it experiences in Olam Haba.

The Sun

The second thing that is a measure of Olam Haba is the sun. This is also not the only time that Olam Haba is compared to the sun. As mentioned in the previous chapter, the Talmud teaches that Olam Haba was inaccessible to all the prophets based upon the verse, "an eye cannot see it." Like the sun, Olam Haba is too bright for even the great visionaries to absorb. Also, the Midrash teaches that the light of Day

One of Creation was hidden away in storage awaiting the Tzaddikim in Olam Haba.[5] A third instance is the Talmud, which states that in Olam Haba the light of the sun will be diminished.[6] *Rashi* explains that the sun's illumination will remain unchanged, but the light emanating from the Tzaddikim will outshine it and, in comparison, the sun will appear fainter.

The Soul is a bright spiritual light. In this world, the Soul is enshrouded in a body that conceals it. Olam Haba is where the Soul in unsheathed from the body and it shines forth with the brightness of a thousand suns. Only Moshe succeeded in mimicking the status of Olam Haba in this world; hence, "the face of Moshe was like the face of the sun."[7]

A Clear World

Olam Haba is aptly compared to the sun when viewed in contrast to this world. In the absence of the sun, darkness and night descend. Fittingly, the Talmud compares this world to darkness.[8] In a fascinating and multifaceted Talmudic teaching, we are taught about the perils of navigating through this dark world. The piece begins with a verse that compares Torah and Mitzvos to different types of light, "A candle is a Mitzvah and Torah is light,"[9] and proceeds to demonstrate the role of Torah and Mitzvos:

> *A man was walking in the black of night, and he was scared of becoming entangled in thorns, falling into holes, tripping over prickly thistles, being attacked by wild animals and bandits, and he does not know which direction he is going. If he gets a fiery torch, he is saved from the thorns, holes, and thistles, but he is still fearful of wild animals and bandits, and he doesn't know which direction he is heading. At daybreak, he is saved from wild animals and bandits, but still does not know*

---

5   Quoted by *Rashi, Bereishis* 1:4.
6   *Sanhedrin* 91b.
7   *Bava Basra* 75a.
8   *Bava Metzia* 83b.
9   *Mishlei* 6:23.

which direction he is heading. If he reaches a crossroads, he is saved from all.[10]

The Soul's journey to Olam Haba occurs in the dark of night. Fumbling through the darkness, man is liable to injure himself in a variety of ways: By tripping over inert obstacles and pitfalls (thorns, holes, and thistles), and by being preyed upon by predators afforded cover by the darkness (wild animals and roving bandits). These refer to sins that can injure the Soul and hamper its progress. With their torch-like quality, Mitzvos remedy the three obstacles. Via adherence to Mitzvos, a person unearths his dormant Soul and restores it to being a path-illuminating headlamp as it was in utero, thus enabling him to sidestep the obstacles in the darkness.

Torah thwarts the danger even more powerfully. It is like daybreak, when the arrival of the sun ushers in a beacon of clarity that disperses all the dangers. That said, even Torah does not comprise a full protection from sin. Though it signals daybreak, nightfall may yet come and the settings for sin will resume.

Olam Haba is like the sun itself. In that world there is no darkness and no potential for sin under any circumstances.

An Upside-Down World

What is the nature of the clarity of Olam Haba that leaves no room for sin? The answer can be found in the first documented near-death-experience as recorded in the Talmud:

> *Rabbi Yosef, the son of Rabbi Yehoshua, became ill and his Soul departed. When he was resuscitated, his father asked him what he saw. He said, "I saw an upside-down world; lofty ones were lowly and lowly ones were lofty." His father responded, "You saw a clear world." His father questioned further, "How are the Torah scholars viewed there?" Rabbi Yosef answered, "The same way they are viewed here they are viewed there."*[11]

---

10   *Sotah* 21a.
11   *Bava Basra* 10b.

Rabbi Yosef temporarily experienced the next world and returned here to tell us what it is like. He described a world that is diametrically opposed to ours. There, the "lofty ones are lowly and the lowly ones are lofty." Initially, the stark differences between these worlds caused him to conclude that he saw an upside-down world. His father, Rabbi Yehoshua, corrected him, saying that in truth he saw a *clear* world and *our world* is upside down.

To someone suspended by their feet from the ceiling, everyone else appears upside down. When we look at Olam Haba, everything seems upside down; *no one is interested in matters of the body, all they want is to partake in Soulful pleasure.* But the truth is that Olam Haba is like the sun: it is a *clear world*; in *our world of darkness, everything* is upside down.

My grandfather drew a powerful lesson from the follow-up exchange: When asked how the Torah scholars are viewed in Olam Haba, Rabbi Yosef answered that they are viewed the same as they are here. The Torah scholars live *here in a clear world.* By doing Mitzvos and studying Torah, we can create a mini Olam Haba in this world; a dose of clarity; a measure of right-side-upness while everyone else is upside-down. To others who have never experienced sunlight, that world is foreign and upside-down; but for the scholars who regularly conjure candles of Mitzvos to illuminate the darkness and evoke daybreak through Torah, they recognize that this world is the one that is upside-down.

Tashmish

The third thing that is comparable to Olam Haba is *tashmish.* Due to the ambiguity of that term, the Talmud must clarify that it does not mean marital relations (which weaken a person), rather it refers to using the restroom. This, too, reveals a deep insight. The sources teach that the pleasure of Olam Haba dwarfs any conceivable pleasure in this world, but Olam Haba pleasure is not merely greater in *quantity*, it is an entirely different *kind of pleasure.*[12] In his treatise, *Rambam* elucidates the difference between the two:

---

12   *Avos* 4:17.

> *We are in the world of the body, and therefore we cannot grasp only its weak and temporary pleasures. But spiritual pleasures are constant, eternal, and ceaseless. These two pleasures have no relation at all.*

The ephemeral body experiences ephemeral pleasures; the eternal Soul experiences eternal pleasures. There is a fundamental reason for this distinction: Bodily pleasures stem from a catalyst. Regardless of what the source of the physical pleasure is—eating, drinking, skiing, etc.—when it ceases, the sensation of pleasure ends as well, frequently leaving a bad aftertaste in its wake. Spiritual pleasures are not a result of something external; they are inherent and internal and therefore never stop.

In this last comparison to Olam Haba, the Sages were looking for a pleasure wherein the good feeling extends beyond the activity or stimulant that triggered it. The Talmud scanned the entire gamut of worldly pleasures and found a small one where the activity of the pleasure ends but the good feeling continues on. To sharpen its point, the Talmud uses the ambiguous term *"tashmish"* to convey this lesson. By noting that the marital relations–variety of the word *"tashmish"* weakens a person, it is clearly an example of pleasure from the bodily world. However, with the other type of *"tashmish,"* the pleasure doesn't end when its catalyst ends. Thus, the point of the Talmud that Olam Haba pleasures continue beyond its stimulant is conveyed both by rejecting the *"tashmish"* of marital relations because it weakens, and by teaching that the other *"tashmish"* is similar to Olam Haba in this small way. Of course, this is not to suggest that using the facilities is comparable to the pleasure of Olam Haba in magnitude or scope; one second of Olam Haba outweighs the collective sum of all physical pleasures combined. The only parallel is with respect to it sharing a scintilla of the type of Olam Haba pleasure in that it is somewhat ongoing.

All told, this short Talmudic teaching offers us (at least) four insights into Olam Haba:

- By comparing it to Shabbos, we learn both that Mitzvos in this world create the spiritual pleasure that is only actualized in Olam Haba.

- Spiritual matters in Olam Haba are as natural and visceral as physical matters here.
- We also learn that in the sun-like clarity of Olam Haba, sin is impossible.
- Finally, this teaching informs us that the spiritual pleasure in Olam Haba is ceaseless.

In the next chapter, we will focus on the interrelationship between this world and Olam Haba, clarify the fundamentally different nature of man's existence in that world, and begin to construct the necessary criteria to secure our coveted entry ticket to that world.

Chapter 28 Takeaways

Olam Haba–pleasure is comparable to three things in this world: Shabbos, the sun, and going to the bathroom. Each of these things help us get a picture of what Olam Haba is all about.

Crossover to Eternity

*B*efore we examine the practical steps needed to ensure eligibility for Olam Haba, we must first clarify the fundamental nature of the relationship between this world and the next, and of the crossover and the handoff between the two.

Resurrection for Judgment

Let us begin by examining the connection between Olam Haba and another pillar of Jewish faith: Resurrection of the dead. What is the nature and purpose of resurrecting the dead? An examination of the sources finds differing answers.

In an intriguing dialogue between Rabbi Yehudah Hanassi and the Roman Emperor Antoninus recorded in the Talmud, we discover that Souls are restored to their body hosts for the purpose of judging sinners for their sins:

> *Antoninus said to Rabbi Yehudah Hanassi: "The body and the Soul can each exonerate themselves from judgment. How so? The body can say, 'The Soul sinned for since the day it departed from me, behold, I am like an inanimate rock in the grave.' The Soul can say, 'The body sinned for since the day I departed from it, behold, I am flying in the air like a bird.'"*
>
> *Rabbi Yehudah HaNassi responded: "Let me explain with a parable: A king had an orchard full of beautiful figs, and he*

stationed two guards to watch it, one crippled and one blind. The crippled guard said to the blind guard, 'I see beautiful figs in the orchard. Come and carry me on your back and we will get them to eat.' The cripple rode on the back of the blind, they collected the fruits and ate them. Some time later, the owner of the orchard returned and asked them, 'Where are the beautiful figs?' The crippled guard said, 'Do I have legs to walk with and retrieve them?' The blind guard said, 'Do I have eyes to see with and retrieve them?' What did the owner do? He placed the cripple on the back of the blind and judged them as one. So too, the Holy One, blessed is He, will bring the Soul and cast it into the body and judge them as one."[1]

Antoninus proposed a brilliant loophole to exonerate people from judgment. After their death, the Soul and body can each independently deflect blame onto the other for their sins. Rabbi Yehudah Hanassi indeed conceded that judgment is not possible so long as Soul and body are separate, and judgment only happens once those two are reunited once more.

This exchange teaches that the purpose of Resurrection is to *facilitate Divine judgment* for the sinners. *All people*[2]—and especially the wicked—must give an accounting and a reckoning before God after they die. How is that done? From the discussion between Rabbi Yehudah Hanassi and Antoninus, we learn that it is done by once again infusing the Soul back into the body:

Olam Haba and Resurrection

A second source shows that Resurrection is not about merely facilitating judgment, but it is a necessary precursor to Olam Haba. The background to this Talmudic teaching is the famous Mishnah:

All of Israel have a portion in Olam Haba, as Scripture (Yeshayahu 60:21) states, "And Your Nation are all Tzaddikim

---

1   *Sanhedrin* 90a–90b.
2   See *Avos* 4:22.

*for eternity they will inherit the land; the shoot of My plant-
ing, My handiwork, for glory." These are the ones who do not
have a portion in Olam Haba: He who says, "Resurrection of
the dead is not Biblically sourced," [he who says] "Torah is not
Divine"; and a heretic ("apikores").*[3]

Why is someone who says, "Resurrection of the dead is not Biblically
sourced" ousted from Olam Haba? The Talmud (ibid.) explains:

*He repudiated Resurrection therefore he has no portion in
Resurrection.*

When asking why someone loses their portion in Olam Haba because
of rejection of Resurrection, the Talmud answers that because he
doesn't believe in it, he doesn't get to participate in it. Olam Haba and
Resurrection are inextricably linked. Without Resurrection, there can
be no Olam Haba, and therefore someone who repudiates Resurrection
has no path forward to Olam Haba and thus he loses his portion.
Evidently, Resurrection is more than just a way to judge people.

Along these lines, the Talmud is unambiguous that Olam Haba—and
the Resurrection that precipitates it—is reserved for the Tzaddikim.
For example, the Talmud states:

*The Tzaddikim that the Holy One, blessed is He, will bring
back to life in the future will never return to their dust.*[4]

Also, the aforementioned Mishnah asserts that all Jews (with a few
exceptions) have a portion in Olam Haba *because all Jews are Tzaddikim*:

*All of Israel have a portion in Olam Haba, as Scripture states,
"And Your Nation are all Tzaddikim."*[5]

---

3   *Sanhedrin* 90a.
4   Ibid. 92a.
5   *Yeshayahu* 60:21.

In addition, we learn that "Olam Haba is exclusively for *Tzaddikim*,"[6] and that "Olam Haba is only *Tzaddikim* sitting with crowns on their heads and enjoying God's presence."[7]

Resurrection and Reanimation

It is thus clear that there are two kinds of resurrection: one as an enabler of judgment and one as a precursor for Olam Haba. The resurrection for the purposes of judgment refers to the reanimation of all people *in the way that humans are constructed in this world*—a Soul submerged in a body. Just as the crippled and blind guards get reunited for judgment *in the same fashion as they were when they perpetrated the crime*, so too, the Soul and body are fused together for judgment in the same way that they were when they sinned. For judgment, the Soul is "cast into the body"; it is again dependent on its body host. In Talmudic parlance, reanimating a person for judgment is referred to as "standing for judgment."

However, the Resurrection that kickstarts Olam Haba exclusively for the Tzaddikim is a total re-creation of man in a completely new paradigm. We tend to think of Olam Haba as "the Afterlife." That implies that after life in this world, a person is whisked away to a different, presumably vastly better world. The truth is more subtle: Olam Haba is not a new *venue* that a person as *he is currently constructed* is brought to. Rather, it is the world that results from the *person* being fundamentally changed. Olam Haba is the world wherein the Soul is dominant and the body is entirely incidental (there is no eating, drinking, etc.).

In this context, Resurrection refers to the reconstitution of man *in the Olam Haba format*. Resurrection is not about throwing the Soul back into a body and constructing the person in the format of this world—a Soul submerged, drowning in a Yetzer-Hara dominated body; it's a total re-creation of man, bringing to life a person whose Soul now dominates his identity with the same suffocating iron grip that in our

---

6   *Yevamos* 46a.
7   *Berachos* 17a.

world the body is man's identity, restoring the equilibrium that existed prior to the Soul being subjected to a Yetzer Hara.

Restoration of Adam

With our understanding of the fundamental nature of Resurrection, let us examine an interesting theological exchange found in the Talmud:

> *Caesar said to Rabban Gamliel, "You say that dead ones will live. But they are dust, and does dust live?!" Caesar's daughter said, "Let me respond: Suppose there are two craftsmen in the city, one creates with water and one creates with plaster. Which of them is more impressive?" Caesar answered, "The one who creates with water." She said, "God creates with water, He can surely create with plaster."*[8]

Caesar's daughter seems to be responding to the question with a clever quip: In our world, people are created from "water," i.e., from the primordial biological fluid. That is a tremendous feat of engineering; creating from the more substantial dust or plaster is relatively easier.

But there is an eye-popping revelation in this answer: Resurrection for Olam Haba is a fundamentally different process of creation than the one that exists in this world. Here we are created with "water"; in Olam Haba we are formed from "dust." One other human in history was made out of dust—Adam—as the verse states, "And Hashem Elokim formed the man from the dust of the ground."[9] When the Talmud says that during Resurrection man will be remade from *dust*, the implication is that *they will parallel Adam in their physiological makeup*. Before his sin, Adam identified entirely as a Soul and was not subjected to a Yetzer Hara. When Tzaddikim are rebuilt for Olam Haba, they are recreated the way Adam was initially: free of a Yetzer Hara[10] and not registering the existence of a body.[11]

---

8   *Sanhedrin* 90b.
9   *Bereishis* 2:7.
10   *Sukkah* 52a.
11   *Berachos* 17a.

This dispels the common misconception that what makes Olam Haba special is that it is a new *venue* distinct from our world. Olam Haba is different from this world because it is a *new reality of self.* With his trademark golden eloquence, *Rambam* explains this point:

> *The fact that the Sages called it "Olam Haba" (lit., the next world) is not because it is not present now, and this world must be destroyed and afterwards that world comes. The matter is not so! Rather, behold it is extant and standing...and it is only called "Olam Haba" because that life comes to man after the life in this world, in which we exist with a body and a Soul, and that it is the origin of every man.[12]*

Olam Haba exists as much today as it ever will, but because it is the world of the Souls, it is inaccessible to anyone whose Soul harbors the ill effects of a body and Yetzer Hara. If man was able to create within himself the conditions of Olam Haba—if he could render himself a duplicate of Adam pre-sin—he could already exist in that world. Only Moshe managed to do that completely. The forefathers got close. They *tasted* Olam Haba because they divested themselves of their Yetzer Hara, but only Moshe transformed himself completely into an Adam-pre-sin-like state.

Dressing Appropriately for Olam Haba

This insight leads us to the key factor that determines whether a person does or does not merit to be remade as a Soul-first entity in Olam Haba. The Mishnah teaches:

> *Rabbi Yaakov said: This world is akin to a corridor before the next world; prepare yourself in the corridor so that you shall enter the palace.[13]*

The objective of man in this world is to prepare himself to crossover and enter Olam Haba. What is the nature of this preparation?

---

12   *Rambam*, Laws of Repentance 8:8.
13   *Avos* 4:16.

The Mishnah's analogy is of someone walking down the corridor leading to the king's palace. Such a venue demands a certain mode of conduct and dress. As such, the nature of the preparation is for the person to render themselves appropriate for the destination. During the crossover to Olam Haba, a person is reconstructed in the inverse way that he is constructed here. There, the Soul is a person's identity, and the body is only its garment. *The requisite preparation in the corridor is for the person to make himself congruent with the norms of the next world by reframing his identity to becoming more Soul-like and thus ensuring that he will "fit in" when he arrives at the palace.* If man arrives at the palace gates and his body is treated merely as a garment for his Soul, he is an ideal candidate to join the feast.

In Jewish literature, the name for someone who has reoriented his life perspective to be in line with Olam Haba is "Tzaddik." People who walk on ceilings and live in an upside-down world are not admitted to Olam Haba. A Tzaddik is someone who, whilst being in the "corridor," has justified and straightened his worldview to be aligned with Olam Haba.

The Midrash expresses this principle using different terminology:

> *Rabbi Yehudah said: Whoever answers "Amen" in this world merits to answer "Amen" in Olam Haba.*[14]

"Amen" is etymologically derived from the word "*Emunah*." Someone who develops and deepens his Emunah is a Tzaddik, as the oft-quoted verse makes clear: "And a Tzaddik lives with Emunah."[15] A man of Emunah is living right-side up; he's living as a Soul and has created here the conditions to exist and thrive in Olam Haba.

Practical Steps to Getting an Invitation

The skeletal structure of entering Olam Haba is now clear: Those who have prepared for that world by adapting themselves to being congruent with it while here will be rebuilt during the Resurrection in the manner of Adam pre-sin—a Soul with an inconsequential bodily

---

14   *Tanchuma, Tzav* 7.
15   *Chavakuk* 2:4.

"garment"—enabling them to partake in Olam Haba. It is time to get down to specifics.

The Talmud declares that entrance to Olam Haba is by invitation-only:

> *Rabbah said in the name of Rav Yochanan: Jerusalem of this world is unlike Jerusalem of Olam Haba: [Regarding] Jerusalem of this world—whoever wants to enter may enter; Jerusalem of Olam Haba—entrance is limited to those who are invited to it.*[16]

We cannot enter Olam Haba unless we are holders of a Golden Ticket. How does one earn that coveted invitation? How do we make ourselves into a Tzaddik that is worthy of Olam Haba? *Ramchal* writes briefly that the means by which we acquire a share in Olam Haba is the observance of Mitzvos, but he does not elaborate on how it works. It seems that there are at least three general paths that a person can follow to earn a portion in Olam Haba. Let us examine them one at a time.

Chapter 29 Takeaways

- Resurrection of the dead occurs in two ways: the reunification of body and Soul in the same way that they existed during life in order to be able to judge them for their misdeeds, and the complete re-creation of man in the Olam Haba paradigm.
- The Resurrection that is a precursor to Olam Haba is when man is made out of "dust" like Adam before his sin.
- In order to be eligible to enter Olam Haba, we must make ourselves congruent with the norms of the next world before we arrive at its gates.

---

16   *Bava Basra* 75b.

A Kernel of Eternity

A Tzaddik is someone who has adopted the identity of his Soul and absorbed its instincts and values. When the Tzaddik arrives at the end of the corridor, he has already harmonized himself with the world of his Soul—he already became a citizen of Olam Haba during his lifetime—and is ready to seamlessly transition into Olam Haba. In our world, the Yetzer Hara entrenches man's identity as a body, and that worldview appears to be unshakable. A Tzaddik who views his body as merely a garment of his Soul is an outlier. Yet, the Mishnah boldly declares that *all of Israel* (with the exception of egregious sinners) merit a portion in Olam Haba *because they are all Tzaddikim.* It seems like a stretch to state that by dint of being part of Israel someone is guaranteed to reinvent themselves and become a Tzaddik. How can the Mishnah suggest that we will all arrive at the doorsteps of Olam Haba compatible to enter into that world?

A Blossoming Kernel of Greatness

In yet another Talmudic dialogue between a non-Jewish monarch and a Sage regarding Olam Haba, we discover that it is not as hard as it looks:

> Queen Cleopatra asked Rabbi Meir: "I know that the dead will
> come alive, as Scripture states, 'People will blossom in the city

as the grass of the land.[1] *But when they emerge will they be naked or clothed?"*

He told her, *"We can deduce the answer from wheat: Wheat is buried naked but comes out with many layers of clothing (chaff); the Tzaddikim who are buried clothed in burial shrouds most certainly will emerge clothed."*[2]

Cleopatra was not questioning the veracity of Resurrection; she was only curious as to the details of *how* people are reborn. In his answer, Rabbi Meir compares a deceased Tzaddik being buried in the ground to a seed of wheat that is planted, and the Resurrection to the Tzaddik blossoming forth as a plant emerging from the ground. This analogy allows him to conclude that a Tzaddik who is buried clothed will certainly emerge clothed.

There are several takeaways from the Talmud's comparison: For one, it might explain why, for many, the notion of Resurrection is too fantastic to be believable. We have previously noted (in chapter 12) that the Talmud uses agriculture as the quintessential example of a process that is only believable after it has been experienced. A person who has never seen a seed from planting to harvest will surely be dubious of the claim that the tiny, inedible seed that is decomposing and withering away under layers of inedible soil will one day sprout as a fruit-bearing tree or plant. To the uninitiated, there can be nothing besides rot and decay in its future. The transformation and rebirth for Olam Haba is equally fantastic to its skeptics and deniers.

Another important takeaway can be gleaned from Rabbi Meir's analogy: A seed contains the DNA for whatever will subsequently emerge from the ground, despite not currently being comparable to, or identifiable with, what it will eventually be. A seed contains the *potential* that gets developed whilst submerged underground. Different seeds yield different fruits, and the health of the seed is reflected in the robustness of the eventual fruit.

---

1   *Tehillim* 72:16.
2   *Sanhedrin* 90b.

That is exactly how the rebirth for Olam Haba works. Our life is our opportunity to formulate what variety and quality of "seed" will get planted at death and consequently what kind of "fruit" will surface for Olam Haba. Indeed, it is neither easy nor common for a person to transform themselves here into a *full-fledged entity* that is primed for Olam Haba, but as a general rule, the Mishnah can say with confidence that all of Israel have a sensitivity and an affinity for the realm of the Soul and nourish its 613 spiritual components with the 613 Mitzvos. Though this will not necessarily transform man into a complete citizen of Olam Haba here, at a minimum he will develop into a *kernel* of the reality of Olam Haba here, and that kernel will be planted in the ground at burial. To the uninformed, it will only rot and decay into oblivion, but like the subterranean germinating seed it is already beginning to be primed to sprout forth. At Resurrection, that spiritual potential is brought to life and the Tzaddik emerges geared up and ready for Olam Haba.

Rabbi Meir's analogy may also explain why the second blessing of the *Amidah* prayer describes the Almighty actively reviving the dead. If Resurrection is a one-time switch that has not yet been flicked, it is inaccurate to say that He *is* currently reviving the dead. But according to our understanding of the Talmud, Resurrection is a process similar to a seed sprouting, and, though the Tzaddikim have yet to surface, the Almighty is already amidst the process of reviving them.

Birthing a Nation

The Talmud extends the comparison between burial and planting a seed:

> *Rav Tevi said in the name of Rav Yashiya: What is the intended meaning of the verse, "The grave and the narrowness of the womb; land unsated from water"?[3] What can be the possible connection between a grave and the narrowness of the womb? Only to teach you that just as in a womb what enters exits, so*

---

3   *Mishlei* 30:16.

> too, in a grave what enters exits…This rebuts those that claim
> that Resurrection is not Biblically sourced.[4]

The Talmud again compares death to the planting of a seed for a future resurfacing, this time to the implanting of the future child in the womb. In this analogy as well, the seed that enters the womb is similar in its *potential* to the "fruit" that later comes forth, though the input and the output cannot be more different.

There are several additional takeaways from this comparison: By likening burial to insertion of the seed into the womb and Resurrection to birth, the Talmud shows a picture of the eternality of Olam Haba. Someone who fulfills the Mitzvah of procreation helps usher a new Soul to the world, who in turn can continue bringing life and vitality to the world. That impact can scale staggeringly quickly: If someone bears seven children, and each of their children also have seven children, and so on, within seven generations the total descendants will number nearly a million Souls. Given that the length of a generation is roughly twenty-seven years, this can be done in less than 200 years. Bringing children into the world can truly create an enduring, eternal legacy, and it can serve as a fitting comparison to the eternal life of Olam Haba.

Comparing a life culminating in death and burial to the activity that engenders procreation also highlights the fundamental conflict of life. Unlike the previous analogy of planting a wheat seed, the motivation for this form of planting is not necessarily to create any new fruit. There can indeed be a procreational motivation—to think about the future world that will result, but there is a diametrically opposing motivation—to render it entirely recreational and not focusing on any other time but the present. On the positive side it can be an act of supreme holiness and a fulfillment of the words of the Talmud, "If they merited,

---

4   *Sanhedrin* 92a. The model of the handoff between this world and Olam Haba being similar to the process of childbirth is hinted elsewhere in the Talmud. Hebrew does not contain proper names for reproductive organs (see *Rambam, Guide to the Perplexed* 3:8), and the Talmud uses euphemisms instead. Quite interestingly, the womb is called "*kever*" in the Talmud (*Niddah* 21a), the same word for "grave," and the narrow part of womb is called "*prozdor*" (ibid. 17b), the word for "corridor," as in our guiding Mishnah, "This world is akin to a *corridor* before the next world."

the Presence of God is between them";[5] alternatively, it can be a great sin. This parallels the broader challenge of living in this world: Are we going to accede to the temptations of our Yetzer Hara who contends that we ought to maximize this physical and materialistic life as an ends unto its own, or are we going to live with Olam Haba as our goal and focus our energies to creating that future? Will we live our life recreationally and have nothing to show for it at the palace gates, or will we live procreationally and create the spiritual portfolio needed to flourish for eternity?

Finally, the Talmud's comparison sheds light on the huge disparity between the costs of Mitzvos and its benefits. In the analogy, the cost of the initial acts is astonishingly minor compared to the benefits of spawning a million descendants. Mitzvos are strikingly easy and doable relative to the eternal dividends that they engender, yet, unfortunately and bewilderingly, despite the endless opportunities for eternity, we tend to fail to appreciate their value and not seize them and stockpile them breathlessly.

When the Gaon of Vilna was on his deathbed, he seized his tzitzis and began weeping. "In this world," he cried, "for pennies you can buy a pair of tzitzis and through it garner eternal reward. Once you leave this world, however, not even all the money in the world can buy you a single Mitzvah."

Mitzvos are the means to lock up a spot in Olam Haba, and in this world, they are (shockingly!) cheap and accessible. For the limited time that our Soul is harbored in a body, we have access to a vending machine that dispenses diamonds for the price of soda cans. We are advised to make hay while the sun still shines, to grab as much as possible before time expires and the golden opportunity vanishes.

Earning the Golden Ticket and Not Losing It

These added insights notwithstanding, the overall position of the Talmud is clear: In this life we are creating a seed to be buried in the ground at death, and an actualized version of that seed will be

---

5   *Sotah* 17a.

resurrected for Olam Haba. The seed is a microcosm of what will later emerge, and hence our objective is to make ourselves into one that is capable of developing into a citizen of Olam Haba. To be re-created out of dust like Adam pre-sin for Olam Haba, you have to make yourself a bit Adam-pre-sin-like by repulsing your Yetzer Hara and tending to your Soul while you are still here. People who believe in the spiritual world and live their lives that way deposit that type of seed into the ground at death, and what will emerge will be ready for Olam Haba.

The Mishnah teaches that all Jews merit Olam Haba with a few exceptions. The first person to lose his portion is someone who doesn't believe in Resurrection. This may seem as a form of punishment. However, it is more likely just a statement of fact: If someone doesn't believe in Resurrection, if he thinks his death marks the absolute end of his existence, his life and priorities will be reflective of that belief. He will live only for this world, embracing—instead of resisting—the Yetzer Hara's ideology. Those choices and behaviors will mold the seed that will be implanted at death. When the time for the new world arrives, the resultant fruit will simply not be a good candidate for Olam Haba.

Next on the list of Jews who lose their portion in Olam Haba are those who say that Torah is not Divine. Torah is the only antidote to the Yetzer Hara.[6] Torah is indispensable if the goal is to shed the Yetzer Hara's worldview and become a seed of a citizen of Olam Haba. Someone who doesn't recognize the divinity of the Torah will not harness its powers to prepare himself to become a worthy seed for Olam Haba.

The third is the *apikores* (heretic), which the Talmud defines thusly:

> *What is an example of an apikores? Rav Yosef said: Those who say, "How have the Sages benefited us?"*[7]

What is so terrible about questioning the contribution of the Sages? Is there even a Mitzvah to laud their impact?

Questioning the contribution of the Sages is not problematic per se, but it is revealing of the opinion-holder's priorities and values. This

---

6   *Kiddushin* 30b.
7   *Sanhedrin* 99b.

world and Olam Haba are opposing worlds.[8] Citizens of this world who identify as a body and chose to ignore and neglect their Soul view the spiritual citizen as upside-down. Our preparation in this corridor is to flip our perspective and align it with the spiritual world. Someone who sees no benefit of spiritual pursuits is obviously someone who has not reoriented their life-perspective to be in line with Olam Haba. Such a seed bears fruit that is ineligible for Olam Haba.

Most Jews do indeed make the spiritual realm a priority and embrace Mitzvos and therefore earn a portion in Olam Haba. This is the first of three paths to Olam Haba. Let's us examine the others.

Chapter 30 Takeaways

- When someone is buried after they die, the kernel of their spiritual purification is planted in the ground, and a fully actualized version of that will emerge at the Resurrection, ready for Olam Haba.
- People who adopt the spiritual mindset, who resist the Yetzer Hara, and who become Soul-like in their time in this world create a seed of a person who is qualified for Olam Haba.

---

8   *Bava Basra* 10b.

CHAPTER 31

Spiritual Shortcuts

*T*here is a second way to get into Olam Haba: In three Talmudic episodes, we learn of the possibility of acquiring Olam Haba in one hour. The subjects of these narratives are individuals who up to that point had not lived lives of scrupulous Mitzvah observance, but made courageous and transformative acts at the end of their lives that catapulted them into the lofty and exclusive fraternity of those invited to Olam Haba. Let's briefly recount their stories and see the secrets of the fast-lane to eternity.

The first to make use of this shortcut was Ketiah Bar Shalom, a non-Jewish advisor to an unnamed Caesar. The Talmud relates that this Caesar had advocated to destroy the Jewish People, and Ketiah Bar Shalom brazenly rebutted his arguments causing Caesar to table his genocidal plans. However, as a result of his one-upmanship of the monarch, he was sentenced to be executed. As he was being led to his death, a spectator heckled him that he had sacrificed himself for the Jewish People despite being uncircumcised. Ketiah Bar Shalom swiftly seized a knife, circumcised himself, and declared that he had paid his dues to join the Jewish nation; soon afterwards, he was executed. The episode concludes:

A prophetic voice announced: "Ketiah Bar Shalom is invited to Olam Haba!" Upon hearing it, Rabbi Yehudah Hanassi wept,

> *saying: "There is one who acquires his world in a single hour; another acquires it after many years."[1]*

Although Ketiah Bar Shalom was only righteous for one final heroic act, he earned an invitation to Olam Haba. As Rabbi Yehudah Hanassi succinctly summed it up, there are two ways to achieve the same goal: some accomplish it in only one hour, for others it takes many years.

The next story tells of an addicted patron of harlots, Rabbi Eliezer Ben Durdai. After a particularly egregious sin, for which he was shamefully reprimanded, he committed to repent and change his ways. First, he sought to have others aid him in his repentance. When those efforts yielded no results, he declared that only he could change himself and he mournfully repented. Being that he had become addicted to his sinful ways, when he stopped cold turkey, he died from the withdrawal. The narrative concludes as above:

> *A prophetic voice announced: "Rabbi Eliezer Ben Durdai is invited to Olam Haba!" Upon hearing it, Rabbi Yehudah Hanassi wept, saying: "There is one who acquires his world after many years; another acquires it in a single hour!"[2]*

The final episode is regarding the Roman executioner of the great Sage, Rabbi Chanina Ben Teradion. At the time, the Romans decreed that Torah study was an executable offense, alongside other anti-Torah edicts. Rabbi Chanina Ben Teradion refused to capitulate and was murdered in a grisly fashion: The barbarians wrapped him in a Torah scroll and encircled him with branches of wood that were lit aflame. To prolong his agony, the Romans soaked tufts of wool in water and placed them on his heart and distanced the flames so that they would not engulf him. Amid his torture, he calmly conducted inspiring conversations with his daughter and his students. To his distressed daughter, he said: "If it was me alone that was being burned, it would be difficult for me. But now that I am being burned with a Torah scroll, He who

---

1   *Avodah Zarah* 10b.
2   Ibid. 17a.

will demand retribution for the shame of the Torah will also extract retribution for me." When his students asked him what he saw, he responded with the haunting words: "I see the parchment [of the Torah scroll] being burnt, but the letters are flying up to Heaven." Moved by this sight, the executioner asked Rabbi Chanina if he would guarantee him a portion in Olam Haba if he hastened his death, and Rabbi Chanina swore to the affirmative. Immediately, the executioner raised the flames, removed the wool from Rabbi Chanina's heart, and himself jumped into the flames and died as well. Yet again the Talmud finishes:

> A prophetic voice announced: "Rabbi Chanina Ben Teradion and the executioner are invited to Olam Haba!" Upon hearing it, Rabbi Yehudah Hanassi wept, saying: "There is one who acquires his world in a single hour; another acquires it after many years!"[3]

These three stories demonstrate the two roadmaps to Olam Haba: The typical, slow and steady grind that takes many years, and the expedited way that takes only a single hour.

For most, achieving a coveted invitation to Olam Haba requires many years of painstaking work. These three martyrs were able to bypass the typical method and achieved the same result with one valorous act of martyrdom. In fact, the prophetic voice equated the invitation to Olam Haba extended to Rabbi Chanina Ben Teradion—who spent his entire life toiling in Torah study—with that given to the executioner—who was righteous for only the last moments of his life.

How is it possible to achieve the result of a lifetime of tireless commitment to all the Mitzvos with one act? Also worth pondering is the fact that the three protagonists who earned entry to Olam Haba in one hour all died. Why must the hour-long path to Olam Haba conclude with death?

---

3   Ibid. 18a.

Condensing a Lifetime of Work into One Act

The first (more typical) path to Olam Haba detailed in the previous chapter requires spending many years earning Olam Haba by becoming a citizen—or at least a kernel of a citizen—of Olam Haba. To become a citizen of Olam Haba requires the use of the 613 Mitzvos to breathe eternal life, vitality, and nourishment into the Soul. Each Mitzvah corresponds to one of the Soul's spiritual limbs and a Tzaddik whose Soul absorbs the vitality of all 613 Mitzvos has given life to a complete and robust spiritual body-double that will flourish in the spiritual world. Our Sages reassured us that we don't need to be fully adapted to that world to gain entry; we only need to internalize a kernel of the Olam Haba attitude before we arrive at the palace doors. That said, earning a Golden Ticket via this method is still the product of a multi-year war with the Yetzer Hara—acquiring Olam Haba Mitzvah by Mitzvah, one spiritual limb at a time.

Not so for the people who died for the Almighty. These martyrs arrived at the same goal all at once. With one act of martyrdom for the Jewish People, with one commitment to repentance, with one triumph over evil, they managed to consecrate *all* their limbs—their very lives—to the Almighty. The result is the same: an entire spiritual existence primed for Olam Haba. These three episodes demonstrate an accelerated process of achieving total transformation all at once.

This can be likened to two different ways to become rich. One way is to start a business, put in the long hours, reinvest profits, seize opportunities when they are available, and expand and grow the business until wealth is achieved. The other path is to win the lottery. The results are identical. This analogy may also explain Rabbi Yehudah Hanassi's lament. It is painful for the person who put in eighty-hour workweeks for decades to achieve great wealth to be on equal footing as someone who correctly guessed six numbers. When he heard about the prophetic declaration inviting these three individuals to Olam Haba, Rabbi Yehudah Hanassi cried when he realized that it is possible to gain such a high degree of greatness so rapidly.

This also demonstrates why we must always be ready to forfeit our lives for God should the opportunity arise. An opportunity to die for

God is like a winning lottery ticket; it is a chance to compress a lifetime of hard work into one act, and it is surely unwise to forgo such a golden opportunity. When the Talmud describes the martyr's death of Rabbi Akiva, it notes that he recited the *Shema* as he was being killed. When pressed by his student to explain this behavior he said:

> *My entire life I was distressed by reading the words of the Shema, which command us to love God "with all our Soul," which teach that we must be willing to give up our life for God, saying, "When will this opportunity come so that I may fulfill it?" Now that the opportunity arrived, I should not fulfill it?!*[4]

Rabbi Akiva's joy at the opportunity to die for God may sound strange initially. However, once we recognize that it is a shortcut to achieving a lifetime's work instantly, his jubilance is quite understandable.

The Loophole in the Shortcut

From the sources, it seems that the only way to achieve Olam Haba in one hour is via self-sacrifice that ends with death. However, there may be a loophole that would allow for instant acquisition of Olam Haba *without actually dying*.

The Talmud lists several people who earn Olam Haba:

> *The Rabbis taught: Those who are shamed by others and do not shame in return; those who hear their disgrace and do not respond; those who perform Mitzvos motivated by love of God and not with intention to receive reward or avoid punishment; and those who are joyous with suffering—regarding these the verse says, "And the lovers of God are like the mighty rising sun."*[5]

This Talmud enumerates four people who earn entry to Olam Haba (recall that the sun is a euphemism for Olam Haba). The commentaries disagree whether this Talmud is only referring to a person who

---

4   *Berachos* 61b.
5   *Gittin* 36b.

incorporates *all* these characteristics,[6] or if it even extends to a person who has a single characteristic of the four.[7] Regardless, these cause a person to merit Olam Haba. Let us analyze them.

The first two are "those who are shamed by others and do not shame in return; and those who hear their disgrace and do not respond." Why does someone who stoically swallows his shame earn a spot in Olam Haba? A suggestion can be made that someone who is embarrassed by another person and does not lash back is equivalent to a martyr who dies for God. The Talmud equates being whitened with shame to being killed, and hence it is preferable to be thrown into a fiery furnace in order to avoid shaming another.[8] By extension, when someone is embarrassed by another person, and has an opportunity to fire back at the perpetrator but instead bites his tongue, it is as if he was killed while doing the great Mitzvah of not shaming another person. This is a grand act of martyrdom for God, and thus the one who performs it earns a Golden Ticket to Olam Haba in one hour without actually dying.

There was once a strident opponent of one of Rabbi Moshe Feinstein's halachic rulings. Not content with quietly disagreeing, this person made disrespectful and disparaging comments in public against the preeminent halachic authority of the late twentieth century. Despite his conduct and without apologies, this individual later approached Rabbi Feinstein and brazenly asked for a favor, to which he obliged. When pressed by the incredulous onlookers to explain his actions—how he could help the person who had unrepentantly disparaged him—Rabbi Moshe Feinstein said, "The Talmud teaches that it is possible to acquire Olam Haba in one hour. Perhaps this is my hour."

From his words, it is apparent that every person will be afforded at least one once-in-a-lifetime chance to catapult himself into Olam Haba in one hour. Perhaps the source for that sentiment is the Mishnah in *Avos*:

---

6   *Rashi, Shabbos* 88b.

7   *Rambam,* cited below.

8   *Sotah* 10b.

Don't be scornful of any person and do not be dismissive of anything, for there is no person who does not have his hour, and there is nothing that does not have its place.[9]

Do not reject any person—even a lifelong sinner—for there is no person who does not have *his hour*, i.e., a possibility to overcome a lifetime of sin and usher themselves into the highest pantheon of Olam Haba in one hour. Invariably, each one of us will have at least one chance to expedite our life objective and acquire Olam Haba in one hour, be it by an opportunity to actually sacrifice our life for God and achieve the goal of all 613 Mitzvos in one fell swoop, or by swallowing our shame and being metaphorically "killed" for God. We must be ready to pounce on the opportunity and seize the hour.

The Joy of Suffering

The Talmud lists two more ways to get in: "those who perform Mitzvos out of love of God [and not to receive reward or because of fear of retribution]; and those who are joyous with suffering." Let's examine these two paths, beginning with one who is "joyous with suffering." The first question we must ask is why would someone in their right mind be happy to have pain? Also, why would that justify them receiving entry to Olam Haba?

Before we answer, it is vital to note that the suffering of the righteous is a difficult issue to grapple with. In fact, the Talmud interprets Moshe's request from God, "Inform me of Your ways,"[10] to refer to, among other things, why bad things happen to good people.[11] *Ramban* writes that the suffering of the righteous is something that we cannot possibly understand.[12]

That said, the Talmud teaches that suffering in this world cleanses a person of sin that they would otherwise need to account for in Olam Haba:

---

9   *Avos* 4:3.
10   *Shemos* 33:13.
11   *Berachos* 7a.
12   *Shaar Hagemul*.

> *What is meant by the verse, "A God of faith with no iniquity"?*[13]
> *"A God of faith"—this teaches that just as punishment is to be exacted in Olam Haba from the Resha'im even for a minor sin, so too, punishment is exacted in this world from the Tzaddikim even for a minor sin.*
>
> *"With no iniquity"—this teaches that just as reward is to be paid to the Tzaddikim in Olam Haba even for minor Mitzvos, so too, reward is paid in this world to the Resha'im even for minor Mitzvos.*[14]

The Talmud teaches that the Almighty treats everyone fairly: The Tzaddikim are also punished for their sins and the Resha'im are also rewarded for their Mitzvos. The only distinction between the two is that the Tzaddikim are punished for their sins in this world and rewarded for their Mitzvos in Olam Haba, and the Resha'im receive the opposite treatment: they are rewarded for their Mitzvos here and punished for their sins in Olam Haba.

Yet the question persists: The Mishnah teaches that the most minute amount of reward in Olam Haba outweighs the cumulative sum of all the feasible pleasures in this world. Therefore, if a Tzaddik and a Rasha both perform the identical Mitzvah, but the Tzaddik is rewarded for it in Olam Haba and the Rasha is rewarded here, their rewards for the same Mitzvah are inequitable. How can the Talmud claim that the Almighty is fair when He dispenses reward and punishment and go on to detail a clearly unfair system?

The answer is that both the righteous and the wicked self-selected to receive their reward in their respective worlds:

- The righteous viewed Olam Haba as the ultimate purpose and prioritized it in their behavior and deemphasized this world, therefore they *chose* to be punished here and rewarded there.
- The wicked lived their life by an opposite system of priorities: They valued this world as a venue for ultimate purpose and

---

13   *Devarim* 32:4.
14   *Taanis* 11a.

ignored the next, and therefore they implicitly chose this world as their preferred venue for reward.

The Almighty indeed rewards and punishes with eminent fairness. Not only is every deed accounted for—even the smallest Mitzvah is rewarded and even the smallest sin results in punishment—but the Almighty even allows the person to choose in which world they want to be rewarded and where they want their punishment. The Rasha chooses this world as his place of reward and the Almighty acquiesces to his wishes.

Perhaps this is the deeper meaning behind the Mishnah:

Envy, lust, and honor remove a person from the world.[15]

The common interpretation of this Mishnah is that these three qualities make life *here* unlivable. With our newfound discovery that man's behavior with respect to choosing which world he prioritizes dictates in which world he is asking God to reward him for his Mitzvos, we can posit that these three character flaws remove a person from the *next* world, from Olam Haba. When someone is envious, they demonstrate that they view material and physical qualities in this world as an ends and not a means. Envy thus exhibits a prioritization of this world as the preferred locale of reward. Lust, similarly, is the pursuit of this world's pleasures, and to seek honor is to crave reward for good deeds in this world. Hence, these three qualities implicitly show a person choosing to be rewarded in *this* world, and God will oblige and allow them to cash in their Mitzvos here, and consequently they are—fairly—removed from Olam Haba.

This would explain why the righteous are happy with suffering in this world. No one is entirely free of sin,[16] and the Almighty operates with an immutable principle that every action—both good and bad, both Mitzvah and sin—must be recompensed with reward or punishment. No matter how great a person may be and how few sins they may have

---

15 *Avos* 4:21.
16 See the deathbed of Rabbi Eliezer episode in the *Sanhedrin* 101a.

committed, they are not granted blanket immunity, and every sin must be atoned for. The only question is in which world will that punishment be meted out. It is preferable to get punishment here—when the intensity of punishment is relatively minor—and arrive at Olam Haba cleansed from sin. If someone must pay a fine of "a hundred," it would be a great blessing to get away with paying a hundred dollars and not a hundred kilograms of solid gold.

Suffering in this world is of course painful, but it is infinitely preferable to punishment in Olam Haba. Those who are joyous with suffering are the people who value Olam Haba over this world and are therefore delighted with the opportunity to disencumber it from the consequences of sin. Their joy with their suffering is reflective of their life's priorities. It demonstrates that though they are in this world, they are already living with the attitude and outlook of Olam Haba. Such a person is clearly preparing himself in the corridor to be compatible with the next world, and when he arrives he will surely be welcomed aboard.

The last person who merits Olam Haba is someone who does Mitzvos out of love of God and not because of fear of punishment. We will examine this third path to Olam Haba in the upcoming chapter.

Chapter 31 Takeaways

- Three Talmudic episodes demonstrate that acquiring an invitation to Olam Haba can be done in a single hour.
- Typically, acquiring Olam Haba in this fashion requires the person to forfeit his life in martyrdom—a worthwhile exchange, of course—but there will be opportunities in every person's life to earn Olam Haba in one hour, with one act, without dying.
- Suffering in this world cleanses a person from their sins and spares them from being punished for those sins after they pass.
- The Almighty dispenses reward and punishment for every deed—but the righteous have their reward stored up for Olam Haba and get their punishment done here, whereas the wicked are rewarded here and punished in Olam Haba.

Just One Mitzvah

*I*n his treatise on reward and punishment, *Rambam* writes that the entire purpose of life is to gain entry to Olam Haba:

> *The ultimate goal is to be included in the lofty society of people who merit Olam Haba, and to be present at this great honor.*

Thus far, we have explored two general ways to get in:

- The first is to become a Tzaddik, meaning one whose mindset is aligned with that of Olam Haba. The Mishnah assumes that all of Israel harbor this attitude and are in. Practically speaking, this attitude is reflected in observance of Mitzvos, saying "Amen," being joyous with suffering, revering Torah scholars, and by not acting in a way that would exclude a person from that world.[1]
- The second way to earn a coveted invitation is via martyrdom, either by literally dying for God, or by figuratively dying for God by absorbing disparagement without responding.

The Talmud, cited in the previous chapter, shows us a third avenue: One who performs Mitzvos solely because he loves the Almighty and wishes to obey His commands, without intending to get reward or to avoid punishment.[2] *Rashi*, in his commentary on the Talmud, writes that this refers to a person who performs *many* Mitzvos with pure intentions.

---

1   See *Rambam*, Laws of Repentance, chap. 3, for a complete list of disqualifiers.
2   *Gittin* 36b.

Rambam maintains a different approach. His position is found on the Mishnah that teaches:

> *Rabbi Chanania Ben Akashia says: The Holy One, blessed is He, desired to benefit the Jewish People, and therefore He increased for them Torah and Mitzvos.*

How do we benefit from the abundance of Torah and Mitzvos? *Rambam* explains:

> *One of the principles of faith is that when a man fulfills one of the 613 Mitzvos properly and perfectly, and does not combine with it any other motivation in the world, [but] rather he does it for its sake and motivated by love of God, behold he will merit Olam Haba through it. Regarding this principle did Rabbi Chanina teach his lesson. The abundance of Mitzvos will make certain that a person will invariably fulfill one of them to perfection, and as a result his Soul will live for eternity.[3]*

Rambam codifies a stunning principle: It is possible to gain an invitation to Olam Haba with performance of a *single* Mitzvah, provided that it is done with utmost perfection—out of love of God and not for any other reason ("*lishmah*" in Talmudic parlance). Therefore, the preponderance of Mitzvos is a boon to us in fulfilling our life mission of accessing Olam Haba.

As proof, *Rambam* cites an episode of Rabbi Chanina Ben Teradion recorded in the Talmud, wherein he asked his teacher, Rabbi Yose Ben Kisma, if he would merit Olam Haba. Upon discovery that Rabbi Chanina had once commingled personal money and charity money and gave it all to the poor, Rabbi Yose Ben Kisma exclaimed that he is assured a spot in Olam Haba in its merit.[4] Rabbi Chanina Ben Teradion was a great Sage who undoubtedly did myriads of Mitzvos, but this particular act was unique because it was sure to be untainted by any

---

3   *Rambam*, commentary on Mishnah, end of *Makkos*.
4   *Avodah Zarah* 18a.

motivations aside from obeying the will of the Almighty, and through this one Mitzvah his eligibility for Olam Haba was guaranteed.

How can *one single* Mitzvah, regardless of its purity, stamp a ticket to Olam Haba? While pure intentions certainly make a Mitzvah more special, how can a single Mitzvah equal the impact of a lifetime of living with the Olam Haba–mindset or an act of martyrdom? What about doing a Mitzvah perfectly causes the seismic transformation of a person to becoming Olam Haba–like? Let us suggest three approaches.

Visiting above the Heavens

The first approach is based upon the Talmud's characterization of Mitzvos that are done with the sole intention of doing God's will:

> *Rava posed a contradiction: It states, "For great until the Heavens is Your kindness,"[5] and elsewhere it states, "For great above the Heavens is Your kindness."[6] How can these two verses be reconciled?*
>
> *When it states that God's kindness extends even above the Heavens, that is referring to when Mitzvos are done with the sole intention of doing God's will, and when it states that God's kindness is only until the Heavens that is when Mitzvos are done for ulterior reasons.[7]*

A Mitzvah done without anticipation of reward or fear of punishment is a Mitzvah done "above the Heavens." It is not merely a better motivation for Mitzvos; rather it is a reflection of its doer ascending above this world, above the body and its petty agenda, above the Yetzer Hara and its lustful desires, and behaving as a Soul would in the spiritual world. When a person does a single Mitzvah in this manner, he momentarily catapults into Olam Haba on a "tourist visa." Perhaps this is why doing one Mitzvah perfectly earns man entry to Olam Haba. Taking a stroll in Olam Haba assures permanent eligibility to that world. When that

---

5   *Tehillim* 57:11.

6   Ibid. 108:5.

7   *Pesachim* 50b.

person dies and arrives at the palace doors of Olam Haba, because he has been there before—he's already been vetted and admitted once before—he is waved in again no questions asked.

A Valiant Act of Self-Sacrifice

A second way to understand why someone who does a single Mitzvah perfectly earns a Golden Ticket to Olam Haba is found in *Rambam's* writings. He dedicates chapter 5 of the Laws of the Foundations of Torah to the guidelines and virtues of *kiddush Hashem* (sanctifying God's Name), and the devastation and irrevocability of *chillul Hashem* (desecrating God's Name). The bulk of the chapter discusses the parameters of mandatory martyrdom: Under what circumstances must someone die in order to not transgress a sin and thereby fulfill the Mitzvah of *kiddush Hashem*, and when must he transgress a sin in order to save his life. In §10, *Rambam* applies the lofty status of *kiddush Hashem* to someone who does a Mitzvah perfectly:

> *Whoever abstains from sin or performs a Mitzvah not because of any motivation in the world, not fear, nor dread, nor to seek honor, only because of the Creator, blessed is He, as in the instance of Yosef refraining from sinning with his master's wife, behold he sanctified God's Name.*

The correlation between actual martyrdom and doing a Mitzvah without worldly motivations seems odd. How can *Rambam* equate someone who chooses to die in order to refrain from committing a sin (when halachah thus warrants) with someone who does one Mitzvah for God and no other reason, but whose life is never threatened?

By combining the notion of doing a Mitzvah perfectly with actual martyrdom, *Rambam* is revealing what it takes to do a Mitzvah without any ulterior motivations: To die for God demands total self-sacrifice. Every fiber of man's body urges him to preserve his life. Yet, the martyr overcomes the comprehensive resistance and forfeits it all for God. Nothing is a more palpable testament of God's existence than a person willing to forgo their most basic instinct of survival in order to uphold that belief, and therefore it is the ultimate act of *kiddush Hashem*.

Doing a Mitzvah without any worldly motivations requires a similar degree of self-sacrifice. By default, we are spurred to act when we can anticipate some tangible, physical benefit from that act. Conversely, we are equally motivated to *not* act when we do not foresee a tangible, physical benefit from that act. When someone does a Mitzvah only for God, they must deny every fiber of their body that resists this action in a similar way to what a martyr must overcome. That too is defined as a *kiddush Hashem*.

The badge of *kiddush Hashem*—regardless if it reflects the doer's disavowal of their body's resistance to die or their body's resistance to a Mitzvah that garners it no benefit—unlocks the doors of the palace at the end of the corridor.

Perfect Reward for a Perfect Mitzvah

There is a third way to explain how a single Mitzvah done perfectly guarantees a spot in Olam Haba. The Talmud establishes a bedrock principle that the Almighty does not withhold reward for even the most minor of Mitzvos, the overall piety of its performer notwithstanding.[8] Even wicked sinners will be fairly rewarded for their few Mitzvos. However, a Tzaddik receives reward for his Mitzvos in his preferred venue—Olam Haba, and the wicked get theirs in their preferred venue—this world. A Mitzvah must be rewarded, but it is not necessarily rewarded in the best and greatest fashion. It could be compensated in an imperfect and inferior manner—in this world.[9]

Perhaps we can suggest that receiving reward for a Mitzvah in this world is only possible when the Mitzvah was done with worldly motivations. The only way a Mitzvah can be rewarded in an imperfect manner *is if the Mitzvah itself was also performed in an imperfect manner*. However, if a Mitzvah is done perfectly, without any flaws of improper motivation, *then the reward must also be flawless*, and flawless reward is only possible in Olam Haba. Thus, even if someone is a Rasha overall who would normally receive reward for their Mitzvos in this world, if

---

8   *Bava Kama* 38b.

9   *Taanis* 11a.

they do a single Mitzvah perfectly, they guarantee themselves a ticket to the abode of perfect reward—Olam Haba.

Beyond the Palace Doors

Thus concludes our study of the various paths to ensure an invitation to Olam Haba. It is important to stress that getting your foot in the door is not all that matters. There are many different levels of Olam Haba—once someone has already gained entry. The Talmud describes the Tzaddikim in Olam Haba being singed with sadness when comparing their friend's "canopy" to their own comparatively smaller one.[10] This is not the product of envy, but rather a deep sadness at their own personal lack of perfection.[11] We ought not to suffice with just gaining a ticket to Olam Haba, we should strive to elevate our status there to the highest realm that it could be.

The Sages tell us that this world is like the time to make Shabbos preparations for consumption in Olam Haba:

> *Whoever toils before Shabbos will eat on Shabbos; whoever did not toil before Shabbos, from what will they eat on Shabbos?*[12]

A Shabbos meal can consist of a hastily prepared sandwich, or it can be a sumptuous, multicourse feast. Similarly, it is possible to access Olam Haba and only have a comparatively small portion, or to have an enormous one. May we all be so fortunate to arrive at the palace gates armed with a Golden Ticket to enter, and with pallets of Torah and Mitzvos so that our Souls merit a high stature in that world for eternity.

Chapter 32 Takeaways

- A single Mitzvah done with flawless motivations will earn its doer eternal life in Olam Haba.
- The preponderance of Mitzvos afford us ample opportunities to do at least one of them perfectly over our lifetimes.

---

10   *Bava Basra* 75a.
11   See *Mesilas Yesharim*, chap. 4.
12   *Avodah Zarah* 3a.

CHAPTER 33

From Adam to Moshe

*T*o conclude and summarize our study of how Torah and its Mitzvos change man, let us examine a pithy teaching in the Talmud:

> *The Torah begins and ends with episodes of Godly kindness: It begins with Godly kindness as Scripture states, "And Hashem made for Adam and his wife leather garments and He clothed them,"[1] and it ends with Godly kindness, as Scripture states, "And [God] buried [Moshe] in the gorge."[2]*

The commentaries explain that by pointing out that the Torah is bookended with instances of God performing acts of kindness, the Talmud is revealing that the *entirety of the Torah*—from the beginning of *Bereishis* until the final chapter of *Devarim*—is a continuous, uninterrupted flow of Godly kindness.[3]

This bold explanation provokes two questions:

- First, the Torah seems to be about many more things than just Godly kindness. A cursory perusal of the Torah reveals numerous narratives about Adam, Noach, Avraham and his descendants, Moshe, etc.; chapters detailing the intricacies of the building of the *Mishkan* and its vessels; myriads of laws relating to sacrifices;

---

1   *Bereishis* 3:21.
2   *Sotah* 14a, quoting *Devarim* 34:6.
3   *Maharsha* and others.

and many other items that do not seem to be examples of Godly kindness in the mold of clothing Adam or burying Moshe. How does the Talmud contend that *all* of Torah falls under the general rubric of Godly kindness?

- A second question relates to the particular examples the Talmud chose to represent God's kindness. While the death, burial, and eulogy of Moshe indeed mark the very end of the Torah, the episode of God making leather garments and clothing Adam and Chavah is found at the end of chapter 3 of *Bereishis*—not exactly at the *beginning* of the Torah. Why does the Talmud resort to that example to prove that "the Torah begins with Godly kindness" when there are ample earlier examples such as God's creation of the world, which Scripture itself attests was a supreme act of benevolence, as the verse states, "The world was built with kindness"?[4]

One may argue that perhaps the Talmud opted to forgo the instances of kindness manifested by creation in order to find an example of direct Divine kindness specifically with *mankind*. Even with that criterion, an earlier example exists: "And God said, 'It is not good for man to be alone, I shall make for him a helper,'"[5] and He proceeded to construct Chavah out of Adam's rib. Afterwards Adam proclaimed joyously, "This time it is a bone from my bone and flesh from my flesh!"[6] Why is the story of God remedying Adam's loneliness by furnishing him with a spouse not a candidate to convey the principle that the Torah begins with Godly kindness? Elsewhere, the Talmud finds nuanced kindness in the manner that the Almighty fashioned a wife for Adam. By plunging Adam into a deep slumber and only then extracting his rib and building Chavah out of it and thereby sparing Adam from witnessing the gory surgery, God ensured that Adam will not lose his appeal for his new wife.[7] This certainly ought to qualify as evidence of the Torah beginning

---

4   *Tehillim* 89:3.
5   *Bereishis* 2:19–24.
6   Ibid. 2:23.
7   *Sanhedrin* 39a.

with Godly kindness. Why does the Talmud skip over this story and feature His kindness with Adam and Chavah after the sin in the Garden of Eden to showcase this precept?

Torah: An Antidote to Venom

Perhaps we can propose an answer that will both demonstrate the precision of the Talmud's examples and reveal its underlying message. Our Sages tell us that the sin in the Garden of Eden physiologically altered Adam and Chavah. Before the sin, the Yetzer Hara was an *external influencer*, portrayed in the Torah as a cunning serpent. As a result of consuming the forbidden fruit, however, they became "knowing good and evil,"[8] meaning that thenceforth the Yetzer Hara infiltrated them, and both good and evil became *internal influences*. In the words of the Talmud, the sin caused the serpent's venom to be injected into them.[9]

The serpent's deadly venom that began coursing through Adam and Chavah as a result of their sin spurred multiple ripple effects. For example, it made them realize and be ashamed of their nakedness, and due to their newfound contamination, they were banished from the Garden of Eden. But a notable result of the sin was that it created the conditions that led the Almighty to convey His Torah to humanity. Our Sages teach us that, "Torah is the antidote for the Yetzer Hara."[10] Before his sin, Adam was not armed with Torah *nor did he need it* to contend with the Yetzer Hara. Prior to the sin, the Yetzer Hara was external and relatively weaker, and even without Torah guiding man's way, victory over it was feasible. Once the venom of the Yetzer Hara began pulsing through man's veins, however, the Torah is the only antidote to its fatal assault.

We can now see why the Talmud chose the episode of God clothing Adam and Chavah to prove that the Torah begins with Godly kindness. Certainly, the Torah begins earlier, and both the creation narrative and providing Adam with a spouse display God's kindness as well, but prior to the sin there was no *raison d'etre* for Torah to be given to mankind. In

---

8   *Bereishis* 3:5.

9   *Avodah Zarah* 22b; *Shabbos* 146a.

10   *Kiddushin* 30b.

that respect, *the beginning of Torah is only after Adam and Chavah sinned* and absorbed the Yetzer Hara's venom. The very first kindness *after* the sin and the need for man to receive Torah was established was that God crafted leather garments and clothed Adam and Chavah.

With this perspective in mind, the Talmud's principal insight that the entirety of Torah is a continuous flow of Godly kindness is now eminently clear. In its entirety, Torah is God's kindness since it affords man the ability to battle the Yetzer Hara harboring within him and ultimately expunge him of all remnants of its venom. Of course, the Torah is composed of many things—Mitzvos, narratives, descriptions, prophetic predictions, etc.—but they are all aspects of the antidote allowing man to resist and destroy the Yetzer Hara within him. The consistent theme threaded throughout the Torah in its totality is Godly kindness, for there is no greater kindness than to offer an antidote to a bitten and dying man.

Man's Origin and Destiny

Another grand insight can be drawn from this Talmudic teaching: *The Torah begins with Adam and ends with Moshe.* Adam consumed the venom that ensured that mankind received Torah; Moshe embodied the culmination of Torah because he deployed it to undo all the effects of that sin. Within Moshe, the antidote was fully administered and the Yetzer Hara was expelled as it was prior to Adam's sin. As a result of the evil operating within him, Adam was evicted from paradise; Moshe employed the Torah as a roadmap to regain admittance. Adam is the *cause* of man getting Torah and Moshe is the *effect* of man harnessing its power completely. Torah spans every stage of the continuum from Adam post-sin to Moshe, and its kindness is exhibited in its ability to propel man down the road from being subject to the venomous Yetzer Hara, like Adam, to being healed from it, like Moshe.

The transformation from Adam pre-Torah to Moshe post-Torah mirrors the journey that the Torah wants us to embark on and complete. Recall the Mishnah outlining our objective in this world:

> *This world is like a corridor before Olam Haba. Prepare (lit., fix) yourself in the corridor so that you may enter the palace.*[11]

We begin our journey in this world in the same state as Adam right after his Sin. Just as he was recently found unfit to reside in the spiritual world and was evicted, we begin life harboring a Soul that was recently booted from *its* spiritual home, and confined to circumstances that render it unfit to return to its place of origin.

Our mission is to use Torah and its Mitzvos to facilitate the Soul's journey home. With Torah and Mitzvos as our guide, we can navigate the corridor of preparation and transform ourselves from being like Adam to being more like Moshe, so that when our Soul arrives home at the gates of Olam Haba, it is granted access.

May we all be so fortunate to be included in the guest list for Olam Haba and be able to thank God and sing to His exalted Name. "To proclaim Your kindness in the morning and Your faith in the night. **Upon a ten-stringed harp...**"

---

11   *Avos* 4:15.

Acknowledgments

As this book goes to press, I want to thank my family, the people who helped me become the person I am, and the people who aided me in the writing and completion of this book.

I have had the good fortune of spending many years in various yeshivos and studying under great Torah scholars. In particular, I had the great privilege to spend several years studying in the great Mir Yeshiva under the tutelage of Rav Asher Arieli. Rav Arieli is the paradigmatic example of a true Torah giant. A man of unparalleled Torah scholarship and diligence, a paragon of the finest, most sterling character and a portrait of princely nobility. Rav Arieli also helped me navigate some critical decisions in my life. I'd like to think that I was influenced by Rav Asher's crystal clear and methodical way of thinking, his tenacious commitment to Torah, and his exemplary character.

I would also like to mention other great heads of yeshivos who have had an influence on my life: Rav Yehoshua Eichenstein, Rosh Yeshivas Yad Ahron; my esteemed uncle, Rav Ezriel Erlanger, Mashgiach of Mirrer Yeshiva; Rav Yitzchak Berkovits, Rosh Yeshivas Aish HaTorah; and Rav Sholom Kamenetsky, Rosh Yeshivas Philadelphia. I also want to mention two other great rabbis who have since passed: Rav Nosson Tzvi Finkel, z"tl, Rosh Yeshivas Mir; and Rav Yisrael Meir Homnik, zt"l, Mashgiach of Yeshivas Yad Ahron. I have been the beneficiary of their wisdom, guidance, and vast wealth of Torah knowledge.

My parents, Mr. and Mrs. Avi and Faige Wolbe, raised us in a warm and loving home, a home that truly embodies both the *emunah* and the *chessed* of Avraham Avinu. They perfected a dexterous approach to parenting consisting of vigorous encouragement and love; imbuing their children with confidence and self-esteem; aiming for long-term instead of short-term results; deflecting suggestions of short-sighted and harmful interventions advocated by breathless (and of course well-intentioned) educators; and incessant, relentless prayer. My grandfather, a universally recognized expert on parenting and pedagogy, described their parenting approach as a model worthy of emulation. I am fortunate to have been raised in their home, and I am eternally indebted to them.

My in-laws, Mr. and Mrs. Yaakov and Pessy Florans, are paragons of *chessed* and *avodas Hashem*. Their generosity, dedication to their children (and grandchildren, of course), fastidious care to fulfilling the Almighty's will, and completely open home are truly worthy of admiration. I am overjoyed to have joined their family and deeply appreciate the support and love that they have and continue to extend to us. I am lucky to have such wonderful in-laws, and my children are lucky to have such fabulous grandparents!

My oldest brother, Rav Eli Wolbe, and his wife, Malky, are remarkable people who elevate and uplift everyone they encounter. They set the gold standard of what it means to take responsibility for Klal Yisrael at large—and for every individual in particular. I was a recipient of their kindness, attention, and care. May the Almighty shower them with blessings of great health, abundant prosperity, and *nachas* from all their descendants, and may they see tremendous success in their manifold holy endeavors.

My wife, Chaya, is my partner in everything I do. I always tell my children that as a young man I did not excel academically, but there was one test on which I scored a perfect 100 percent—the test of who I would marry. I am fortunate to share my life with such an exquisite woman. Thank you for all the joy, blessing, and goodness that you bring to my life. Thank you for helping me conceive and sharpen some of the book's ideas, for transcribing and editing early versions of the manuscript, for countless tips and suggestions to improve the book, and for your support during the homestretch of its publication. Without you, this book would not exist, nor would any of my other projects. May the Almighty bless you with happiness and harmony, peace and prosperity, stellar health and longevity, may He give you the strength to continue using your prodigious skills in all your sacred work, and may we have *nachas* from our children, Akiva, Yehoshua, Miriam, Shlomo, Yitzy, and Rivka.

Since 2012, I have had the honor of serving as Director of Outreach for TORCH. TORCH is an organization that is on the cutting edge of the sacrosanct mission of connecting Jews and Judaism. I hereby extend my appreciation to my brilliant and fantastic TORCH colleagues, Rabbi Yaakov Cohen (who helped me with some of the sources in the book) and Rabbi Chaim Bucsko, and to the president of the TORCH Board, my dear friend, Dan Kullman. I am quite fortunate to work alongside such gifted and talented people.

In particular, I want to acknowledge the Executive Director of TORCH, my esteemed brother, Rabbi Aryeh Wolbe. TORCH is fortunate to have such a visionary and bold leader. Thank you for believing in me, and supporting and encouraging me in everything I do. When it comes to dedication and self-sacrifice to the betterment and advancement of our people, Rabbi Aryeh and Zehava Wolbe are in a class of their own. May the Almighty bless them with incredible success in all their endeavors.

I view the generous benefactors who support the wonderful work of TORCH as our partners in all our efforts. Without the friendship and generosity of our partners, this book would not exist. Thank you for your support and partnership. Your dedication and generosity are truly an inspiration!

Writing this book has been a long, grueling, and largely solitary experience. The first draft was completed in 2016, and it was admittedly rough and unpolished. Ultimately, the manuscript underwent more or less twenty rounds of revisions and rewrites wherein the material was organized, edited, and refined. There were many people along the way who helped bring the book to fruition.

The ideas of the book were not developed in a vacuum. I want to thank all the people who were participants in my classes and who are listeners of my podcasts. These audiences were the first to hear many of the ideas presented in the book, and thanks to the feedback that they shared, served as a (perhaps unwitting) sounding board to sharpen them.

I also want to mention all the kindhearted listeners who have taken out the time to reach out to me (rabbiwolbe@gmail.com) and share their feedback. There is nothing more gratifying to me than to hear from my listeners. In addition, I'd like to specifically thank the podcast listeners who have recommended the podcasts to their friends. I have been astounded by the organic growth of the podcast audience over the years, and much of the growth is due to these podcast ambassadors who spread the word. May it be the will of the Almighty that the podcasts continue to grow and impact the Jewish world.

I also want to thank the following people who read parts of the manuscript and provided valuable feedback that enhanced the finished product: My dear friends Danny Katz, David Fleischmann, Bill Koen, Dr. David Genecov, Max Genecov, Dr. Jeffrey Yarus, Rabbi Yaakov Nagel, David Borowsky, and my esteemed brother-in-law, Rabbi Yitzy Caplan. These eagle-eyed readers spotted typos, caught many mistakes, sharpened arguments, suggested reformulations, helped me remove repetitions and redundancies and write with better clarity and precision. I deeply appreciate your friendship and help.

I would also like to thank the dedicated staff of Mosaica Press for their adroitness and patience. The Jewish world is fortunate to have such a professional and high-level publishing house.

Above all, my greatest thanks goes to the Almighty for all the goodness He has bestowed upon me and my family. Our Sages tell us that we must thank God for every breath that we inhale. How much more must we thank Him for giving us an elevated life, for selecting us to study and teach His Torah—for giving us breaths of Torah.

Writing and publishing this book gave me a palpable sense of Divine assistance. Throughout this entire process I felt the Almighty's guiding hand shepherding me. Many times I would stumble upon Talmudic teachings that plugged in gaps in the complete picture that the book seeks to paint. Whenever I confronted a seemingly intractable problem, as if by Divine mandate, a solution or a clarification would suddenly materialize. May this book serve as a *kiddush Hashem*, and may we all witness the ingathering of the exiles speedily in our days.

About the Author

*R*abbi Yaakov Wolbe is a prolific and innovative Torah teacher and podcaster. Since pioneering Jewish and Torah podcasts in 2013, Rabbi Wolbe has released more than 1,000 episodes across six shows (The Jewish History Podcast, The Parsha Podcast, This Jewish Life, The Ethics Podcast, The Mitzvah Podcast, and TORAH 101), which have cumulatively earned more than a million and a half downloads. Rabbi Wolbe and his family live in Houston, where he serves as Director of Outreach for TORCH. Author of multiple Hebrew-language works on advanced Talmudic inquiry, *Upon a Ten-Stringed Harp* is Rabbi Wolbe's first in English.

Subscribe and Listen to Rabbi Wolbe's Podcasts

R abbi Yaakov Wolbe is the host of six acclaimed and chart-topping podcasts. Since pioneering Jewish and Torah podcasts in 2013, Rabbi Wolbe has released more than 1,000 episodes, which have cumulatively earned more than a million downloads.

The podcasts can be found on Apple Podcasts, Google Podcasts, Spotify, and all the other podcast apps. To simplify matters for listeners who want to listen to all of Rabbi Wolbe's podcasts, you can find all the episodes from all six channels on one feed: All Rabbi Yaakov Wolbe Podcasts. Please email any questions, comments, or feedback to rabbiwolbe@gmail.com.

"This Jewish Life" with Rabbi Yaakov Wolbe

"This Jewish Life" is Rabbi Yaakov Wolbe's flagship podcast. Since its founding in January of 2013, "This Jewish Life" has featured a delightful potpourri of podcast episodes on a myriad of Jewish subjects. In its current incarnation, the podcast focuses on exploring the deeper elements of Jewish life and philosophy. In each episode our objective is to go a bit deeper into subjects that we may be familiar with, to plumb the depths and uncover the essence of the beauty and sublimity of Jewish life and customs, and to bask in the warmth and the beauty of Torah wisdom.

"The Parsha Podcast" with Rabbi Yaakov Wolbe

"The Parsha Podcast" was started in 2016 with the goal of making the weekly *parsha* accessible and useful. Every Sunday, "The Parsha Podcast" will feature an hour-long podcast outlining the story, narratives, and major themes of that week's *parsha* and offer a selection of valuable and interesting insights from it. Towards the end of the week, a second episode that focuses deeply on specific ideas, themes, or comments on the *parsha* will be released.

"The Jewish History Podcast" with Rabbi Yaakov Wolbe

Rabbi Yaakov Wolbe started "The Jewish History Podcast" in 2016 with the goal of making Jewish history interesting and accessible. Over the course of the years, episodes have covered the vast expanse of Jewish history, from Abraham to Moses and Joshua, to the giants of the Mishnaic and Talmudic times, to great sages in modern times, to modern Israeli politics and conflicts. Each episode is dedicated to either a theme of Jewish history, a great personality of Jewish history, an era of Jewish history, or a transcendent event of our people's history. We learn about our people's triumphs and high-points, and of course, our nadirs. The chosen people have experienced an unprecedented 4,000-year story, and it is gloriously retold in "The Jewish History Podcast."

"TORAH 101" with Rabbi Yaakov Wolbe

"TORAH 101" is aptly described as "an intellectual's introduction to Torah." If you are a person who wants to understand the foundations of Torah in a logical and cogent fashion; if you don't want to subsist with the juvenile perception of Torah of your youth; if you want to wrestle with the deeper questions of theology, eschatology, theodicy, and Jewish philosophy; TORAH 101 is the podcast for you. We will delve into the weighty topics in Jewish philosophy: the divinity of Torah—the interrelationship of Written and Oral Torah, the multidimensionality of Torah, a critical examination of Bible criticism, Torah and science, why bad things happen to good people, and we will thoroughly explore Maimonides' Thirteen Principles of Jewish Faith.

"The Ethics Podcast" with Rabbi Yaakov Wolbe

"The Ethics Podcast" is dedicated to exploring the authoritative book of Jewish Ethics, the book of Mishnah titled *Ethics of our Fathers*. This book, called *Pirkei Avos* in Hebrew, is nearly 2,000 years old, and it is a compendium of the ethical aphorisms of the great Sages of Jewish History, circa 300 BCE–200 CE. Each episode begins with a biographical sketch of the Mishnah's author culled from the Mishnaic, Talmudic, and Midrashic literature, and shares some of the timeless lessons and applications of the teaching.

"The Mitzvah Podcast" with Rabbi Yaakov Wolbe

The Torah contains 613 mitzvos, commandments. Many of the mitzvos are quite familiar to us, such as loving our fellow as ourselves and eating matzah on Passover, but many are more obscure and unfamiliar. "The Mitzvah Podcast" is a project to offer a snapshot of each mitzvah, in the order in which they appear in the Torah. Each episode will be dedicated to a single mitzvah or a bunch of mitzvos, if they are closely related, and offer an overview of said mitzvah, together with anecdotes and vignettes and interesting questions that arise in the Talmud and other books of Jewish literature.

MOSAICA PRESS

BOOK PUBLISHERS

Elegant, Meaningful & Bold

info@MosaicaPress.com
www.MosaicaPress.com

The Mosaica Press team of
acclaimed editors and designers
is attracting some of the most
compelling thinkers and teachers
in the Jewish community today.
Our books are available around
the world.

HARAV YAACOV HABER
RABBI DORON KORNBLUTH